Schriften zum Umweltenergierecht

edited by
Prof. Dr. Helmuth Schulze-Fielitz
Thorsten Müller
Prof. Dr. Sabine Schlacke

in cooperation with
Stiftung Umweltenergierecht

Volume 32

Fabian Krause

U.S. Emissions Trading and what it can teach us for a Post-Kyoto World

Nomos

The Deutsche Nationalbibliothek lists this publication in the Deutsche Nationalbibliografie; detailed bibliographic data are available on the Internet at http://dnb.d-nb.de

a.t.: Köln, Univ., Diss., 2021

ISBN 978-3-8487-8390-8 (Print)
978-3-7489-2780-8 (ePDF)

British Library Cataloguing-in-Publication Data
A catalogue record for this book is available from the British Library.

ISBN 978-3-8487-8390-8 (Print)
978-3-7489-2780-8 (ePDF)

Library of Congress Cataloging-in-Publication Data
Krause, Fabian
U.S. Emissions Trading and what it can teach us for a Post-Kyoto World
Fabian Krause
280 pp.
Includes bibliographic references.

ISBN 978-3-8487-8390-8 (Print)
978-3-7489-2780-8 (ePDF)

Onlineversion
Nomos eLibrary

1st Edition 2021

Table of Contents

Table of abbreviations

AAU	Assigned Amount Unit
AB 32	California Assembly Bill 32
ACES	American Clean Energy and Security Act
ACMA	Alternative Compliance Market
APA	American Power Act
ARP	Acid Rain Program
ATU	Allotment Trading Unit
BAU	Business as Usual
C&C	Command and control
CAA	Clean Air Act
CAAPP	Clean Air Act Permit Program
CARB	California Air Resources Board
CBA	Cost Benefit Analysis
CCR	Cost Containment Reserve
CDM	Clean Development Mechanism
CDM EB	Clean Development Mechanism Executive Board
CER	Certified Emissions Reductions
CO_2	Carbon dioxide
CO_2e	Carbon Dioxide equivalents
COATS	RGGI CO_2 Allowance Tracking System
CoP	Conference of the Parties
EPA	Environmental Protection Agency
ERC	Emission Reduction Credits
ERG	Emission Reduction Generator
ERMS	Emissions Reduction Market System
EUR	Euro
EUTS	European Union Emissions Trading System
FESOP	Federally Enforceable State Operating Permit
GDP	gross domestic product
GGRF	California's Greenhouse Gas Reduction Fund
GHG	Greenhouse Gases

ICJ	International Court of Justice
ICJ	International Court of Justice
IEPA	Illinois Environmental Protection Agency
iNDC	Intended nationally determined contribution
IPCC	Intergovernmental Panel on Climate Change
ITMO	Internationally transferred mitigation outcomes
MGGRA	Midwest Greenhouse Gas Reduction Accord
MOU	Memorandum of understanding
MRR	Mandatory Reporting Requirements
MWe	Megawatt electrical
MWh	Megawatts per hour
NDC	Nationally determined contribution
NO_X	Nitrogen Oxide
OECD	Organisation for Economic Co-operation and Development
OSHA	U.S. Occupational Safety and Health Administration
PDD	Project Design Document
R&D	Research and development
RGGI	Regional Greenhouse Gas Initiative
RGGI MR	Regional Greenhouse Gas Initiative Model Rules
SO_2	Sulphur Dioxide
Source	Emissions source as covered by a program
U.S.	United States
UNEP	United Nations Environment Programme
UNFCCC	United Nations Framework Convention on Climate Change
USD	United States Dollar
USD	United States Dollar
VOM	Volatile Organic Material
WCI	Western Climate Initiative

A. Introduction

I. Introduction to the topic

1. The topic

The topic of this thesis is environmental regulation relating to climate change. While environmental law is an established and highly dynamic field with an increasing importance, some topics remain subject to ongoing, often controversial debate. The relationship between the increasing threat of climate change and economic concerns is at the center of this. As our knowledge of climate change continues to grow, we have identified economically sensitive sectors, such as the energy and transportation industry, as its main cause. As it became clear that the emission reductions required to at least halt climate change would only be possible at considerable economic costs, politicians and regulators have put a focus on using so-called "economic instruments," such as emissions trading.

At the same time, policymakers have tried to answer the global nature of climate change and global pollution's character as a "tragedy of the commons,"[1] with international treaties like the Kyoto Protocol or the Paris Agreement. This brings two aspects of environmental regulation into focus: the current status and future of emissions trading as the "economic instrument" used in many countries nowadays, and the methods of international cooperation regarding environmental pollution, especially regarding climate change. This thesis examines both topics and their relationship with each other.

This thesis also contains an analysis of the major emissions trading systems in the United States of America and thus concerns itself with emissions trading as a regulative compliance tool used to achieve emissions reductions. Apart from providing data-based case studies on the status and performance of such emissions trading systems, this thesis aims to review the lessons we can learn from such systems, both relating to the idea of emissions trading as environmental regulation as well as, more generally, environmental regulation on a national or international level. To that end, this thesis reviews emissions trading systems from two perspectives: as a

1 *Cf.* page 101 for definition and discussion of this term.

regulative compliance tool and as a sample concept for the development of environmental regulation as a whole, regardless of its specific regulative type.

In connection with that, this thesis reviews the state and the methods of international cooperation against climate change. In view of the shift in policy between the Kyoto Protocol and the Paris Agreement, which can be understood as *caesura* in the international cooperation regarding climate change, this thesis aims to study lessons from the reviewed United States emissions trading systems relating to this policy shift from a "top-down" to a "bottom-up" approach. This is appropriate as while the Member States of the European Union have chosen to ratify the Kyoto Protocol and subsequently created an international "top-down" regulative approach to environmental regulation, the United States has chosen to go a different route. Instead of following most of the international community in its "top-down" approach to pollution utilized in the Kyoto Protocol, some North American federal states developed grassroots "bottom-up" environmental regulation in lieu of, or to supplement, federal policy.

This thesis aims to analyze this step in the broader context of a general policy shift away from multinational agreements with "top-down" regulation to a "bottom-up" approach, focusing on whether bottom-up regulation based on emissions trading is indeed an alternative to international regulation and whether such a system is likely to emerge on the global stage within the extremely short timeframe required to attack pollution and climate change.

2. Research context

This topic was chosen for multiple reasons.

For one, much has been written on the performance of the European Trading System. Comprehensive and independent, data-driven, legal case studies on the much smaller trading systems in the United States are less common, especially from a European perspective. More importantly, the few case studies available limit themselves to the analysis of an individual system and do not analyze the potential interaction between systems and their respective linking dynamic, which given the shift away from international binding approaches (such as the Kyoto Protocol) towards national approaches (as displayed in the Paris Agreement) is particularly interesting to analyze.

The topic was chosen because of the possibility of comparing and making cross-references between the systems. Such cross-references are valuable for multiple reasons, but two stand out in particular: Cross-references can suggest whether issues with individual trading systems are specific to that individual trading system, or whether such issues are systematic to emissions trading as a whole. It can also address whether the possible linkage between systems and regulative regimes has the potential to form a drastic counterapproach to the (arguably) failed approach taken in the Kyoto Protocol, thus allowing us to academically test the theory of a replacement of international level regulations by local regulations—an approach taken by the Paris Agreement—which as a method, marks a *caesura* in international cooperation.

3. Research objectives and questions

This thesis aims to contribute to the understanding of environmental regulation, specifically of emissions trading systems. Despite the failure of most emissions trading systems—empirically proven by the data reviewed in the course of this thesis—and the subsequent academic discussion in opposition of emissions trading, further research and discussion of emissions trading as the "economic instrument" of choice in many countries is still relevant, especially relating to the root causes for the failure of emissions trading. In the United States, recent polls still show large public support for emissions trading.[2] The European Union, which considers itself a world leader in fighting climate change,[3] still relies heavily on emissions trading as a compliance instrument in order to achieve designated emissions reductions and continues to discuss emissions trading as a main component of its legal climate change approach. This is exemplified by the fact that despite the shortcomings of the European Emissions Trading System discussed later in this thesis, which are mirrored by the systematic issues of the emissions trading systems implemented in the United States, the European Union has chosen to enter a fourth trading period until

2 *Americans Support Strong Climate, Energy Policies* YALE CLIMATE & ENERGY INSTITUTE (Sept. 9, 2019), https://www.climatechangecommunication.org/wp-content/uploads/2019/09/American-Voters-Support-Climate-Action.pdf.

3 Cornelia Klugman, *The EU, A World Leader in Fighting Climate Change*, EUROPEAN PARLIAMENT (May 2018), http://www.europarl.europa.eu/RegData/etudes/BRIE/2018/621818/EPRS_BRI(2018)621818_EN.pdf.

2030[4] and even discusses expanding the scope of the European Union Emissions Trading System (EUTS). Other major emitters have shown a tendency towards emissions trading systems as well, leading with China or Mexico, both of which in 2017 chose to adopt its own emissions trading system. Other Latin American states, such as Brazil, are discussing implementation of emissions trading systems.[5]

This tendency of state actors to observe other emissions trading systems leads to the second research question discussed in this thesis: In addition to an analysis of emissions trading systems in the United States, this thesis looks at the possibility of using emissions trading as growing "bottom-up" regulation as an alternative to the international "top-down" approach. This is a relevant research question, as the "top-down" approach that was previously chosen by international actors in the Kyoto Protocol has been replaced by a "bottom-up" approach in the Paris Agreement. Given these two interacting factors, legal science must address the question of whether the combination of emissions trading and a "bottom-up" approach can replace an international "top-down" system.

a. Analysis of emissions trading in the United States

Once a highly innovative concept resulting from ideas from some of the world's leading scholars, emissions trading systems are now amongst the most disputed types of environmental regulation, with opinions ranging from treating emissions trading as a "silver bullet" for reducing carbon pollution to viewing cap-and-trade systems as a "carbon carousel" mostly catering to industry interests.[6] In legal and environmental scholarship, emissions trading is highly disputed as well. Many scholars believe it to be ineffective at its main objective: reducing emissions. Despite that, it continues to play an essential role in international environmental policy and remains at the core of most nation states environmental regulation. In

4 EU Directive 2018/410 of the European Parliament and of the Council of March 14, 2018 amending Directive 2003/87/EC to enhance cost-effective emission reductions and low-carbon investments, and Decision (EU) 2015/1814.

5 For a comprehensive list of enacted and discussed systems *see Emissions Trading Worldwide: Status Report 2019* International Carbon Action Partnership, https://icapcarbonaction.com/en/icap-status-report-2019 (last visited March 18, 2020).

6 For an introduction, *see* Joseph Goffman, *Title IV of the Clean Air Act: Lessons for Success of the Acid Rain Emission Trading Program*, 14 Penn St. Envtl. L. Rev. 177 (2005-2006).

view of this debate, this thesis chooses to analyze enacted emissions trading systems, with the aim of answering the following questions:

(i) Is this criticism warranted relating to systems in the United States, i.e., how did enacted systems perform environmentally and economically?
(ii) If emissions trading is indeed found to be ineffective, what are the lessons that can be learned from this going forward?

The review is first and foremost a legal review. However, additional insight is gained by using a quantitative review approach rooted in an economic analysis of the law. The value of this reveals itself in the following pages. For example, legal scholarship has often been content with stating that a given emissions trading system is overallocated and thus environmentally inefficient, i.e., it misses its main legal objective. While this is sufficient from a legal perspective, the root causes for the overallocation remain obscure, which hinders scholars from gaining a complete understanding of the regulative structure. A further quantitative review can be of value to supplement legal conclusions.

Pollution, especially pollution causing climate change, is a problem of international scale. Hence, this thesis seeks to explore how local carbon markets relate to a global environmental regulation regime, especially against the backdrop of the shift away from the "top-down" approach taken in the Kyoto Protocol towards the "bottom-up" approach of the Paris Agreement.

The United States was chosen as the main reviewed jurisdiction for multiple reasons. For one, they are one of the major contributors to global pollution and environmental damage around the world. But they also have more individual trading systems on a state level designed to address this problem than any other country and were amongst the first countries worldwide to address environmental pollution with legal regulation. In this way, they share a unique characteristic with some Canadian and Mexican states: climate regulation on a state level rather than on a federal or even international level. In addition to this, the United States has the longest experience with emissions trading, with the first emissions trading system having been enacted in the 1970s.

b. Grassroots environmental regulation as a potential solution to the Kyoto shortcomings: Policy shift from Kyoto to Paris

Based on the above, a further focus of this thesis is the development of "bottom-up" markets in the United States. This is an interesting development, especially as some of these systems have established links with other systems or have otherwise grown their jurisdiction. This thesis looks at this "bottom-up" movement and analyzes its lessons for a world after the Kyoto Protocol regarding the possibility of a shift from the current international "top-down" approach to a grass-roots regulative regime and whether such a policy could be efficient if based on emissions trading as compliance tool.

Such a shift could be important for many reasons. For example, results of the Kyoto Protocol were disappointing. One may argue that this follows directly from the regulative tool of choice used by some states, i.e., emissions trading. However, this thesis argues that at least some of the reasons lie in the nature of international agreements. Consequently, it is interesting to examine if local grassroots environmental regulation can solve the international problem that is pollution.

This question remains relevant given that states and some scholars seem to favor such a "bottom-up" approach going forward, for reasons later discussed herein.

II. Methods

This thesis uses both a qualitative and quantitative research approach to answer the research objectives detailed above. Qualitatively, much of the research is done as doctrinal research, i.e., "research which asks what the law is,"[7] or as defined by Hutchinson, "Research which provides a systematic exposition of the rules governing a particular legal category, analyzes the relationship between rules, explains areas of difficulty and, perhaps, predicts future development."[8]

Of course, it is doubtful whether doctrinal research can be understood as qualitative research, at least when seen from a western standpoint[9] as this would imply that "the law" is found and not reasoned. Consequently, the doctrinal research employed here is modeled after the rigorous research template designed by Fink[10] and adopted for legal research by

---

7 Research Methods for Law 17 (Mike McConvill & Wing Hong Chui, eds., 2017).

8 Terry Hutchinson, Researching and Writing in Law 7 (2nd ed. 2006).

9 *Cf.* Legal Hermeneutics: History, Theory, and Practice (Gregory Leyh ed., 1992); also the 52 Duq. L. Rev. (Winter 2014).

10 Arlene Fink, Conducting Research Literature Reviews: From the Internet to Paper 3 (2nd ed. 2005).

Ian Dobinson and Francis Johns,[11] which emphasizes selection of, *inter alia,* research questions, search questions, and review. For this purpose, the review is primarily focused on the body of law providing rules on the subject (referred to as primary sources) such as the legislation and any case law on the subject—for example, state and federal legislature on a given emissions trading system as well as case law concerning its application. In addition to analyzing primary sources, this thesis uses a library-based review of secondary literature, such as legal dictionaries, textbooks, journal articles, case digests, and legal encyclopedias.[12] Both German and English secondary literature is consulted. Due to the connection to public policy, this thesis also heavily relies on material released by government authorities or governing bodies, such as opinions, statements and press releases, that are often available online only. Such material is identified correspondingly in the references.[13]

The regulatory framework of a given emissions trading system is summarized and its application to a set of real-world facts are synthesized. This doctrinal research is supplemented with non-doctrinal research, often referred to as "law reform" research, aimed at identifying issues and proposing changes to the law.

In an effort to identify issues susceptible to "law reform" research, this thesis heavily relies on quantitative research. "The term 'quantitative method' refers in large part to the adoption of the natural science experiment as the model of scientific research, its key features being quantitative measurement of the phenomena studied and systematic control of the theoretical variables influencing those phenomena."[14] The topic discussed in this thesis is very conducive to this research method as the success of emissions trading systems can, according to their objective, be measured in emissions reductions, which makes it necessary to analyze emission reduction data. In addition to that, other implications of a legal rule found after the doctrinal research discussed above can be measured in data as well. This will be detailed later in this thesis and concerns data relating to, for example, market volume or market revenue, which according to economic theory allows inferences to certain results caused by a given legal rule. Especially when reviewing market failures, this economical approach

---

11 RESEARCH METHODS FOR LAW, *supra*, at 23.

12 HUTCHINSON, *supra*, at 7.

13 *Cf. infra* at 7, 8 regarding the implicit possibility of biased opinion in such material.

14 MARTYN HAMMERSLEY, WHAT IS SOCIAL RESEARCH? 39 (1993).

can add valuable information to a qualitative analysis. For example, when analyzing the root causes of an overallocation of allowances in a given market scheme, one must look at the quantitative market data to gain a full understanding of the causes of overallocation.

In the context of an "economic analysis of the law," this approach can be understood as a *descriptive* economic analysis of the law—i.e., an analysis concerning the effects of a legal rule. A *normative* economic analysis of the law, i.e., an analysis pertaining to the social desirability of the legal rule,[15] seems less significant in the environmental context as any reduction in pollution is desirable by itself. The analysis in this thesis therefore uses a descriptive economic analysis of the law especially pertaining to the cost-efficiency of such reductions. Of course, the reliance on provided data produces a problem inherent to most quantitative research: the collection and selection of data will inadvertently influence the results of the qualitative analysis. To avoid any possible data bias, this thesis follows the research rules suggested by King and Epstein that

> *(i) identify the population of interest; (ii) collect as much data as is feasible; (iii) record the process by which data come to be observed; and (iv) collect data in a manner that avoids selection bias.* [16]

To that end, all publicly available data for the years leading up to the year 2015 are used, with the respective data provider and any possible bias resulting from their role being duly noted and taken into account.

However, in many data reviews conducted in this thesis, usage of biased data is inevitable, as available data are often limited to what is provided by interested parties, such as a state's environmental protection agencies. In addition to that, in some cases specific data was not obtainable, which inherently reduces the value of a comparison between systems. This thesis accounts for that in its quantitative analysis.

Another challenge arose due to the transition of administrations on January 20, 2017. Before this date, both the federal as well as the state Environmental Protection Agencies published extensive data on their respective websites, thus allowing in-depth review. After the transition, most of this data was no longer publicly accessible. However, most of the data review in this work was finished prior to that. The respective data being affected by this are marked in this thesis.

---

15 Steven Shavell, Foundations of Economic Analysis of Law 1 (2004).

16 Lee Epstein & Gary King, *Empirical Research and the Goals of Legal Scholarship: The Rules of Inference* 69 U. Chi. L. Rev. 99 (2002).

III. Structure and contents

This thesis is divided into multiple chapters.

Chapter B briefly introduces pollution and its consequences for the environment. It discusses root causes and some environmental effects of pollution, with an emphasis on global climate change as a result of the introduction of pollutants, such as "greenhouse gases," into earth's atmosphere and the corresponding need for legal regulation as an answer to the issue of climate change.

Chapter C provides an in-depth discussion of the international response to climate change. The nature of global pollution causing climate change as (in economic terms) a "free rider" problem is presented and the resulting implications for a concerted international response are discussed. Consequently, Chapter C describes history and the current status of international treaties regarding climate change, from the United Nations Framework on Climate Change to the Paris Agreement. It also analyzes the codified and noncodified legal principles in international law as they relate to climate change with the intent of demonstrating the existence of a binding legal framework that obliges national actors in their approach to climate change.

Chapter D presents and analyzes the debate on the usage of legal regulation. Following from the topic of this thesis, this chapter focuses on the usage of economic instruments as regulative tools to reduce pollution. In analyzing economic instruments, this thesis focuses on two proposed economic instruments: Pigouvian taxes and emissions trading. Key regulative features of emissions trading systems are reviewed in detail, and the chapter ends with an analysis of design features theoretically necessary for an effective emissions trading system. Bottom-up trading and top-down regulation are introduced as opposing concepts and as the subject of this thesis.

Chapter E analyzes past and current emissions trading systems in the U.S. After a discussion of present U.S. regulation governing climate change, individual emissions trading systems are analyzed. Following the discussions in the previous chapters, the analysis has several focal points: Are there examples for effective emissions trading systems? Can U.S. experiences with emissions trading help us gain a better understanding of the development of bottom-up regulation? How have they affected other trading schemes? What can we learn going forward? Subsequently, chapter E contains detailed quantitative and qualitative research on the Acid Rain Program, the Illinois Emissions Reduction Market System, the Regional

Greenhouse Gas Initiative, and the California Global Warming Solutions Act of 2006. The review is divided into multiple research questions and points. Each system is approached with the same research questions to ensure comparability: First, a brief history of each program is provided. This is followed by a detailed description of the relevant regulation. Then a detailed environmental and economic analysis is provided for each system. Relating to the theories discussed in Chapter D, this is followed by a subsequent review pertaining to whether and to what extent the respective system can be used as an example for bottom-up regulation and how results and experiences with the system relate to a post-Kyoto regulative system.

Based on the reasons discussed for the Kyoto Protocol's failure in Chapter C, Chapter F provides a conclusion of the lessons learned from U.S. experiences with emissions trading and considers alternative policy approaches with a focus on the development of bottom-up regulation as an alternative to top-down approaches like the Kyoto Protocol. Scholarship on the requirements of effective regulative policy and on coalition forming is presented and reviewed. This chapter asks: In theory, could the development of an international policy on pollution happen "from the ground up", i.e., by the development and linking of local regulation?

The last Chapter G serves as a final synthesis of findings and conclusions drawn in the previous chapters, especially Chapter E.

IV. Terms

In theory, two types of emissions trading programs exist: cap-and-trade programs and credit trading programs. "Emissions cap-and-allowance trading programs impose a strict regulatory standard that reduces pollution—a permanent cap on the amount of allowable emissions—as well as an allowance trading program, whereas 'emissions credit trading programs are grafted onto existing regulatory programs, and allow sources that emit below their baseline levels to trade the resulting credits once they receive regulatory approval.'"[17]

In this thesis, the terms emissions trading and cap-and-trade are used synonymously, acknowledging that the concept of trading pollution rights does not necessarily require a cap on emissions.

---

17 Byron Swift, U.S. *Emissions Trading: Myths, Realities and Opportunities*, 20 Nat. Res. & Envt. 3, 4 (2005).

In reviewing emissions trading, the term "property rights" is used to describe, *inter alia,* emissions credits. The term is used to stay consistent with the traditional usage of terms and does not suggest that there is a "right to pollute."[18]

18 *See* Kirk W. Junker, *Ethical Emissions Trading and the Law*, 13 U. BALT. J. ENVTL. L. 149 (2005-2006).

B. Climate change and the necessity of regulation

Climate change has been called the defining environmental issue of the twenty-first century.[1] This is drastic but not surprising given its nature as a worldwide environmental problem that endangers not only humankind and its natural resources, but the earth itself and all species on it. Climate change can be defined as the process of "change in the state of the climate that can be identified (e.g., using statistical tests) by changes in the mean and/or the variability of its properties, and that persists for an extended period, typically decades or longer. It refers to any change in climate over time, whether due to natural variability or as a result of human activity."[2] The main cause of climate change is pollution. Pollution is generally defined as the introduction of contaminants into the natural environment that causes adverse change.[3] This sounds rather unassuming upon first sight, and indeed, the introduction of such contaminants is a cultural phenomenon that has accompanied human development from the beginning. Every life form on this planet is dependent on using its environment in some way or another. For humans, the usage of the environment was not only *condition sine qua non* for their existence, but also for their cultural advancement, which started as early as 5,000 years BCE with the first dammed rivers and irrigation systems in Mesopotamia, i.e., the start of human manipulation of the environment. Consequently, the idea of humankind "co-existing" with nature is a rather novel concept in human history. For example, in 1678 citizens of the alpine community of Fiesch in Switzerland applied to Pope Innozenz XI for permission to

---

1 David Hunter, James Salzman & Durwood Zaelke, International Environmental Law and Policy 607 (4th ed. 2011).

2 Definition used by the International Panel on Climate Change (IPCC) *cf.* International Panel on Climate Change (IPCC), *Climate Change 2013: The Physical Science Basis. Contribution of Working Group I to the Fifth Assessment Report of the Intergovernmental Panel on Climate Change* Annex III: Glossary (T.F. Stocker, D. Qin, G.-K. Plattner, M. Tignor, S.K. Allen, J. Boschung, A. Nauels, Y. Xia, V. Bex & P.M. Midgley, eds., 2013). The UNFCCC defines climate change as "a change of climate that is attributed directly or indirectly to human activity that alters the composition of the global atmosphere and that is in addition to natural climate variability observed over comparable time periods," *cf.* Article 1 para. 2 of the Convention.

3 Marquita K. Hill, Understanding Environmental Pollution 8 (3rd ed. 2010).

conduct a prayer procession for the retreat of the nearby Aletsch glacier, which was threatening the village. In 2010, 332 years later, the community reversed course and received the Pope's verdict allowing them to change their prayer as the glacier has almost fully melted,[4] much like many other glaciers in the European Alps.[5]

Science has shown that humans are using more of the earth's resources than the earth can endure.[6] A 1997 article found that among other impacts, humans have transformed up to 50 percent of the earth's land surface. Over 20 percent of the concentration of atmospheric greenhouse gases resulted from human action. Humans also put almost 60 percent of the world's accessible fresh water to use.[7] Since then, human influence has increased even more. Nowadays, there is a clear consensus in the scientific community that human influence in the form of environmental pollution is not only affecting biodiversity and the health of eco-systems, but it is also changing the global climate. For example, "[t]he Intergovernmental Panel on Climate Change (IPCC) is now 95 percent certain that humans are the main cause of current global warming. In addition, the SYR [Synthesis Report] finds that the more human activities disrupt the climate, the greater the risks of severe, pervasive and irreversible impacts for people and ecosystems, and long-lasting changes in all components of the climate system."[8] In 2005, the Millennium Ecosystem Assessment, a first of its kind four-year study carried out by 1,400 scientists with a $20 million USD budget found that at least 60 percent of services supporting life on earth[9]

---

4 *Cf.* Tagesanzeiger, Walliser beten für den Gletscher, 27.07.2012, available online at http://www.tagesanzeiger.ch/panorama/vermischtes/Walliser-beten-fuer-den-Gletscher/story/31501391 (last checked January 11, 2020).

5 *Cf.* Deutscher Alpenverein, Gletscherrückgang und tauender Permafrost, available online at https://www.alpenverein.de/natur/klimaschutz/ausstellung-klimawandel-klimaschutz/gletscherrueckgang-und-tauender-permafrost_aid_28388.html (last accessed January 11, 2020).

6 Of course, this thesis is not a work in natural science, and a law thesis is hardly the right place to discuss current scientific debates. The author is aware of the very controversial discussion relating to scientific findings regarding climate change.

7 Sandra L. Postel, Gretchen C. Daily & Paul R. Ehrlich, *Human Appropriation of Renewable Fresh Water*, 271 Science 785 (1996).

8 International Panel on Climate Change (IPCC), *Climate Change 2014: Synthesis Report. Contribution of Working Groups I, II and III to the Fifth Assessment Report of the Intergovernmental Panel on Climate Change* 5 (R.K. Pachauri & L.A. Meyer eds., 2014).

9 This includes fresh water, fisheries, forests and vital species.

are being used in an unsustainable fashion.[10] This includes consumption of resources as well as the introduction of pollutants.

Almost any chemical or material from human (and natural) sources can be a pollutant. Scientists class pollutants into organic chemicals, inorganic chemicals, organometallic chemicals, acids, physical, radiological, and biological pollutants.[11] The results of pollution sometimes are blatantly obvious. For example, Ohio's Cuyahoga River had such a high amount of oil on its surface in 1959, that it caught fire and burned for eight days straight. At least thirteen such fires are recorded.[12] However, they are sometimes invisible and less obvious, such as the increasing concentration of pollutants in the earth's atmosphere, which leads to the topic of climate change.

Climate change is usually defined as a change in weather patterns. One of these changes is the warming of the earth's atmosphere, often referred to as "global warming." Responsible for this warming process is the so-called greenhouse effect: Solar radiation passes through Earth's atmosphere and heats its surface. Non-absorbed heat energy is reflected upon the earth's surface and emitted back to space. However, scientific research suggests that pollution has altered the atmospheric composition, which has caused its capacity to absorb heat energy to increase. As a consequence, the atmosphere's capacity to emit heat energy not absorbed by the earth's surface is lowered; non-absorbed energy cannot be emitted back into space, but is instead trapped under the atmosphere similar to heat being trapped under a greenhouse roof, hence the term greenhouse effect.[13] As a consequence, the earth's surface is warming.

There are a multitude of pollutants responsible for this effect. These gases are classified as "greenhouse gases." Considered to be responsible for atmospheric changes are carbon dioxide (CO^2), methane (CH^4), nitrous oxide (N^2O), tropospheric ozone (O^3), and CFC-11. Most of these gases are emitted in connection with industrial activity. For example, the concentration of CO_2 in the northern hemisphere has increased by 109 parts per million compared to pre-industrial revolution levels; the CH4 levels increased

10 Millennium Ecosystem Assessment Board, *Living Well Beyond Our Means: Natural Assets and Human Well-being Statement of the MA Board*, (March 2005), http://www.millenniumassessment.org/documents/document.429.aspx.pdf.

11 Hill, *supra* note 3, at 11.

12 Jonathan H. Adler, *Fables of the Cuyahoga: Reconstructing a History of Environmental Protection*, 14 Fordham Envtl L. rev. 103–104 (2002).

13 Kirstin Dow & Thomas E. Downing, *The Greenhouse Effect* in Atlas of Climate Change (2011).

by 1170 parts per billion.[14] Causes are, amongst others, emissions from the combustion of fossil fuels, the industrialized mass-husbandry of livestock, as well as other industrial land use and forestry.[15]

Naturally, no scientific knowledge is written in stone. Knowledge changes and adapts. As such, our understanding of the non-refutable process of climate change is subject to change. However, the scientific community as of today considers rising temperatures on Earth as virtually certain. "By the 2050s, the global average temperature is almost certain to be more than 1°C higher than that for 1960 to 1990, and may be as much as 6°C higher by the end of this century."[16] One of the results of such warming is the retreat of glaciers, polar ice caps, and snow reserves around the globe. For example, the average temperature in the state of Alaska has risen by 3°C in the past thirty years, four times greater than the average global increase. As a result, Alaskan glaciers have melted at an alarming rate. This is a global phenomenon. Since satellite measurements began roughly thirty-five years ago, the Arctic has lost more than 20 percent of its ice.[17] This is dramatic for many different reasons, including the loss of habitat for many species and rising sea levels. Another reason is that this decrease in glaciers, which reflect heat due to their surface composition, itself contributes to climate change, as less heat energy is reflected off Earth's surface.

The relationship between human development and pollution has been discussed above. However, at least theoretically, there is no necessary connection between development and pollution: Pollution was defined as the introduction of contaminants into the natural environment that cause adverse change. Contaminants themselves are not pollutants. "Oil enclosed within a tanker is not a pollutant. Spilled into the environment, it is."[18]

These environmental effects strongly support the assertion that the destructive human influence on the environment has grown too large. As mentioned previously, humans are part of the ecological system; consequently, their activities (such as economic activity) are limited to what the globe's ecological system can support—i.e., its "carrying capabilities."

---

14 *Cf.* Adler, *supra* at 13.

15 *Cf.*, for example, data provided by the United States Environmental Protection Agency, *Sources of Greenhouse Gas Emissions* http://www3.epa.gov/climatechange/ghgemissions/sources.html (last visited January 11, 2020).

16 Kirstin Dow & Thomas E. Downing, *Forecasting Future Climates* in ATLAS OF CLIMATE CHANGE (2011).

17 HILL, *supra* note 3, at 179.

18 HILL, *supra* note 3, at 8.

These carrying capabilities put a limit on the scope, size, and intensity of human activity—i.e., the "scale" of human activities.[19] Especially in the course of the industrial revolution, the scale of human activity has outgrown the globe's carrying capabilities and continues to further outgrow them.[20] Economic growth is (still) related to resource consumption and pollution even though, in the past decades, the economy has undergone a process of "dematerialization, i.e., a reduction of resources needed to upkeep economic performance." As a result of such dematerialization, the economic growth rate has become higher than resource consumption and pollution.[21] However, the scale of economic growth continues to outgrow global carrying capabilities to a point where growth is "overwhelmingly likely to increase costs more rapidly than it increases benefits, thus ushering a new era of 'uneconomic growth' that impoverishes rather than enriches."[22] Consequently, a paradigm shift in our perception of economic growth may be necessary. Any regulative answers to pollution will have to take this into account. They will also have to address the urgency of the issue of climate change. To date, the international community remains committed to restricting the absolute increase in global temperature to below 2°Celsius. Such a threshold results from concern for small island and shore communities that might be over proportionally affected by a rise in sea level as well as scientific research that considers a 1.5°C increase as the "tipping point," after which the process of climate change becomes irreversible.[23] Holding such an increase requires that the current increase in global emissions must peak by 2020 and must be reduced by at least 50 percent by the year 2050.[24]

---

19 Hunter et al., *supra* note 1, at 34.

20 Herman E. Daly & John Cobb, For the Common Good: Redirecting the Economy toward Community, the Environment, and a Sustainable Future (Revised ed. 1994).

21 James Gustave Speth, The Bridge at the End of the World: Capitalism, the Environment, and Crossing From Crisis to Sustainability 50–51 (2009).

22 *Cf.* Hunter et al., *supra* note 1, at 34.

23 IPCC, Climate Change 2007: Synthesis Report. Contribution of Working Groups I, II and III to the Fourth Assessment Report of the Intergovernmental Panel on Climate Change (2007).

24 *Cf.* Hunter et al., *supra* note 1, at 34.

C. International response to climate change

For the longest time, both scholars and policymakers considered a concerted international approach as fundamental to fighting climate change. Given the global nature of climate change as well as emissions leakage issues, this response is intuitive. Additionally, climate change is, speaking in economic terms, a "free-rider" or "collective action" problem.[1] Consequently, the majority opinion tended towards considering a globally unified approach as fundamental.

However, especially in view of what some considered shortcomings in the Kyoto Protocol architecture and a change in political perception, scholars and policymakers called for a bottom-up approach to climate change.[2] The following chapter examines the history and current status of international environmental law and discusses this policy shift in the context of emissions trading.

In reviewing the international objectives and principles of international environmental law relating to climate change, one can differentiate between general principles of international environmental law[3] and the climate change regime as created by nation state actors[4] in the 1992 United Nation's Framework Convention on Climate Change (UNFCCC), the Kyoto Protocol, the Cancun Adaption Framework, the Paris Agreement, and various Conference of the Parties (CoP) decisions. The following is a discussion of the governance agreements and related processes in fulfilling the UNFCCC objective.

---

1 *See* next section for a detailed discussion of these terms.

2 *See*, for example, Gwyn Prins & Steve Rayner, *Time to Ditch Kyoto?* 449 NATURE 937 ff (2007).

3 Discussed in Chapter C.V.

4 This thesis uses the term "nation states" as reference to sovereign nations and "state" as a reference for federal states within a nation state.

I. Global pollution as a free-rider problem

It is intuitive to seek global scale solutions for global issues. In the case of climate change, this is supported by economic scholarship, [5] which characterizes. clean air or an intact atmosphere as a "public good." Such public goods are generally defined as goods that are both non-excludable and non-rivalrous, meaning that individuals cannot be effectively excluded from use of the goods and that use by one individual does not reduce availability to others.[6] Because of the non-excludability and non-rivalrous use of public goods, the market fails at appropriately producing and protecting public goods.[7] In the case of global pollution, an additional unique characteristic of the common good, "clean air," exacerbates this. Clean air as a common good has, in economic terms, a "stock" character. This means that the impact of a behavior depends upon "a stock of a capital-like variable that accumulates over time."[8] This means that climate change is caused by pollution of the global atmosphere, but only after the accumulation of a certain amount of pollutants in the atmosphere, whereas the introduction of an amount under this threshold is harmful, but does not cause climate change. This uncertainty complicates any free market approach to the protection of the common good, as actors exploiting the common good might not anticipate its imminent depletion.

This provides a strong incentive for "free-riding" behavior on the part of individuals and market participants. In this context, free-riding[9] "occurs when a party receives the benefits of a public good without sharing the

---

5 As a root cause of climate change is economic activity causing pollution, it is useful to consult economic scholarship.

6 Tyler Cowen, *Public Goods* in THE CONCISE ENCYCLOPEDIA OF ECONOMICS (David Henderson, ed., 2008).

7 First established in Paul A. Samuelson, *The Pure Theory of Public Expenditure*, 36 REV. ECON. & STAT. 387 (1954).

8 William D. Nordhaus, *Paul Samuelson and Global Public Goods: A Commemorative Essay for Paul Samuelson* in SAMUELSON ECONOMICS IN THE TWENTY-FIRST CENTURY (Michael Szenberg, Lall Ramrattan & Aron A. Gottesman, eds., 2006).

9 The free-rider problem is a concept in behavioral economics developed in the context of the "tragedy of the commons." A free-rider problem occurs when a market participant benefits from services but does not bear the costs. In the context of climate change, substantial emissions reductions by a few countries could reduce global warming. As emission reductions come at a price, countries are incentivized to avoid reductions and profit from other countries' reductions or from their knowledge gain achieved by cost-intensive research and development. *Cf.* WILLIAM BAUMOL, WELFARE ECONOMICS AND THE THEORY OF THE STATE (1952).

costs." In the case of the international climate change policy, countries have an incentive to rely on the emissions reductions of others without taking proportionate domestic abatement.[10] In the context of climate change, this causes two cumulative implications: For one, free-riding nation states have no (economic) incentive to enact emission abatement regulations. As this generally imposes costs on economic actors, market participants located in a free-riding country have a locational advantage against participants in regulated markets. As a consequence, nation states enacting desirable regulations are punished. In a globalized world with globalized markets and commerce, this causes inherent resistance against impactful national regulation. Since nation states are self-interested actors, they would rather be the free-rider than the regulator. This results in a deadlocked situation where no nation state enacts the required regulation.

A solution to this dilemma[11] is the formation of clubs to eliminate free-riding. "A club is a voluntary group deriving mutual benefits from sharing the costs of producing a shared good or service. The gains from a successful club are sufficiently large that members will pay dues and adhere to club rules to gain the benefits of membership."[12] In theory, such "climate clubs" could penalize free-riding non-members, for example, by excluding them from free trade to offset the benefits gained from free-riding and thus provide an incentive to join the club. Consequently,

> *[a]n important aspect of the climate club, and a major difference from current proposals, is that it creates a strategic situation in which countries acting in their self-interest will choose to enter the club and undertake high levels of emissions reductions because of the structure of the incentives.*[13]

Necessary for establishing such a club is an international agreement that compromises a critical mass of potential club members. This emphasizes the importance of international law and international cooperation to combat climate change. However, the free-rider character of climate change not only means that club-forming is necessary, but it simultaneously complicates the process of club-forming as it needs to provide enough pull-factors—i.e., factors that incentivize a certain behavior—to eliminate the incentive to free-ride. As summarized by Hare et al.,

---

10 William D. Nordhaus, *Climate Clubs to Overcome Free-Riding*, 105 Am. Econ. Rev. 1339 (2015).

11 Also *cf.* the "tragedy of the commons" discussed on page 101.

12 *Cf.* note 9.

13 *Cf.* note 9.

> *The participation of more countries, each with their own interests, increases the complexity of negotiations; the incentive to free-ride is high; and a de facto veto power is created, because individual countries know that their lack of participation will decrease the effectiveness of the regime and they can therefore negotiate concessions in return for their participation.*[14]

This is exacerbated by the nature of international law under the "Westphalian rules," which as a result of nation states' sovereignty rights,[15] prevent any legal means by which nation states "can coerce reluctant, free-riding countries into mechanisms that provide for global public goods."[16] Consequently, interested nation states cannot enact a legal structure in which non-participant states are legally obligated to follow the rules enacted by other states, thus forcing them to comply with, for example, climate change regulation.

II. Climate change and its international response: From UNFCCC to Kyoto and Doha

As a response to climate change, 154 UN- and non-UN Nation States signed the UNFCCC in 1992.[17] The UNFCCC went into force in 1995 and, as of now, has 192 signatory and observer countries, amongst them the USA and China.[18] The UNFCCC differentiates between so called "Annex I" parties, the industrialized countries, and "Non-Annex I" parties, non-industrialized and emerging countries. A separate grouping of parties is shown as "Annex II," which refers to all industrialized countries (i.e., Annex I countries) with the exception of the former Soviet Union. While the UNFCCC, as one scholar points out, "may have been short on substantive commitments, it did establish an institutional framework for the progressive development of the regime through protocols and frameworks."[19]

---

14 William Hare et al., *The Architecture of the Global Climate Regime: A Top-down Perspective*, 10 Climate Policy 600-614 (2010).

15 *Cf.* page 69.

16 *Cf.* note 9.

17 United Nations Framework Convention on Climate Change, 1771 UNTS 107, reprinted in 31 ILM 849 (May 29, 1992).

18 United Nations Framework Convention on Climate Change, *Parties to the Convention and Observer States*, https://unfccc.int/process/parties-non-party-stakeholders/parties-convention-and-observer-states (last visited January 11, 2020).

19 David Hunter, James Salzman & Durwood Zaelke, International Envtl. Law & Pol'y 683 (4th ed. 2011).

According to Article 2 of the Convention, the ultimate objective of the UNFCCC is

> *to achieve, in accordance with the relevant provisions of the Convention, stabilization of greenhouse gas concentrations in the atmosphere at a level that would prevent dangerous anthropogenic interference with the climate system. Such a level should be achieved within a time-frame sufficient to allow ecosystems to adapt naturally to climate change, to ensure that food production is not threatened and to enable economic development to proceed in a sustainable manner.*[20]

The language used here is noteworthy. The Convention uses the term "stabilization." The parties to the Convention thus are "prepared to tolerate some degree of climate change."[21] The main objective, therefore, is not reversal, but rather stabilization to allow for adaption. Article 2 also states that such an objective is not just intended by the Convention itself, but also any "related legal instruments that the Conference of the Parties may adopt" (Article 2).

Consequently, the UNFCCC follows the Vienna Convention model by establishing a general framework approach to climate change, which may be "addressed through different legal policies, instruments and measures."[22] Based on that, the modern international response to climate change is organized in a hierarchical fashion, with the UNFCCC as the top level of contractual international law on climate change. While the Convention states in Article 4, para. 2, that the developed parties (i.e., the Annex I parties) shall adopt national policy measures in order to mitigate climate change, it does not set out specific requirements. The Convention does provide for a timeline in which the environmental standards defined

---

20 United Nations Framework Convention on Climate Change, *supra* note 18.

21 Marauhn, Thilo, A Global Energy Strategy as a Viable Means for Redressing Climate Change?, Zeitschrift für ausländisches öffentliches Recht und Völkerrecht (ZaöRV), 2003, 281.

22 Rowena Maguire, *Foundations of International Climate Law: Objectives, Principles, and Methods* in CLIMATE CHANGE AND THE LAW 85 (Erkki Holler, Kati Kulovesi & Michael Mehling, eds., 2013).

by Article 2 must be met,[23] but does not set a specific target or mandatory emissions reductions, mostly due to concerns voiced by the United States, Japan, and the former Soviet Union. This *modus operandi* has shaped the subsequential agreements as well. As Mehling puts it:

> *At the international level, nations seeking to cooperate on climate change have always been forced to navigate a fine line between substance and process, general principles and specific rules, formal obligations and political commitments. Many of the core issues have been so divisive that progress has only been possible at the expense of specific and binding normative outcomes. As the negotiations on a future climate regime unfold, it is becoming increasingly evident that international cooperation itself is undergoing fundamental change.*[24]

According to Article 4, para. 2 lit d) of the Convention, the developed parties to the agreement are required to conduct "Conference of the Parties" (CoP) meetings to review the national policy measures that member states have enacted to mitigate climate change. Such CoP meetings have taken place every year since the UNFCCC was signed. The soft targets used in the original Convention wording were at the center of the first CoP meeting in Berlin in the year 1995, where environmental interest groups, governments, and experts discussed the intensification of, specifically, the Annex I parties' commitment levels.[25] Subsequently, the CoP signed the so-called "Berlin Mandate" proposed by some emerging economies. This report displays the national attempts at climate change abatement as mandated by the Convention but, more importantly, creates a hard timetable for the developed countries to "set quantified limitation and reduction

23 An interesting, albeit very academic, question is whether this a soft timeline as often implied by scholars, *cf. supra* at 85. Article 2 states that emission levels must be stabilized "within a time-frame sufficient to allow ecosystems to adapt naturally to climate change, to ensure that food production is not threatened and to enable economic development to proceed in a sustainable manner." This is only a "soft" non-defined timetable as our scientific environmental data is insufficient. If it were sufficient, a time-frame could easily be defined. This is especially interesting as in the course of the UNFCCC, the United States, Japan, and the former Soviet Union opposed fixed time-frames, arguing that scientific data was insufficient.

24 Michael Mehling, *Implementing Climate Governance: Instrument Choice and Interaction* in CLIMATE CHANGE AND THE LAW 12 (Erkki Holler, Kati Kulovesi & Michael Mehling, eds., 2013).

25 *Cf.* HUNTER ET AL., *supra* note 19, at 683.

objectives within specified timeframes, such as 2005, 2010, and 2020, for their anthropogenic emissions," Art. II.2 FCCC/CP/1995/7/Add.1.

III. The Kyoto Protocol

1. History of the Kyoto Protocol

As a response to emerging scientific data supporting the need for action regarding impending climate change, the controversial discussion at the 1995 CoP in Berlin, and the lack of clear and quantifiable emissions reductions achieved so far, the UNFCCC parties negotiated the Kyoto Protocol in December 1997. Except for the U.S., Australia, and Canada, which signed but did not ratify, the Kyoto Protocol was ultimately signed and ratified by most industrial nations.

To incentivize ratification by a sufficient number of developed countries, significant concessions were made to particular countries. As Victor et al., point out, the Russian Federation and the Ukraine in particular were allowed to join the Protocol with "commitments of a zero percent reduction below 1990 levels, although by the time of the negotiations their actual emissions were already far below the 1990 baseline because of the post-Soviet economic contraction."[26] This provided a strong economic incentive to join as the countries would (i) not have to reduce emissions and (ii) were enabled to sell their excess emissions allowances to other Kyoto parties.[27]

While no immediate emission reductions were achieved by countries joining the Protocol, this process can still be considered useful. For one, this is consistent with the UNFCCC's intention to "gain the largest possible number of adherents."[28] Amongst other factors, such as the "pull-factor" resulting from a significant number of signatories, the effect of such institutionalization of legal processes can cause a further development of the field. As Kreuter-Kirchhof points out, the institutionalization achieved by the Intergovernmental Panel on Climate Change (IPCC) has stimulated

---

26 David G. Victor et al., *The Kyoto Protocol Emission Allocations: Windfall Surpluses for Russia and Ukraine*, 49 CLIMATIC CHANGE 263, 264 (2001); Michael Wara, *Measuring the Clean Development Mechanism's Performance and Potential*, 55 UCLA L. REV. 1768 (2008).

27 Colloquially known as "hot air."

28 Donald Goldberg, *As the World Burns: Negotiating the Framework Convention on Climate Change*, 5 GEO. INT'L ENVTL. L. REV. 239, 244-51 (1993).

the international climate change regime, as the findings of the IPCC were not only the basis for the adoption of the UNFCCC and the Kyoto Protocol, but also the foundation for future commitments.[29]

The Protocol, considered the first international response to the problem of climate change and "likely the largest and most expensive international effort to combat a global environmental commons problem,"[30] went into force in 2005, almost a decade after its signing. It, *inter alia,* defined emission reduction targets for signatory parties: they agreed on a reduction in greenhouse gas (GHG) emissions of 5 percent below 1990 levels during the 2008 to 2012 period. To achieve this, the Protocol followed a regime of "common but differentiated responsibilities," *cf.* Art. 3.1 UNFCCC. The Bush Administration decided to withdraw from this regime and enacted a mixture of local, mostly non-compulsory, initiatives and bilateral cooperation agreements.

2. The Kyoto Protocol Regime

In the Kyoto Protocol, the Annex I parties commit to limit their emissions to a defined baseline. Countries' emission reduction commitments are defined on the basis of the agreement, in a so called "top-down" approach.[31] The reductions to be achieved by the parties reflect a binding commitment of the parties, according to Article 3 of the Protocol. The initial commitment of the Annex I parties was to reduce greenhouse gas emissions to 5 percent under 1990 levels in the first so-called "commitment period" from 2008 to 2012 as designated in the UNFCCC. Following the Principle of Common but Differentiated Responsibilities,[32] the respective parties undertook individual commitments following their individual capabilities, which, however, have been criticized as somewhat arbitrary.[33] The European Union initially undertook a reduction of 8 percent under 1990 levels while other parties undertook no commitments. This will be discussed

---

29 Kreuter-Kirchhof, Charlotte, Dynamisierung des internationalen Klimaschutzregimes durch Institutionalisierung, Zeitschrift für ausländisches öffentliches Recht und Völkerrecht (ZaöRV), 2005, 967.

30 Wara, *supra* note 26, at 1760.

31 Kati Kulovesi, *Exploring the Landscape of Climate Law and Scholarship: Two Emerging Trends* in CLIMATE CHANGE AND THE LAW 46 (Erkki Holler, Kati Kulovesi & Michael Mehling, eds., 2013).

32 *infra.* page 76 for a detailed discussion of this principle.

33 *Czarnecki*, Verteilungsgerechtigkeit im Völkerrecht, 2008, S. 155 ff.

further later in the text. The reduction commitments were initially set out in phases or "commitment periods."

The Kyoto Protocol allowed participating member states to use three[34] flexible mechanisms to achieve the emissions reduction goal. These were included, *inter alia,* with the intention "to reduce the cost of meeting the emission targets—and therefore increase the likelihood that the Protocol will be ratified and the targets met."[35] The flexibility instruments discussed below, such as emissions trading, have to be supplemental to domestic actions for the purpose of meeting the emission limitation and reduction commitments under Article 3 of the Kyoto Protocol. For the purpose of implementing these mechanisms, which are highlighted below, the Kyoto Protocol differentiates between the "developed" parties listed in an Annex to the Protocol and the "non-developed" parties.[36] Only the developed parties may engage in certain "flexibility" mechanisms such as emissions trading.

Although the flexibility mechanisms mentioned previously are only supplemental to the primary national mitigation measures, this thesis focuses on these flexibility mechanisms as they fall within the category of economic instruments reviewed herein and can therefore contribute to the research objective of this thesis.

---

34 Hunter et al. consider the "Article 4 bubble-approach" as the fourth emissions reductions mechanism. The bubble-approach set out in Article 4 allows for a joint fulfillment of emission-reduction commitments by two or more parties, *cf.* HUNTER ET AL., *supra* note 19, at 690. For that purpose, Article 4 allows parties to create a "bubble" around the parties' reduction obligations, provided that the parties do not exceed their aggregate allowances under the Protocol. This is was utilized, *inter alia,* by the European Union as a prerequisite for the European Emissions Trading System.

35 ORGANIZATION FOR ECONOMIC CO-OPERATION AND DEVELOPMENT (OECD), ACTION AGAINST CLIMATE CHANGE: THE KYOTO PROTOCOL AND BEYOND (OECD Publications, 1999).

36 Most scholars identify the Annex I parties as "industrialized" or "developed" countries, whereas the non-Annex I parties are often identified as "developing" *cf.* HUNTER ET AL., *supra* note 19, at 690. Arguably, this characterization is not entirely correct, as countries such as Saudi-Arabia, which is commonly perceived as a high-income economy and is part of the G-20, is characterized as a non-Annex I party. Other non-Annex I countries are economies such as Israel, China, Qatar, *cf.* the United Nations Framework Convention on Climate Change, *List of Non-Annex I Parties to the Convention*, https://unfccc.int/process/parties-non-party-stakeholders/parties-convention-and-observer-states (last visited June 10, 2018).

a. International emissions trading

Article 17[37] allows the parties to define relevant "principles, modalities, rules and guidelines, in particular for verification, reporting and accountability for emissions trading," i.e., a legal framework that allows parties to transfer parts of their emissions contingent to other parties. This feature is commonly known as "cap-and-trade;" aggregate allowable emissions are defined and the allowable emissions are "capped" at a certain level. Within this aggregate cap, participants are free to transfer parts of their "emissions allowance" to other parties, in theory allocating the "permission" to emit to parties that value it the most, making the emissions abatement cost effective. Correspondingly, the developed Kyoto parties are allowed to participate in emissions trading for the purposes of fulfilling their emissions reduction commitments under Article 3. However, any such trading must be supplemental to domestic actions for the purpose of meeting quantified emission limitation and reduction commitments under Article 3.

In the course of negotiating the Kyoto Protocol and subsequent amendments, the negotiators repeatedly stated that climate change in its suspected form can only be approached on the "international stage," i.e., using a top-down approach. Indeed, given the global scale of the externality and the significant "free-rider" problem associated with the solution to the problem of global emissions, an international approach seems preferable as a solution to the "tragedy of the commons." While the Protocol is often considered a failure, much of the international focus still rests on facilitating an international policy response.

However, given the response to the Kyoto Protocol and the rather underwhelming results, a national "bottom-up" approach has been be considered as well. As of today, many nation states have enacted emissions trading systems on a federal or state level. Besides the EU with its European Union Emissions Trading System (EUTS), emissions trading also takes place in various U.S. and Canadian states, China, Kazakhstan, New Zealand, and South Korea. Brazil intends to establish "market-based" environmental regulation. Japan drafted an emissions trading system, but deferred its implementation as a result of U.S. and Australia's opposition to the Kyoto Protocol—another manifestation of the free-rider issue.

---

37 The "Kyoto Protocol to the United Nations Framework Convention on Climate Change" is available online in multiple languages at https://unfccc.int/process/the-kyoto-protocol (last visited on January 11, 2020).

b. Joint implementation

Article 6 allows for the "joint implementation" of emissions reduction obligations by developed parties. It allows "[f]or the purpose of meeting its commitments […], any [developed] Party [to] transfer to, or acquire from, any other such Party emission reduction units resulting from projects aimed at reducing anthropogenic emissions by sources or enhancing anthropogenic removals by sinks of greenhouse gases in any sector of the economy." This stands under the condition that (a) any such project has the approval of the Parties involved; (b) any such project provides a reduction in emissions by sources, or an enhancement of removals by sinks, that is additional to any that would otherwise occur; (c) it does not acquire any emission reduction units if it is not in compliance with its obligations under Articles 5 and 7; and (d) the acquisition of emission reduction units shall be supplemental to domestic actions for the purposes of meeting commitments under Kyoto Protocol.

c. The Clean Development Mechanism

The third Kyoto flexibility mechanism is the Clean Development Mechanism (CDM) under Art. 12 of the Kyoto Protocol. Art. 12 § 2 defines the CDM's purpose as assistance to the non-Annex I Parties in "achieving sustainable development and in contributing to the ultimate objective of the Convention"[38] as well as to assist Annex I Parties "in achieving compliance with their quantified emission limitation and reduction commitments." Article 12 § 3 sets out the CDM's method of operation: the developed Annex I Parties can facilitate emissions reduction projects in non-Annex I countries. The Annex I Parties can subsequently use the resulting "certified emissions reduction" for compliance with their own quantified emissions limitation and reduction under the Kyoto Protocol. This conceptual mechanism, employed in a national or trans-national cap-and-trade context, is often defined as "offset credits" and is implemented into nearly every U.S.

38 The principle of "sustainable development" has been introduced into the canon of international law by the ICJ in its *Gabčíkovo–Nagymaros* decision, *cf.* ICJ Gabcikovo-Nagymaros Project (*Hung. v. Slovk.*), 1997 I.C.J. 140 (Sept. 25, 1997), hereinafter Gabcikovo-Nagymaros. Also *cf.* Stephen A. Roosa, Sustainable Development Handbook (2010).

market-based cap-and-trade system.[39] Although the CDM is not an emissions trading program, it is based on the same rational as emissions trading: by allowing emission reductions to occur where marginal abatement costs are the lowest, total abatement costs—and thus costs of compliance with the Kyoto Protocol—are reduced. However, the CDM features an interesting special design element: while it is largely based on experiences with emissions trading under the preceding U.S. Clean Air Act, the CDM was the first market-based mechanism to encompass multiple pollutants instead of just one.

aa. Basic framework

The CDM's regulatory framework has been extended dramatically since the Kyoto Protocol first came into force. Despite the high number of standards, rules, guidelines, and procedures, the basic design can be traced to a few core design elements:

The CDM features Certified Emissions Reductions (CERs) which, in comparison to the general cap-and-trade design explained above, take the function of allowances and are commonly referred to as "carbon credits." Each CER is equivalent to one metric ton of pollutants.[40] Annex I Parties, or companies with registered offices in those countries, can obtain CERs by facilitating emissions reduction projects located in a non-Annex I country. Such projects need to be proposed to the CDM Executive Board (CDM EB) in a Project Design Document (PDD), a standardized form that explains the project and details how it will satisfy the requirements set out in the grant of CERs. Parties must especially explain how the emissions reductions intended with the project are "voluntary, real, additional" and

39 *Cf.* Illinois Administrative Code, tit .35 § 205.500 establishing an offset credit system for the Illinois Emissions Reduction Market System (ERMS); Section 9.2 of the Western Climate Initiative and 17 CCR § 95856(h)(1)(A) for the California's cap-and-trade program, Section 20-10.3(a)(1) of the Regional Greenhouse Gas Initiative Model Rules for the Regional Greenhouse Gas Initiative. The only U.S. cap-and-trade program to not implement offset credits is the Acid Rain Program, which can thus be characterized as a "true" cap-and-trade program as opposed to the programs above, which have been characterized as "hybrid" cap-and-trade programs.

40 United Nations Framework Convention on Climate Change, *Clean Development Mechanism, Glossary CDM Terms, Version 08.0*, https://unfccc.int/process-and-meetings/the-convention/glossary-of-climate-change-acronyms-and-terms (last visited January 11, 2020).

specify how they will not facilitate emissions leakage.[41] In addition to that, the PDD must detail the method used to measure emissions.

Voluntary emissions reductions in the above sense are reductions that are not compelled by national or provincial law or regulation. Real emissions reductions are monitored with sufficient care under the method approved by the CDM EB to ensure that they actually occur, something that proved to be a problem in the years following implementation. Additional emissions reductions are those that are in addition to reductions that would have occurred absent the CDM subsidy. Emissions leakage occurs when emissions reductions that would have occurred from a CDM project absent the CDM subsidy are displaced to another location because of the subsidy.[42]

The Annex to Decision 3/CMP.1[43] specifies the exact required modalities and procedures for the CDM as defined in Art. 12 of the Kyoto Protocol. Chapter C. of the Annex allows the CDM EB, *inter alia,* to approve new measuring technology relating to baselines, monitoring plans etc. Under paragraph 20(a), the CDM EB, which is made up of ten members of the Kyoto Protocol, paragraph 7, accredits operational entities, which meet the accreditation standards. Paragraph 26 specifies rules regarding designated operational entities, which answer to the COP/MOP and are, *inter alia*, responsible for the validation of proposed CDM projects. Further rules regarding validation, verification, and certification of projects can be found in paragraph 27(b) and (e).

Paragraph 35 defines validation as the process of independent evaluation of a project activity by a designated operational entity against the requirements of the CDM as set out in decision 17/CP.7, the present annex and relevant decisions of the COP/MOP, on the basis of the project design document, as outlined in appendix B below. According to paragraph 43, a CDM project activity is additional if anthropogenic emissions of greenhouse gases by sources are reduced below those that would have occurred in the absence of the registered CDM project activity. The additionality of

41 United Nations Framework Convention on Climate Change, *Clean Development Mechanism (CDM) Executive Bd., Guidelines for Completing the Project Design Document (CDM-PDD), The Proposed New Methodology: Baseline (CDM-NMB) and the Proposed New Methodology: Monitoring (CDM-NMM) (Version 04, 2005),* http://cdm.unfccc.int/Reference/Guidclarif/index.html#proj_cycle (last visited January 11, 2020).

42 Wara, *supra* note 26, at 1771.

43 Available online at https://cdm.unfccc.int/Reference/COPMOP/08a01.pdf#page=6 (last visited January 11, 2020).

projects has been one of the major controversies related to the CDM. Another criticism relates to the reliability of the emissions baseline employed for CDM projects. Under paragraph 44, the baseline for a CDM project activity is the scenario that reasonably represents the anthropogenic emissions by sources of greenhouse gases that would occur in the absence of the proposed project activity. A baseline covers emissions from all gases, sectors, and source categories listed in Annex A within the project boundary. Paragraph 47 regulates that the baseline shall be defined in a way that CERs cannot be earned for decreases in activity levels outside the project activity or due to *force majeure*. Under paragraph 48, in choosing a baseline method for a project activity, project participants must select, from certain approaches, the one deemed most appropriate for the project activity. Baseline methods are existing actual or historical emissions or emissions from a technology that represents an economically attractive course of action, taking into account barriers to investment or the average emissions of similar project activities undertaken in the previous five years in similar social, economic, environmental, and technological circumstances, and whose performance is among the top 20 percent of their category. This is, *inter alia*, used to avoid leakage, defined as the net change of anthropogenic emissions by sources of greenhouse gases that occurs outside the project boundary and that is measurable and attributable to the CDM project activity.

The last step is verification and certification of the project under Paragraph 61. Verification is the periodic independent review and ex-post determination by the designated operational entity of the monitored reductions in anthropogenic emissions by sources of greenhouse gases that have occurred as a result of a registered CDM project activity during the verification period. Certification is the written assurance by the designated operational entity that, during a specified time period, a project activity achieved the reductions in anthropogenic emissions by sources of greenhouse gases as verified.

For the second commitment period, the Doha parties extensively debated[44] the possibility of CER carry-overs, i.e., the second period usage of CERs created in the first commitment period. In the context of cap-and-trade systems, this mechanism is usually called "banking" and is generally considered to be desirable as it increases market participant's certainty

44 The debate was led with an East against West axis, as eastern states such as Poland were afraid of losing the many surplus units with which they were incentivized to join the Protocol.

as to future usage and prices of credits. The compromise reached in the amendment allows for limited carry-over. Paragraph 24 of the amendment allows for carry-over of unretired credits for a maximum of 2.5 percent of a country's assigned emissions amount. Parties may acquire surplus units from other parties for up to 2 percent of their assigned emissions amount (para. 26).

bb. CDM economics

The following graphs 1 and 2 display data of CDM projects and credits.

Graph 1: Second compliance period registered projects, projects issuing CERs and issued CERs[45]

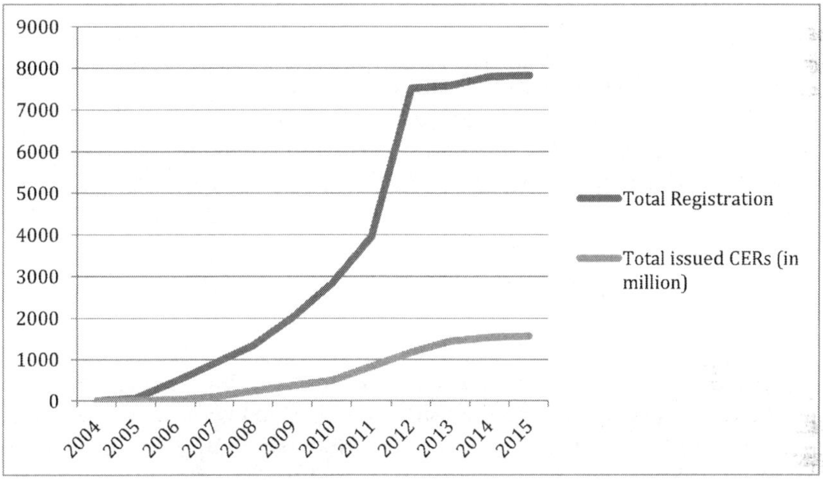

45 Data compiled from United Nations Climate Change Network, *Clean Development Mechanism,* https://cdm.unfccc.int/Statistics/Public/index.html (last visited January 11, 2020).

Graph 2: Second compliance period registered projects, projects issuing CERs and issued CERs[46]

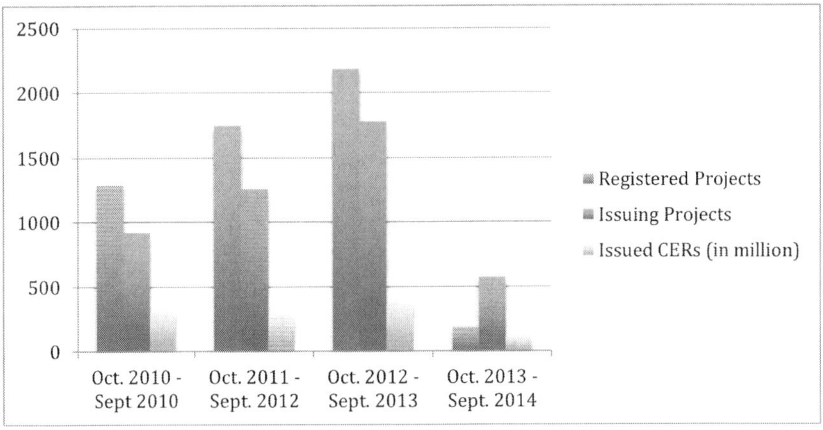

As of 2015, projects in China accounted for 48 percent of the expected CERs from registered projects; projects in India accounted for 15 percent, Brazil 9 percent, South Korea 8 percent, and projects in 45 other countries accounted for the remaining 20 percent.[47]

cc. CDM as linking instrument

Linking provisions allow for the linking of cap-and-trade systems. This can be achieved via direct linking, as established in California's cap-and-trade program, for example. Direct linking works by allowing participants of one cap-and-trade program to purchase and use allowances created in other programs to fulfill their compliance obligations. Direct linking provisions are complicated and therefore rare. Of all currently enacted U.S. cap-and-trade programs, only California's cap-and-trade system and, to

46 Market data compiled from Conference of the Parties serving as the meeting of the Parties to the Kyoto Protocol, *Annual Report of the Executive Board of the Clean Development Mechanism to the Conference of the Parties serving as the meeting of the Parties to the Kyoto Protocol* (November 6, 2014), http://unfccc.int/resource/docs/2014/cmp10/eng/05.pdf.

47 Judson Jaffe & Robert N. Stavins, *Linking U.S. Cap-and-Trade System for Greenhouse Gas Emissions: Opportunities, Implications, and Challenges* 6 (Reg-Markets Center, Working Paper 08-01, January 2008).

some degree, the Illinois Emissions Reduction System provides for direct linking. Weisbach identifies three general obstacles to the implementation of linking provisions: loss of political autonomy due to a loss of regulatory control over the respective emissions trading scheme, lobbying, and compatibility issues.[48]

However, links between cap-and-trade systems can also be established by indirect linking. The CDM establishes such indirect linking on an international level.

dd. The theoretical benefits of linking in the Kyoto context

In theory, linking has many advantages. Linking creates a bigger market for emission allowances and thus theoretically reduces abatement costs. For example, Trotignon[49] found that in the first two years of the Phase II (Kyoto) compliance period from 2008–2009, participants in the European Union Emissions Trading system saved at least 280 million Euro by purchasing emissions credits from other Kyoto countries instead of investing in higher-cost abatement technology.

In addition to that, bigger markets with more participants allow for more trading, which increases the market's liquidity.

Those advantages can even be extended: In theory, an international linking system could provide mechanisms "for countries to coordinate and harmonize their emissions caps, price controls, and other design features. By encouraging systems to work together through decentralized negotiations, linkage could, in principle, take the place of a centralized top-down climate agreement.[50] One objective of this paper is to evaluate and review whether an international linking system could be an alternative approach to the Kyoto Protocol, which is widely considered a failure; this is discussed in the next section. Amongst other conditions, this would, of course, require sufficient evidence indicating that linkage could cause the emission reductions necessary for combating climate change.

---

48 STEFAN WEISHAAR, EMISSIONS TRADING DESIGN: A CRITICAL OVERVIEW 193 (2014).

49 Raphael Trotignon, *Combining Cap-and-Trade with Offsets: Lessons from the EU-ETS*, 12 CLIMATE POLICY 280 (2012).

50 Matthew Ranson & Robert N. Stavins, *Linkage of Greenhouse Gas Emissions Trading Systems: Learning from Experience* 2. (Harvard Project on Climate Agreements, Discussion Paper ES 2013-2, November 2013).

4. Why the Kyoto Protocol failed

The Kyoto Protocol used a centralized top-down approach. It divided its signatories into "developed" and "non-developed" parties with different responsibilities regarding emissions abatement, which has been criticized. According to some scholars, "[t]he Kyoto Protocol is a symbolically important expression of governments' concern about climate change. But as an instrument for achieving emissions reductions, it has failed."[51] And indeed, while some countries have reduced their emissions after signing the Kyoto Protocol, data shows that no significant measurable emissions reductions related to the Protocol were achieved across all member countries.[52]

As discussed above, the parties to the Kyoto Protocol relied heavily on the flexibility mechanisms permitted by the Protocol, specifically on international emissions trading under Article 17. However, the top-down creation of an international market for emissions has seemingly failed as "[…] there is little sign of a stable global carbon price emerging in the next 5–10 years. Even if such a price were to be established, it is likely to be modest—sufficient only to stimulate efficiency gains."[53]

Leal-Arcas, for example, argues that to be effective, a post-Kyoto policy needs to include all major emitters, irrespective of GDP. He does not consider the Kyoto Protocol's focus on involving developing countries as a plausible approach to climate change.[54] And, indeed, especially the U.S. maintained that the regulative focus on "developed countries," as questionably defined in the Protocol, gave non-Annex I Parties an unfair commercial advantage. This might have been a factor in the decision by the U.S. not to ratify the Protocol.[55] Australia did not ratify the Protocol for similar reasons.[56]

The Kyoto Protocol was modeled after the Montreal Protocol on Substances that Deplete the Ozone Layer.[57] Yet, while the Montreal Protocol

---

51 Prins & Rayner, *supra* note 2, at 973.

52 *Cf.* Exhibit 3.

53 *Cf.* note 50.

54 Rafael Leal-Arcas, *Top-Down Versus Bottom-Up Approaches for Climate Change Negotiations: An Analysis*, 6 The IUP Journal of Governance and Public Policy 8 (December 2011).

55 *Cf.* Hunter et al., *supra* note 19, at 689.

56 *Cf. infra* p. 87 and the discussion of "non-minimizing" behavior.

57 Available online at http://ozone.unep.org/pdfs/Montreal-Protocol2000.pdf (last visited July 8, 2015).

is widely considered a successful program, the Kyoto Protocol failed at achieving its goals. This is not entirely surprising as the premises of these protocols are very different: ozone depletion can be considered a relatively simple issue compared to climate change. Ozone depletion is caused by a relatively small class of artificial gases used by a relatively small class of industries. Through research and development, alternatives for such gases were found and widely utilized shortly after enactment of the Montreal Protocol, a relatively simple solution that would not be feasible for climate change, which can be traced to the usage of a variety of greenhouse gases emitted across various industries and private households. In contrast to gases causing ozone depletion, alternative technology replacing the combustion of fossil fuels is hard to utilize. Indeed, "[o]n present trends, for another 20 years, the world will continue installing carbon-intensive infrastructure, such as coal power plants, with a 50-year lifetime."[58] A national bottom-up approach has the potential to be more flexible and efficient, especially as national emissions trading has shown a tendency to move towards more stringent caps. A regime addressing climate change must necessarily be flexible as on the one hand, perception and understanding of climate change evolves, and on the other hand, impact assessment for industry and sources change. This is a similar idea to the argument made by the authors of the Hartwell Paper, who propose an alternate understanding of the climate change paradigm. To illustrate their point, they borrow from urban planning terminology and refer to climate change as a "wicked" problem,[59] as opposed to "simple" pollution as a "tame"[60] problem.[61] In this paradigm, ozone depletion is a well understood problem with a more or less straightforward solution, whereas

> *[r]ather than being a discrete problem to be solved, climate change is better understood as a persistent condition that must be coped with and can only be partially managed more—or less—well. It is just one part of a larger complex of such conditions encompassing population, technology, wealth disparities, resource use, etc. Hence it is not straightforwardly an "environmental" problem either. It is axiomatically as much an energy problem, an economic*

58 Prins & Rayner, *supra* note 2, at 974.

59 "Comprising open, complex and imperfectly understood systems."

60 "Complicated, but with defined and achievable end-states."

61 Prins et. al., *The Hartwell Paper: A New Direction for Climate Policy after the Crash of 2009* 15 (Institute for Science, Innovation & Society, University of Oxford; LSE Mackinder Programme, London School of Economics and Political Science, 2010).

development problem or a land-use problem, and may be better approached through these avenues than as a problem of managing the behaviour of the Earth's climate by changing the way that humans use energy.[62]

This understanding would suggest a different approach to climate change: from the aim to preventing climate change to the aim of a sustainable management of climate change, especially considering the growing access to electricity in developing countries (*cf.* Graph 4), which corresponds with an increasing demand leading to higher emissions.

Graph 4: Greenhouse Gas Emissions Growth Projections[63]

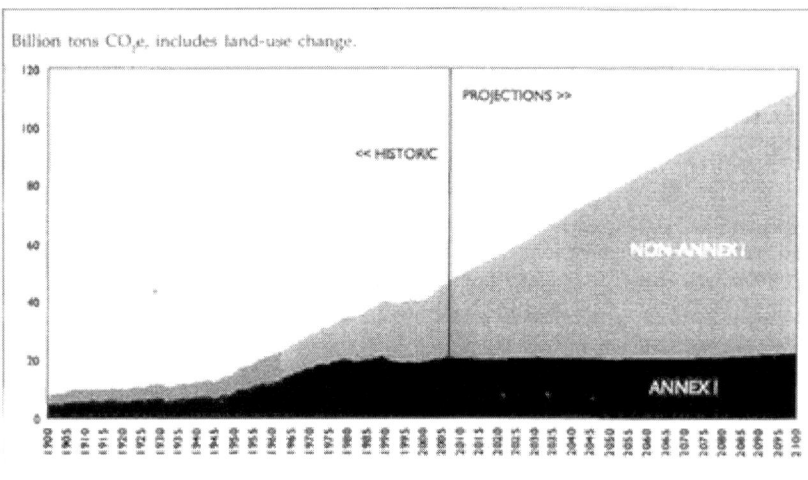

Source: Historic Emissions from Carbon Dioxide Information Analysis Center (2009); and Projected Emissions Growth from International Energy Agency (2009)

In addition to climate change being a significantly more complex issue than ozone depletion, the approach modeled after the Montreal Protocol had one significant issue. Unlike the Montreal Protocol, the Kyoto Protocol was not able to establish a club in the meaning defined above. As discussed,

[t]he major conditions for a successful club include the following: that there is a public-good-type resource that can be shared [...]; that the cooperative

62 Prins et. al., *supra* note 61, at 16.
63 Leal-Arcas, *supra* note 54, at 09.

> *arrangement, including the dues, is beneficial for each of the members; that non-members can be excluded or penalized at relatively low cost to members; and that the membership is stable in the sense that no one wants to leave.*[64]

Since the Montreal Protocol targeted a relatively small class of pollutants and products that are connected with such pollutants, regulators were able to include trade sanctions into the Protocol. These trade sanctions functioned, *inter alia,* as a non-compliance tool and, more importantly, as a club-building tool: for example, the Protocol forbid parties to the Protocol to engage in commerce relating to any of the controlled pollutants with non-parties.[65] In the context of club-building as displayed above, such trade-sanctions ensured that cost of membership was lower than the cost of non-membership, as no country wanted to lose access to other markets. Thus, the Montreal Protocol effectively built a club in order to eliminate the free-rider issue. In contrast, the Kyoto Protocol did not contain related provisions. Any relevant club-building efforts were limited to climate finance and the CDM, which can work as incentives but do not establish a penalty for non-members.

5. Kyoto results and the Copenhagen Accord

Subsequent to the issues with the Kyoto Protocol discussed above, a diplomatic effort to maximize the Protocol's potential ensued. The attempt to include the major emitters like the U.S. and potentially India and China, *inter alia,* led to the Copenhagen negotiations, which in the course of the fifteenth CoP meeting resulted in the non-binding "Copenhagen Accord," a document containing non-binding "general approaches for cooperation in financing, foresting and reporting of emissions, all in an effort to limit global average temperature increase to less than 2°C above pre-industrial levels."[66] The U.S. was a party to the Copenhagen Accord.

The Kyoto Protocol's first commitment period started in 2008 and ended in 2012 with limited results.[67] Subsequently, the Kyoto Parties drafted the "Doha Amendment to the Kyoto Protocol" on December 2008 following the understanding reached in Bali. Amongst other commitments,

---

64 *Cf.* note 9.

65 Montreal Protocol on Substances That Deplete the Ozone Layer, art. 4 1, Sept. 16, 1987, 522 U.N.T.S. 3; *see also* note 56.

66 Hunter et al., *supra* note 19, at 610.

67 *Cf.* Exhibit 3.

some of the Kyoto Parties agreed on a second commitment period from January 1, 2013 to December 31, 2020.[68] Some countries (e.g., Canada, Japan, and New Zealand[69] have not agreed to new targets. Amongst this group of countries is also the Russian Federation, which has been incentivized to participate in the first commitment period. The Ukraine, which was also incentivized to join with a zero abatement obligation, has stated that it will not reduce emissions in the second commitment period.[70] However, while not agreeing to any emissions reductions, China became a party to the Doha Amendment by depositing its instrument of acceptance on June 2, 2014.[71]

Collectively, these excluded countries produce 70 percent of all emissions within the OECD (Organization for Economic Co-operation and Development} and Russia.[72] (*Cf.* Exhibit 3.)

Ultimately, the free-rider nature of climate change shown in the excluded countries and the corresponding conflicting interests may be too diverse to reach an effective agreement from the top-down. As discussed above, state sovereignty rights and the "Westphalian rules" provide that nation states cannot be forced into entering a global legal regime against their will.

Consequently, for any future climate change regime to be effective, it must be able to address different expectations and problem sets as well as develop strong pull-factors for nation states to form a "climate club." In view of this paradigm, a "bottom-up" approach could be potentially more efficient at accommodating diverse interests while still maintaining environmental integrity and efficiency and could be a valid alternative approach to the current regime. As one scholar said, "[i]nternational pledges grow out of, and reflect, domestic policies, rather than being superimposed on them."[73]

---

68 UNFCC (2012), art. 1 (A), Doha Amendment to the Kyoto Protocol http://unfccc.int/files/kyoto_protocol/application/pdf/kp_doha_amendment_english.pdf (last visited January 11, 2020).

69 New Zealand instead implemented national measures, such as a national emissions trading system with linking potential.

70 Commentary, *Environmental Issues: Time to Abandon Blame-games and become Proactive*, The Economic Times, December 15, 2012.

71 United Nations Treaty Collection, Chapter XXVVII *Environment*, 7.c Doha Amendment to the Kyoto Protocol, December 8, 2010.

72 OECD Library, *Greenhouse Gas Emissions Data* from OECD Environment Statistics (2014), DOI: http://dx.doi.org/10.1787/data-00594-en (last visited January 11, 2020).

73 Daniel Bodansky, *A Tale of Two Architectures*, 43 Ariz. St. L.J. 16 (2011).

This theory will be reviewed in the following pages and tested against experiences gained from enacted emissions trading systems.

Exhibit 3: OECD and Russia greenhouse gas emissions (in tons)[74]

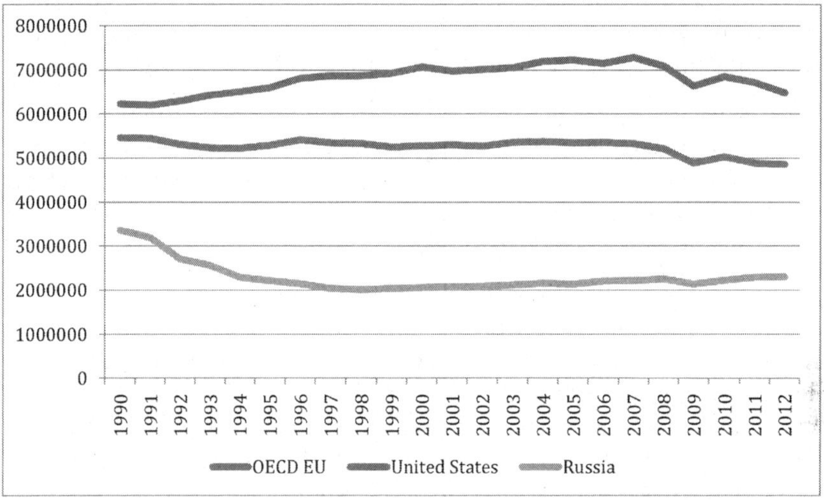

IV. The Paris Agreement

1. Basic content

Inter alia, following the Copenhagen Accord and the 2011 United Nations Climate Change Conference in Durban (the so called "Durban-Mandate"), in which the parties agreed to "launch a process to develop a protocol, another legal instrument or an agreed outcome with legal force under the Convention applicable to all Parties," FCCC/CP/2011/9/Add.1 preamble, the Paris Agreement was created in 2015.

Signed by 197 countries, the Paris Agreement went into force on November 4, 2016, after the ratification by at least fifty-five countries, which together account for roughly 55 percent of worldwide GHG emissions.[75] One hundred seventy of the 197 signatory countries have ratified

74 *Cf.* note 71.
75 *Cf.* UNFCCC, Information on Ratification Status, http://unfccc.int/paris_agreement/items/9444.php (last visited January 11, 2020).

the Agreement as of November 2017, among them China and the U.S., although the U.S. subsequently decided to leave the agreement.[76] Russia has signed the Agreement, but has not ratified it yet.[77]

Some scholars consider the Paris Agreement a "new era" of international environmental regulation.[78] Indeed, the Paris Agreement is the first internationally binding agreement to specify a global warming limit while at the same time eschewing binding emission reductions. The Agreement aims to hold

> *the increase in the global average temperature to well below 2°C above pre-industrial levels and pursuing efforts to limit the temperature increase to 1.5°C above pre-industrial levels, recognizing that this would significantly reduce the risks and impacts of climate change.*[79]

The 2°C temperature limit reflects the current scientific consensus on the "tipping-point," after which climate change becomes irreversible. It therefore substantiates the UNFCCC objective of "preventing dangerous anthropogenic interference," Article 2 UNFCCC. To achieve this binding target, each party agreed to prepare, communicate, and maintain successive nationally determined contributions that it intends to achieve. The parties shall pursue domestic mitigation measures with the aim of achieving the objectives of such contributions, Article 4, para. 2 of the Agreement. This contains a binding obligation of the participating states to achieve emission reductions.[80] However, these emission reductions, defined as intended nationally determined contributions (iNDC) in the Agreement, are voluntarily defined by the member states themselves.

These iNDCs are recorded in a public registry maintained by the UNFCCC secretariat. As of March 27, 2017, a total of 134 parties have submitted

---

76 An expressly permitted possibility under art. 28 of the Paris Agreement.

77 *Cf.* United Nations Treaty Collection, https://treaties.un.org/pages/ViewDetails.aspx?src=TREATY&mtdsg_no=XXVII-7-d&chapter=27&clang=_en (last visited January 11, 2020).

78 Morgenstern, Lutz, Dehnen, Milan, *Eine neue Ära für den internationalen Klimaschutz: Das* Übereinkommen von Paris, Zeitschrift für Umweltrecht (ZUR), 2016, 131; Kreuter-Kirchhof, Charlotte, Das Pariser Klimaschutzübereinkommen und die Grenzen des Rechts - eine neue Chance für den Klimaschutz, Deutsches Verwaltungsblatt (DVBL) 2, 2017, 97.

79 Art. 2 para. 1 Paris Agreement.

80 *Cf.* Morgenstern , Lutz, Dehnen, Milan, Eine neue Ära für den internationalen Klimaschutz: Das Übereinkommen von Paris, Zeitschrift für Umweltrecht (ZUR), 2016, 131, 133.

their NDCs to the secretariat.[81] For example, the U.S. initially submitted an economy-wide NDC of a GHG emissions reduction of 26-28 percent below its 2005 level in 2025 and pledged to make best efforts to reduce its emissions by 28 percent. The U.S. initially announced that it does not intend to use international emissions trading to achieve this reduction.[82] In comparison, the European Union has announced an NDC of "at least 40 percent domestic reduction in greenhouse gas emissions by 2030 compared to 1990, to be fulfilled jointly."[83] As such targets are generally considered insufficient for the two-degree limit specified in Article 2 of the Agreement,[84] Article 4, para. 9 provides that each party shall communicate a further nationally determined contribution (NDC) every five years. Under Article 4, para. 3, each NDC "will" fall below the previously communicated NDC,[85] thus effecting a progressive reduction of emissions by all parties. Article 4, para. 3 states that "[e]ach Party's successive nationally determined contribution will represent a progression beyond the Party's then current nationally determined contribution and reflect its highest possible ambition, reflecting its common but differentiated responsibilities and respective capabilities, in the light of different national circumstances." It is therefore important to differentiate between the iNDCs under Article 4, para. 2 and the NDCs under Article 4, paras. 3 and 9.

An important and disputed question is whether this establishes an emissions reduction obligation of the parties, i.e., whether the iNDCs or the NDCs stipulated in the Agreement are binding.

---

81 *See* UNFCCC Secretariat, Interim NDC Registry, http://www4.unfccc.int/ndcregistry/Pages/Home.aspx (last visited January 11, 2020).

82 *Cf.* Morgenstern & Dehnen, *supra* note 78, at 81.

83 *Cf.* note 80.

84 *Cf.* note 80.

85 *Cf.* below for a discussion of this wording and whether this effects a binding obligation.

2. Legal character

Most scholars understand both iNDCs and NDCs as self-commitments made by the parties, not binding reduction obligations.[86] While some scholars do not further explain this reasoning,[87] the technical argument advanced in favor of the non-binding characteristic is that the emission reduction contributions are not part of the Agreement, but rather a separate registry and can therefore not be binding obligations.[88] In international law scholarship, this is characterized as an "obligation to conduct" as opposed to an "obligation of result."[89] This is correct, but requires further examination. The iNDCs, of course, are not part of the Agreement. However, the NDCs are. Under Article 4, para. 3, parties "will represent a progression beyond the Party's then current nationally determined contribution." The Agreement therefore does provide wording on successive emissions reductions. The question is, therefore, not whether the nationally determined contributions are part of the Agreement, but rather whether the mechanism established by Article 4, para. 3 is binding. The Vienna Convention on the Law of Treaties, as recognized binding legal framework for international treaties,[90] states that the legal principle of *pacta sunt servanda* is also recognized in international treaties. Under Article 26 of the Vienna Convention, every treaty in force is binding upon the parties to it and must be performed by them in good faith.[91] However, international treaties contain a multitude of different provisions, and not all them are intended to be binding by the parties. Whether this is the case depends on the wording chosen by the parties, especially on the choice of verbs. While "shall," as in Article 4, para. 2 of the Agreement relating to the preparation of iNDCs, generally produces a legal obligation, verbs such as "will" iden-

---

86 *Cf.*, for example, Meinhard Doelle, *The Paris Agreement: Historic Breakthrough or High Stakes Experiment?* 6 CLIMATE LAW 1-20 (Special Issue, 2016); Kreuter-Kirchhof, Charlotte, Das Pariser Klimaschutzübereinkommen und die Grenzen des Rechts - eine neue Chance für den Klimaschutz, Deutsches Verwaltungsblatt (DVBL) 2, 2017, 97.

87 *Cf.* note 86.

88 *Cf.* Morgenstern & Dehnen, *supra* note 80.

89 *Cf.* note 80.

90 The Vienna Convention was ratified by 114 states. Nation states that did not ratify the Convention, such as the U.S., view it as customary international law and therefore consider it as binding, *cf.* U.S. Department of State, Statement regarding the Vienna Convention on the Law of Treaties, https://www.state.gov/s/l/treaty/faqs/70139.htm (last visited January 11, 2020).

91 Vienna Convention on the Law of Treaties, 1155 U.N.T.S. 331, 8 I.L.M. 679.

tify a statement "by the parties about their goals, values, expectations, or collective opinions."[92] Article 4, para. 3 uses the verb "will." The successive NDCs are therefore, just like the iNDCs, not a binding emissions reduction obligation, but rather an intended goal shared by the parties. It refers to an "obligation to conduct" and not an "obligation of result." Frank considers this as an intended regulatory gap and proposes the application of international environmental law to fill the gap.[93] By application of, *inter alia*, the no-harm rule and the "highest possible ambitions"-standard,[94] Frank argues that the Paris Agreement parties are obliged to achieve their iNDCs and NDCs. In the language of international law, this would be a "wrongful act" allowing nation states harmed by climate change, such as small island countries, to request emission reductions from other parties.[95] While this reasoning is attractive from an environmental point of view, the record shows that the non-binding character of the emission reduction rules was not an unintended result but rather an intentional choice by the parties. For example, the U.S. delegation expressly advanced concerns regarding binding obligations, arguing that the U.S. Congress's majority ratios would not allow a binding obligation.[96] Accordingly, the non-binding character is not a regulatory gap and does not allow for such interpretation. However, that does not mean that international law becomes inapplicable. The "obligation to conduct" established in the Agreement has to be understood in the context of international law, which can help to substantiate the concrete obligations of the parties. For example, the general principles of international law as well as the obligation to prevent dangerous anthropogenic interference under Article 2 of the UNFCCC binds the parties in their realization of the Agreement's obligations. How-

---

92 Daniel Bodansky, *The Legal Character of the Paris Agreement*, 25 Review of European, Comparative and International Environmental Law 142-150 (2016).

93 Frank, Will, Anmerkungen zum Pariser Klimavertrag aus rechtlicher Sicht - insbesondere zu den „(I)NDCs", der 2°/1,5° Celsius-Schwelle und „loss and damage" im Kontext völkerrechtlicher Klimaverantwortung, Zeitschrift für Umweltrecht (ZUR), 2016, 352.

94 The international environmental law and how it relates to global change" is discussed *infra* in Chapter C.

95 *Cf.* note 93.

96 *See*, for example, Morgenstern, Lutz, Dehnen, Milan, Eine neue Ära für den internationalen Klimaschutz: Das Übereinkommen von Paris, Zeitschrift für Umweltrecht (ZUR), 2016, 131, 133 on the process of defining NDCs, starting with the Warsaw COP.

ever, the practical implications of such are limited as they do not exceed the already binding obligations in Articles 2 and 4 of the Agreement. [97]

While the enforcement mechanism of any given clause does not allow conclusions on the legal character of the clause,[98] the non-binding character of the emissions reductions intended in the Agreement ultimately also follows from the "reporting and compliance" mechanism in the Agreement, called "global stocktaking." Under Article 14, the CoP shall periodically take stock of the implementation of the Paris Agreement to assess the collective progress towards achieving the purpose of the Agreement and its long-term goals. Article 15 of the Agreement establishes an expert committee as a mechanism to facilitate implementation and promote compliance with the provisions of the Agreement. However, the Agreement expressly classifies this as a non-punitive compliance instrument, Article 15, para. 2 of the Agreement.

3. The Paris Agreement and emissions trading

Under Article 4, para. 2 of the Paris Agreement, the parties shall pursue domestic mitigation measures with the aim of achieving the objectives of the NDCs. This gives parties full discretion regarding their national policy approaches in order to achieve desired emissions reductions. Emissions trading on a national level is therefore still allowed without any further express restrictions from the Agreement, subsequent to the following.[99]

In addition, the Paris Agreement contains additional rules for international emissions trading. Article 6, para. 2 states that

> *[p]arties shall, where engaging on a voluntary basis in cooperative approaches that involve the use of internationally transferred mitigation outcomes*

---

97 For a discussion regarding the influence of international environmental law on the binding nature of targets in the Paris Agreement, *see* Ekardt, Felix, Das Paris Abkommen zum globalen Klimaschutz, Chancen und Friktionen - auf dem Weg zu einer substantiellen EU-Vorreiterrolle?, NVwZ 2016, 355.

98 "As with justiciability, enforcement is not a necessary condition for an instrument or norm to be legally binding. If a norm is created through a recognized law-making process, then it is legally binding, whether or not there are any specific sanctions for violations. Conversely, enforcement does not depend on legal form, since non-legal norms can also be enforced through the application of sanctions." *Cf.* note 92.

99 Whether another result follows from international environmental law is discussed *infra* in chapter C.V.

> *towards nationally determined contributions, promote sustainable development and ensure environmental integrity and transparency, including in governance, and shall apply robust accounting to ensure, inter alia, the avoidance of double counting, consistent with guidance adopted by the Conference of the Parties serving as the meeting of the Parties to this Agreement.*

While this Article itself does not establish an international carbon market due to its conditional wording, the creation of "internationally transferred mitigation outcomes" (ITMOs), i.e., national emission reduction credits, allows the parties to create a national or even regional carbon market or to link their existing markets.[100] Most of the details on the creation and transfer of such ITMOs are still subject to debate.[101] Besides those open questions, the concrete result of Article 6 remains unclear. Given the non-binding character of emission reduction obligations in the Agreement and the lack of clear accounting rules, the parties have no real incentive to engage in international trading.

However, with a reference to environmental integrity, the article reads as a direct response to the shortcomings of international emissions trading and the CDM discussed above, particularly the lack of environmental integrity. This may also limit the parties' discretion regarding the use of (international) emissions trading: they may only continue to engage in international trading if environmental integrity is ensured. This will be discussed in depth later and used as relevant criteria for emissions trading going forward.

4. Summary: The Paris Agreement

The approach taken in the Paris Agreement differs from the Kyoto Protocol mainly in five aspects. One main aspect is the lack of binding emissions reductions. While the Kyoto Protocol mandated 2 percent emission reductions below pre-industrial levels with certain countrywide defined emissions allowances, the Paris Agreement leaves emissions reductions

---

100 Böhringer, Ayşe-Martina Das neue Pariser Klimaübereinkommen - Eine Kompromisslösung mit Symbolkraft und Verhaltenssteuerungspotential, Zeitschrift für ausländisches öffentliches Recht und Völkerrecht (ZaörV) 2016, 753 (770).

101 *Cf.*, for example, Nicolas Kreibich and Wolfang Obergassel, *Carbon Markets After Paris - How to Account for the Transfer of Mitigation Results?* JIKO Policy Paper 01/2016. Wuppertal Institut für Klima, Umwelt, Energie. Wuppertal, 33. S. 2.

to its parties' discretion. The 2°C goal can therefore be understood as a political goal with a symbolic character, especially since global emissions would have to be reduced to zero before 2070 in order to achieve this target.[102] Related to this is the second main aspect of the Paris Agreement, which focuses on an expansive large-scale applicability. While the Kyoto Protocol also tried to incentivize large emitters to join, the Paris Agreement achieved this, but at the expense of binding targets. The Agreement achieves an even broader range of application by extending mitigation efforts to developing countries. The third aspect is the shift away from binding emissions reductions to binding limits on temperature increases. The reporting and transparency rules are the fourth aspect. Such rules build on the self-commitment undertaken by the parties in the Paris Agreement and establish a non-legal system encouraging emissions reduction. Finally, the Paris Agreement introduces an adaption framework into the body of internal law.

To sum up, the approach taken by the Paris Agreement can be classified into two systematic groups. For one, the Paris Agreement uses an "obligation to conduct" as opposed to an "obligation of result" approach as well as a "bottom-up" approach as opposed to a "top-down" approach. The strict bottom-up approach is supplemented by some top-down elements, such as a mandated reporting obligation.

In this context, an "obligation to conduct" as opposed to an "obligation of result" means that the parties only are mandated to perform a certain action but do not have to achieve a specific result.[103] Therefore, no binding emission reduction obligations follow from the Paris Agreement. Instead, the Agreement relies on the parties' self-interest regarding emission reductions. This "name-and-shame" or "name-and-encourage" in the official language[104] approach is certainly a paradigm change in international law.[105] Instead of a top-down binding emissions limit or other binding rules, the Paris Agreement relies on its parties' self-commitment as well as reporting and transparency rules to achieve the intended emissions.[106]

These rules introduce a top-down component to the bottom-up character of the self-commitment undertaken by the parties. Chapters F and G

102 Böhringer, *supra* note 100, at 761.
103 *See* note 80.
104 Janos Pastor, "Climate Negotiators Strike Deal to Slow Global Warming." CBS News, CBS Interactive Inc., December 12, 2015.
105 Whether past experiences with emissions trading suggest that this paradigm change is sensible will be discussed *infra* at Chapter F.
106 *Cf.* Böhringer, *supra* note 100, at 753.

will discuss this approach considering the experiences with U.S. emissions trading and will evaluate whether this supposed "pragmatic and innovative" approach can be successful.[107]

V. International legal principles relating to climate change

The emissions trading programs reviewed in this thesis are generally compliance tools within an overlying, higher ranking, regulation; i.e., they are tools permitted by the respective regulators to fulfill certain emission reduction targets or other regulative goals. Consequently, the success of such trading programs can be measured in how effective they are at achieving the desired or mandated reduction results.

In addition to fulfilling targets set out by their overlying regulation—i.e., national law that is discussed within the context of the respective systems, emissions trading systems, even those that are independent regulations and not a compliance tool in an overlying national regulation—must be understood not within a legal vacuum, but within the requirements of international environmental law. They must therefore comply with binding principles of international environmental law, as the highest-ranking applicable law. And, as will be shown later, even the non-binding principles of international law can have a substantial impact on national climate regulation.

The following is a discussion of the binding and non-binding principles and ideas that govern international environmental law and how they relate to the practice of emissions trading.

1. Introduction to international environmental law

International environmental law has two main points of relevance for the emissions trading systems reviewed in this thesis. As the highest-ranking law relating to the topic of pollution and emission control, any (nation-) state action must generally be compliant with the rules of contractual

107 Morgenstern & Dehnen, *supra* note 80, at 131, 134.

international environmental law, such as any international treatises and contracts it is a party to.[108]

Consequently, any domestic environmental regulation or compliance tool must be compliant with it as well. Emissions trading can therefore be reviewed against the principles set out by binding international environmental law.[109] As contractual environmental law is discussed above, the following discussion focuses mostly on customary international law, which is—other than contractual international law that is based on treatises, agreements, and contracts—created by custom (*longa consuetudo*) and recognition (*opinio juris*).[110] It should be noted that the differentiation between contractual and customary law is somewhat arbitrary as individual customary principles of international environmental law are codified in agreements and vice-versa.

2. Principles of international environmental law[111]

International law is, if not codified, often vague and unclear. As a result, the actual legal status of many principles of international environmental law is uncertain and subject to scholarly discussion. Hunter, Salzman, and Zaelke put forward the following thematic classification of binding and non-binding principles:[112]

I. Principles shaping global environmental and sustainable development instruments:
   (1) Right to life and a healthy environment
   (2) State sovereignty
   (3) Right to development
   (4) Sustainable development
   (5) Common heritage of mankind
   (6) Common Concern
   (7) The obligation not to cause environmental harm

108 The consequences of non-compliance with international environmental law and its enforceability are separate topics. *Cf.* Frank, Will, Überlegungen zur Klimahaftung nach Völkerrecht, Neue Zeitschrift für Verwaltungsrecht (NVwZ)-Extra, 2014.

109 Maguire, *supra* at 91.

110 Durner in Landmann/Rohmer, Umweltrecht, Umweltvölkerrecht, Rn. 18

111 The term "principles" is used for both binding and non-binding principles of international law.

112 Hunter et al., *supra* note 19, at 441.

(8) Intergenerational and intragenerational equity
(9) Common but differentiated responsibilities
(10) Precautionary principle
(11) Duty to assess environmental impacts
(12) Principle of subsidiarity
(13) Right of public participation
(14) Prior informed consent

II. Principles relating to transboundary environmental disputes
(1) Peaceful resolution of disputes
(2) Good neighborliness and duty to cooperate
(3) The duty not to cause environmental harm
(4) State responsibility
(5) Duty to notify and consult
(6) Duty to assess environmental impacts
(7) Equitable utilization of shared resources
(8) Non-discrimination of environmental harms
(9) Equal right of access to justice
(10) Prior informed consent
(11) Duty to enact and ensure compliance with effective environmental laws

III. Principles for developing national environmental laws
(1) Duty to implement effective environmental laws
(2) Polluter and user pays principle
(3) Pollution prevention
(4) Precautionary principle
(5) Duty to assess environmental impacts
(6) Principle of subsidiary
(7) Public participation
(8) Access to information
(9) Access to justice
(10) Free, prior informed consent

IV. Principles governing international institutions
(1) Duty to assess environmental impacts
(2) Public participation
(3) Access to information and transparency
(4) Sustainable development
(5) Free, prior informed consent

Not all of the mentioned principles have a clear status. Others have overlapping areas of application with other environmental or general international law principles. For example, the principle of good neighborliness and the obligation to resolve disputes peacefully can just as well be seen as a reflection of the application of general international law principles to environmental issues.[113]

The following discussion therefore focuses on a few core fundamental principles with special importance, especially relating to the law of climate change.

a. The Principle of Sustainable Development

Given its scope and applicability, the Principle of Sustainable Development is one of the most fundamental principles[114] in international environmental law.

aa. History of the Principle of Sustainable Development

Several new theories were developed in the 1980s as a result of growing attention to environmental issues. Amongst others,[115] the "school of ecological economics," founded in the 1980s as a multidisciplinary school of thought with the aim of addressing the world's growing environmental problem more efficiently,[116] proposed a shift in the perception of economic activity as it pertains to the environment. This resulted mostly in the insight that all economic activity must also be environmentally sustainable. In contrast to traditional economic scholarship, which treated natural resources as limitless,[117] environmental economics proposed that natural resources are finite. As a consequence, natural resources must be considered as capital alongside manufactured capital, e.g., infrastructure and social capital, education and institutions. This natural capital is defined as

113 Hunter et al., *supra* note 19, at 439.

114 Scholars argue whether Sustainable Development is a fixed principle of international environmental law. This argument is discussed below.

115 International Union for Conservation of Nature and Natural Resources, *World Conservation Strategy: Living Resource Conservation for Sustainable Development*, (1980), https://portals.iucn.org/library/sites/library/files/documents/WCS-004.pdf (last visited January 11, 2020).

116 Hunter et al., *supra* note 19, at 117.

117 *Cf.* A.D. Basiago, *Economic, Social, and Environmental Sustainability in Development Theory and Urban Planning Practice* 19 The Environmentalist 146 f. (1999).

"the stock of environmentally-provided assets that provides a useful flow of goods or services."[118]

Referring to the general economic definition of sustainability as the "maintenance of capital," this economic scholarship considers the state of environmental sustainability to be achieved when such natural capital is maintained.[119] One implication of this insight is that any development may only occur within this limit.

Building onto this academic discussion, the United Nations World Commission on Environment and Development (WCED) published a report titled "Our Common Future in 1987."[120] The report, mostly referred to as the "Brundtland-Report" after the Commission's chairwoman, former Norwegian Prime Minister Gro Harlem Brundtland, coined the term "sustainable development." The report defines sustainable development as

> *development that meets the needs of the present without compromising the ability of future generations to meet their own needs. It contains within it two key concepts:*
> - *the concept of "needs," in particular the essential needs of the world's poor, to which overriding priority should be given; and*
> - *the idea of limitations imposed by the state of technology and social organization on the environment's ability to meet present and future needs.*[121]

The 1992 United Nations Conference on Environment and Development (UNCED), often referred to as the "Earth Summit," took up the term. The conference resulted (amongst other things) in the "Rio Declaration on Environment and Development," whose Annex I established the Principle of Sustainable Development as a core principle.[122] Accordingly, the Principle of Sustainable Development was integrated into international and domestic legislation concerning environmental law,[123] and it can therefore

118 Robert Goodland & Herman Daly, *Environmental Sustainability: Universal and Non-Negotiable*, 6 Ecological Applications 1002–1017 (1996).

119 *Cf.* note 118

120 The report is available online under http://www.un-documents.net/wced-ocf.htm (last visited February 25, 2017).

121 Chapter 2; see note 120.

122 Available online at http://www.un.org/documents/ga/conf151/aconf15126-1annex1.htm (last visited February 25, 2017).

123 *See* Epiney/Scheyli, Strukturprinzipien des Umweltvölkerrechts, 1998, S. 36 ff, for a list.

be considered a fixed principle of international environmental law.[124] German national constitutional law (Section 20a of the German Constitution), for example, refers to the protection of the environment as a "responsibility to future generations," which national legal scholarship considers as a referral to the Principle of Sustainable development.[125] The Principle also plays a significant role in international and national jurisprudence. For example, in its famous Gabcikovo-Nagymaros case,[126] the International Court of Justice (ICJ) relied on the Principle of Sustainable Development as both parties argued over a dam in the river Danube. They pointed to the need to evaluate the environmental effect of the dam in order to "reconcile economic development with protection of the environment [as] aptly expressed in the concept of sustainable development."[127] Citing the Gabcikovo-Nagymaros case, the Permanent Court of Arbitration (PCA) at The Hague subsequently confirmed the Principle of Sustainable Development in its 2005 Iron Rhine arbitration award[128] as a principle of general international law.[129] In 2010, the ICJ again relied on the Principle of Sustainable Development in its Pulp Mill on the River Uruguay decision.[130]

bb. Definition

Despite this consistent usage in international legislation, legal scholarship is divided on the exact meaning of the Principle of Sustainable Develop-

124 Epiney, Astrid, Zur Einführung - Umweltvölkerrecht, JuS 2003, 1066; Sands, Philippe and Jaqueline Peel, *Principles of International Environmental Law*, 3. Edition (2012), p. 208.

125 *Durner* in Landmann/Rohmer, Umweltrecht, Umweltvölkerrecht, Rn. 57.

126 ICJ, Gabčíkovo–Nagymaros, *supra* note 38.

127 ICJ, Gabčíkovo–Nagymaros, *supra* note 38, at 7, 78.

128 Permanent Court of Arbitration, Iron Rhine Arbitration (Belgium v Netherlands), Award, 2005, ICGJ 373 (PCA 2005), May 24; see also Christian Djeffal, The Iron Rhine Case - A Treaty's Journey from Peace to Sustainable Development, Zeitschrift für ausländisches öffentliches Recht und Völkerrecht (ZaöRV) 2011, 569.

129 Permanent Court of Arbitration, Iron Rhine Arbitration, *supra* note 128, at 67.

130 International Court of Justice (ICJ), Pulp Mills on the River Uruguay (Argentina v Uruguay), Order, Provisional Measures, 2006 ICJ GL No 135 ICJ Rep 113 (July 13).

ment outside of its contractual usage. Some scholars use this as an argument against the status of the principle as customary international law.[131]

According to a majority in legal scholarship, the principle demands a balancing of ecological, economic, and social interests.[132]

The reference to economic development is an important, albeit easily overlooked component of the Principle of Sustainable Development. As we still live in a largely carbon-based economy, the best outcome for the environment would most likely be achieved with a "Club of Rome" no-growth scenario. As this would conflict with the "Right to Development," another principle of international environmental law under which "every human person and all peoples are entitled to participate in, contribute to, and enjoy economic [...] development [...],"[133] the Principle of Sustainable Development includes a reference to development, thus expressly allowing economic development even at the expense of environmental integrity. The Rio Declaration recognizes this tension between economic development and environmental protection and states:

> *Principle 3*
> *The right to development must be fulfilled so as to equitably meet developmental and environmental needs of present and future generations.*

> *Principle 4*
> *In order to achieve sustainable development, environmental protection shall constitute an integral part of the development process and cannot be considered in isolation from it.*

In short, the Principle of Sustainable Development demands reconciliation between economic development and environmental protection. The exact balancing process is not defined and hard to generalize outside of individual cases. Instructive language on the application of the principle can be found in the ICJ's decision on the Gabcikovo-Nagymaros case cited above. Herein, the ICJ argues:

> *Throughout the ages, mankind has, for economic and other reasons, constantly interfered with nature. In the past, this was often done without consideration of the effects upon the environment. Owing to new scientific*

---

131 *Cf.* for example, *Durner* in Landmann/Rohmer, Umweltrecht, Umweltvölkerrecht, Rn. 57.

132 *See* Epiney, Astrid, Zur Einführung - Umweltvölkerrecht, JuS 2003, 1066; c.f. also Sieben, Peter, Was bedeutet Nachhaltigkeit als Rechtsbegriff?, Neue Zeitschrift für Verwaltungsrecht (NVwZ), 1173.

133 G.A. Res. 41/128, Declaration on the Right to Development (Dec. 4, 1986).

> *insights and to a growing awareness of the risks for mankind—for present and future generations—of pursuit of such interventions at an unconsidered and unabated pace, new norms and standards have been developed, set forth in a great number of instruments during the last two decades. Such new norms have to be taken into consideration, and such new standards given proper weight, not only when States contemplate new activities but also when continuing with activities begun in the past. This need to reconcile economic development with protection of the environment is aptly expressed in the concept of sustainable development.*[134]

For the Gabcikovo-Nagymaros power plant, this meant that the construction of the plant and the corresponding damming of approximately 200 km of the Danube (a measure of economic development) was not prohibited. Rather the ICJ obliged the parties to further consider the effects of the proposed construction on the environment and find solutions to mitigate adverse effects. In this context, the Principle of Sustainable Development becomes essentially a procedural right, similar to the Precautionary Principle.[135] In addition to this procedural dimension, the Rio Declaration's focus on the needs of present and future generations results in another very practical application of the principle: economic usage of natural resources may only occur to the point where the need of future generations for such a resource is secured.[136] Other scholars argue that a concept focusing on balance between ecological, economic, and social interests as equal parts is too arbitrary and unclear to contain any practical legal content. They argue that consequently, in order to deliver the legal content implied by its status as customary law principle, the Principle of Sustainable Development must be primarily focused on ecological protection.[137] This conclusion is not compelling. While a balance of seemingly opposing concepts (such as economic development and ecological protection) is hard to achieve, it is only unclear if one concept is given priority over another. Compared to other cases where a balancing of legally protected interests is required, such as data protection, free speech laws etc., the principle is a very straightforward one: economic development is allowed,

---

134 *See* note 126.

135 *See* in this document, section g. The Due Diligence Principle, for a discussion of this principle.

136 *Durner* in Landmann/Rohmer, Umweltrecht, Umweltvölkerrecht, Rn. 57

137 *Kahl* in *Bauer/Czybulka/Kahl/Voßkuhle*, Umwelt, Wirtschaft und Recht, 2002, S. 111 ff. (122 ff.); Epiney, Astrid, Zur Einführung - Umweltvölkerrecht, JuS 2003, 1066 with further citations.

but only to the extent that it does not harm the environment in an unsustainable fashion. Moreover, its value as procedural right as seen in the Gabcikovo-Nagymaros case should not be underestimated.

b. The Principle of Sovereignty and Territorial Integrity

State sovereignty is a general principle of international law not limited to international environmental law. However, many fundamental international environmental law principles, such as the Precautionary Principle and the Principle of Prevention discussed below, are rooted in the general Principle of State Sovereignty and territorial integrity.

(Territorial) sovereignty means that nation states may exercise sovereign power within the borders of their jurisdiction with full discretion to the extent that it does not conflict with international law.[138] The Principle of Territorial Integrity protects nation states from any adverse effects resulting from other state's jurisdiction.[139]

c. The Precautionary Principle and Principle of Prevention

The Precautionary Principle and the Principle of Prevention are both concepts of customary international law resulting from sovereignty rights.[140] Both have a somewhat overlapping area of application and will therefore both be discussed in this section.[141]

aa. The Precautionary Principle

The Precautionary Principle is a (disputed) principle of customary international environmental law.[142] It obliges nation states performing an action with potential adverse environmental impact to take all required measures to avoid environmental harm, even if there is no absolute scientific cer-

---

138 Epiney, *supra* note 124, at 1066, 1070.

139 *Cf.* note 138.

140 *See* Epiney, *supra* note 124.

141 Frank, Will, Schwarte, Christoph, Klimawandel und Völkerrecht - Anmerkungen zu den „Legal Principles Relating to Climate Change“ der International Law Association, Zeitschrift für Umweltrecht (ZUR) 2014, 643.

142 *Cf. Durner* in Landmann/Rohmer, Umweltrecht, Umweltvölkerrecht, Rn. 60;

tainty that environmental impact might occur or that there is causality between the state action and the environmental impact.[143] Read strictly, this effectively results in a shift of the burden of proof, as the nation state undertaking a potential harmful measure is obliged to act as though such a measure is harmful, unless it can prove otherwise.

While some scholars[144] consider the principle to be customary law, the ICJ has not yet confirmed this principle's status as customary law and has instead referred to it as relevant in the interpretation and application of the provisions of law, but not as operational in reversing of the burden of proof.[145] Therefore, although it may not be customary law, the principle has a significant governing effect. [146]

The Precautionary Principle seems to get less attention than, for example, the Principle of Sustainable Development, but it nevertheless has great significance in situations where scientific data is unclear or disputed. It is therefore especially important in the context of global warming, where some scientific data is still subject to debate. Under the Precautionary Principle, unclear data or lack of scientific consensus cannot be an argument against environmental regulation, something that politics and industry lobbying often overlook. This is also relevant for the emissions trading programs reviewed in this thesis. If the review of any given program shows that program design cannot ensure an actual and measurable reduction of emissions, the program must be considered non-compliant with international law within the applicability of the principle.

bb. The Principle of Prevention

Under the Principle of Prevention, nation states must ensure that activities within their jurisdiction and control respect the environment of other states or of areas beyond national control.[147] It obliges states to exercise

143 *See* Epiney, *supra* note 124.
144 *Id.* at 1066.
145 Pulp Mills on the River Uruguay, (Argentina v Uruguay), Judgement, 2010 ICJ Rep. 14, at 61 (April 20).
146 *Cf. Durner* in Landmann/Rohmer, Umweltrecht, Umweltvölkerrecht, Rn. 60.
147 *See* definition in ICJ, Legality of the Threat or Use of Nuclear Weapons, Advisory Opinion, 1996, I.C.J. Rep. 227, 226, 229 (Jul 8). The reference to "areas beyond national jurisdiction" is important as it refers to environmentally significant areas such as the Arctic or the high seas.

due diligence in order to prevent environmental damage in other states.[148] The Principle of Prevention is a core principle of customary international environmental law.[149] Culpable non-compliance, i.e., damage to another nation state's environment, results in a liability of the state causing the damages, as the affected state may demand compensation from the acting state.[150]

The principle originates from the 1930 Trail Smelter arbitration between the United States and Canada. Cause for the arbitration was a dispute between the operators of a smelter in British Columbia, Canada and landowners in the United States. Smoke from the smelter, located in Trail, B.C., just a few miles away from the U.S. border in Washington State, was blown into communities on the U.S. side of the Washington border. Their damage claims against the smelter gave reason for the arbitration after an interesting, thirteen-year-long procedural development.[151] The arbitration tribunal held that,

> *under the principles of international law, […] no State has the right to use or permit the use of its territory in such a manner as to cause injury by fumes in or to the territory of another or the properties or persons therein, when the case is of serious consequence and the injury is established by clear and convincing evidence.*

A similar concept, albeit not related to an environmental case, was confirmed in the ICJ's 1949 decision in the Corfu Channel case. The ICJ confirmed "every State's obligation not to allow knowingly its territory to be used for acts contrary to the rights of other States" as a principle of international law.[152] While the facts of the case had no relation to environmental issues and the decision seems to be rooted in general international law concerning state sovereignty rights, it has great significance for international environmental law as it further established principles governing territorial influences on other state's territories, which more often than not, have environmental significance.

---

148 *See Durner* in Landmann/Rohmer, Umweltrecht, Umweltvölkerrecht, Rn. 46.

149 ICJ, Legality of the Threat or Use of Nuclear Weapons, *supra* note 147.

150 *See supra* note 148.

151 *See* Martiin van de Kerkhof, *The Trail Smelter Case Re-examined: Examining the Development of National Procedural Mechanisms to Resolve a Trail Smelter Type Dispute*, 27 Utrecht Journal of International and European Law 68-83 (2011).

152 Corfu Channel Case (United Kingdom and Northern Ireland v Albania); Assessment of Compensation 15 XII 49 I.C.J. (December 15, 1949).

After the Nuclear Weapons Advisory Opinion mentioned above, the ICJ subsequently referred to the Principle in the Pulp Mill case[153] where it reassured the principle's status as customary international environmental law and pointed out

> *that the principle of prevention, as a customary rule, has its origins in the due diligence that is required of a State in its territory. It is every State's obligation not to allow knowingly its territory to be used for acts contrary to the rights of other States.*
> *A State is thus obliged to use all the means at its disposal in order to avoid activities, which take place in its territory, or in any area under its jurisdiction, causing significant damage to the environment of another State. This Court has established that this obligation is now part of the corpus of international law relating to the environment.*[154]

This language used by the ICJ shows that the Principle of Prevention in its modern form has, similar to the Principle of Sustainable Development, both substantive and procedural elements. For once, the principle obliges nation states to prevent actions within its territory from causing harmful influences on another nation states territory. In addition to such a substantive element, it also obliges nation states to "use all the means at its disposal in order to avoid activities which take place in its territory, or in any area under its jurisdiction, causing significant damage to the environment of another State."[155] This obligation to use all disposable means to avoid environmental damage in other states has a clear procedural dimension relevant for, *inter alia*, domestic environmental regulation.

Scholars have argued that this principle, which originated in cross-border fumigation cases, cannot be applied to environmental change.[156] They correctly argue that climate change as a phenomenon does not fit into the traditional legal and factual conception of transboundary pollution. Unlike "traditional" environmental damages resulting, for example, from fumigation, climate change is caused by a cumulative reaction to a multitude of possible sources and is therefore more complex and difficult to trace to a single nation state or state. Therefore, any harm resulting from climate change can be considered a result of joint failures of nation

153 *Cf.* note 130.
154 *Cf.* note. 130, at 101.
155 *Cf.* note 130 at 101.
156 Frank et al., *supra* note 141; also Christoph Schwarte, *"No Harm" Rule and Climate Change* (Legal Response Initiative, Briefing paper 42, July 2012).

states rather than the actions of an individual nation state.[157] While it is true that climate change challenges many traditional legal concepts, not just in international law, there are arguments against this reasoning. For one, nation states are obliged under the Precautionary Principle to avoid environmental harm, even if there is no absolute scientific certainty that environmental impact might occur or that there is causality between state action and environmental impact.[158] Consequently, it is not necessary to establish an unequivocal connection between cause (pollution) and result (climate change) to establish a legal duty to avoid environmental harm. In fact, a situation where only factual factors outside the nation state's influence cause a situation to be damaging to another state is not unknown in international law. For example, in the Trail Smelter case, only an interaction between the smelter's fumes and the specific weather conditions of the area causes the fumes to transgress boundaries.

Furthermore, the principle focuses on the nation state's actions rather than their impact on another nation state, as shown by the ICJ's reference to "areas beyond national jurisdiction." As "areas beyond national jurisdiction" are only an object, not acting subject of environmental law, such reference shows that the principle focuses more on a nation state's obligation to contain environmentally harmful activity to their own jurisdiction rather than on the effects of such on another object or subject to international law. Consequently, the International Law Association[159] considers the principle as applicable to climate change, noting that

> *application of the customary law principle of prevention of environmental damage to the situation of climate change damage is supported by State practice and the writings of international jurists. [The Principle] is repeated in its entirety in the preamble of the [United Nations Framework Convention on Climate Change].*
>
> *While it might be argued that [the Principle] does not apply to climate change as it falls outside the traditional concept of transboundary pollution, neither the decades of ILC debates on the issue of prevention of environmental harm nor international jurisprudence provide evidence that complex*

157 *Cf.* note 156, at 3. f.

158 *See* Epiney, *supra* note 124.

159 As a non-governmental organization, the International Law Association (ILA) has no authority to shape international law. However, the ILA's codifications are generally considered a source of fundamental customary principles, *cf.* Herdegen, Völkerrecht, 13. Auflage Heidelberg/Berlin 2014, S. 165.

> *instances of environmental change are not to be covered by the general duty to prevent harm and minimize the risk thereof.*[160]

Frank argues that in addition to the undoubtable acceleration of climate change by GHG emissions,[161] applicability of international environmental law to climate change only requires an element of imputability, i.e., a causal relation between a nation state's GHG emissions and damage to another nation state as a result of climate change. He considers this to be the case here and argues that damages resulting from climate change have the character of "distance and summation-damages." For these types of damages, an individualized causal relation between harmful act and damage might be hard to prove. However, for damages relating to climate change, this is not the case, since all GHG emissions increase the harmful concentration of GHG in the atmosphere, which constitutes climate change. Therefore, no nation state can argue that their emissions did not contribute to climate change.[162] Under general German legal dogmatism, this argument is correct: causation means the damage would not have occurred in a situation without the individual harmful action, i.e., the harmful action is *conditio sine qua non* for the damage. At least according to the current scientific knowledge, one nation state's emissions are not enough to effect climate change. However, the cumulative emissions can. This concept is called "cumulative causality" in German law.[163] Climate change would likely not occur without the cumulative emissions from most nation states. The question, therefore, then becomes whether an individual nation state is accountable for a result that only occurred due to cumulative action with other nation states.[164] Again referring to German law dogmatism, it would be accountable as the nation states emitting

---

160 International Law Association, Legal Principles Relating to Climate Change (2014).

161 This also appears to be the opinion of the Paris Agreement Parties, *cf.* Decision, 1/CP.21 Adoption of the Paris Agreement, FCCC/CP/2015/10/Add.1, Preamble: Recognizing that climate change represents an urgent and potentially irreversible threat to human societies and the planet and thus requires the widest possible cooperation by all countries, and their participation in an effective and appropriate international response, with a view to accelerating the reduction of global greenhouse gas emissions.

162 Frank, *supra* note 93.

163 "*Kumulative Kausalität*" in German law.

164 "*Objektive Zurechnung*" in German law.

GHG know that their emissions together with other nation state's emissions cause climate change.[165]

In U.S. tort law, the causation issue relating to climate change is more complicated. Similar to causation in German law, U.S. tort law requires the plaintiff to establish a causal connection between the injury and the defendant's action. Historically, this causal connection was, similar to the German *condition sine qua* non-test referred to above, established using a "but-for-formula." Under this formula, causation is established if the event would have not occurred but for the action performed by the defendant.[166] In many situations, such as toxic torts (i.e., torts in which plaintiff alleges an injury due to a toxic substance or chemical used by the defendant), this but-for test's application is limited, which is why courts tend to supplement it with different and often inconsistent causation tests.[167] Many of the issues present in establishing causation between action and injury in climate change litigation are also present in toxic torts[168] but with the added difficulty of establishing judicial standing. Generally, causation between a polluter's action and climate change seems to not be recognized in traditional U.S. legal scholarship.[169] Following this viewpoint, U.S. courts dismissed the village of Kivalina's lawsuits against Exxon and several other energy companies in which the Alaskan Native community of Kivalina sought monetary compensation for damages caused by flooding as a result of climate change. The courts ruled that (i) Kivalina did not have standing, as the issue of climate change is too abstract; and (ii) this issue is a political rather than a judicial one.[170]

Aside from the more dogmatic legal arguments against an exclusion of climate change from the applicability of the principle, the reference to the principle in the Preamble of the United Nations Framework Convention

---

165 For a discussion of these criminal law principles unrelated to climate change, *see* Kudlich, Hans, Objektive und subjektive Zurechnung von Erfolgen im Strafrecht – Eine Einführung, Juristische Arbeitsblätter (JA) 2010, 681, 687

166 RESTATEMENT (THIRD) OF TORTS: LIABILITY FOR PHYSICAL AND EMOTIONAL HARM, § 29 (AM LAW INST 2005).

167 *See* discussion in Note, *Causation in Environmental Law: Lessons from Toxic Torts*, 128 HARV. L. REV. 2256 (2015).

168 *See*, for example, Koehn v. Ayers, 26 F. Supp. 2d 953, 955 (S.D. Tex. 1998) or Georgia v. Tenn. Copper Co., 206 U.S. 230, 236 (1907) relating to acid rain.

169 *See* also Eduardo M. Peñalver, *Acts of God or Toxic Torts? Applying Tort Principles to the Problem of Climate Change* (Cornell Law Faculty Publications, Paper 730, 1998).

170 See Native Village of Kivalina v. ExxonMobil Corp., 696 F.3d 849, 854 (9th Cir. 2012).

on Climate Change, [171] an international treaty entered into by 197 nation states, is a strong argument in favor of the principle's character as fundamental customary law also relating to climate change as the parties, by way of *opinio juris*, assumed the Principle's applicability.

In this context, a recent decision of The Hague District Court is notable. In its *Urgenda Foundation v. The State of Netherlands* case,[172] The Hague District Court required the Dutch Government[173] to increase its efforts in reducing GHG. The court found that based on the current Dutch emissions policy, which is largely based on the common European approach, the Netherlands will achieve a reduction of 17 percent at most in 2020, which is below the norm of 25 percent to 40 percent for developed countries deemed necessary by the IPCC. However, the court based its decision on a "duty of care" (*zorgpflicht* in Dutch) and on the "doctrine of hazardous negligence" (*leerstuk van gevaarzetting*), both following from Dutch law. The court held that international law, such as the Kyoto Protocol or the No-Harm Principle, was not binding towards individual citizens but must be considered in interpreting law as stated above.[174]

cc. Differentiation between the Precautionary Principle and the Principle of Prevention

Both the Precautionary Principle and the Principle of Prevention are closely related and have an overlapping area of application. Indeed, some scholars have suggested that the differentiation between the principles is predominately a distinction originating in German scholarship without root in international law.[175]

---

171 United Nations Framework Convention on Climate Change, 1771 UNTS 107, reprinted in 31 ILM 849, preamble (May 29, 1992).

172 Rechtbank Den Haag, Judgment dated 24.6.2015, C/09/456689, HA ZA 13-1396, ECLI:NL:RBDHA:2015:7145. English language translation available under http://uitspraken.rechtspraak.nl/inziendocument?id=ECLI:NL:RBDHA:2015:7196 (last checked on January 11, 2020).

173 The Dutch Government appealed the decision, Saurer, Johannes, Purnhagen, Kai, Klimawandel vor Gericht - Der Rechtsstreit der Nichtregierungsorganisation „Urgenda" gegen die Niederlande und seine Bedeutung für Deutschland, Zeitschrift für Umweltrecht (ZUR) 2016, 16.

174 *Cf.* note 173.

175 Rehbinder, Eckard, Das Vorsorgeprinzip im internationalen Vergleich, in: Schlacke, Sabine, Franzius, Claudio (Hrsg.),Umweltrechtliche Studien vol. 12, 2000.

However, it is possible to make a distinction between these principles based on the wording of the ICJ on both principles. The Precautionary Principle obliges nation states performing an action with potential adverse environmental impact to take all required measures to avoid environmental harm, even if there is no absolute scientific certainty that environmental impact might occur or that there is causality between state action and environmental impact.[176] Under the Principle of Prevention, nation states must ensure that activities within their jurisdiction and control respect the environment of other states or of areas beyond national control.[177] The difference therefore lies in the scientific certainty of environmental harm following from a nation state's conduct. If it is unclear that their conduct may cause harm to other nation states or areas beyond national jurisdiction, they act within the parameters of the Precautionary Principle. If environmental risks are known, the Principle of Prevention is applicable.[178]

d. The Principle of Common but Differentiated Responsibilities

"According to the idea of common but differentiated responsibilities, all nation states have common responsibilities to protect the environment and promote sustainable development, but because of different social, economic and ecological situations, countries must shoulder different responsibilities."[179]

The idea of common but differentiated responsibilities[180] goes back to the concerns of developing countries in relation to the prevention of climate change. In view of the relationship between the Principle of Sustainable Development and the protection of the environment discussed above, the idea of common but differentiated responsibilities treats environmental protection not as an isolated principle, but rather tries to balance it

---

176 *See* Epiney, *supra* note 124.

177 *See* definition in ICJ, Legality of the Threat or Use of Nuclear Weapons, Advisory Opinion, 1996 I.C.J. 2 at 226, 29 (Jul 8). The reference to "areas beyond national jurisdiction" is important as it refers to environmental significant areas such as the Arctic or the high seas.

178 *Cf. Durner* in Landmann/Rohmer, Umweltrecht, Umweltvölkerrecht, Rn. 60; International Law Association, *supra* note 160, at 22.

179 Hunter et al., *supra* note 19, at 464.

180 Sometimes referred to as "common but differentiated responsibilities and respective capabilities;" *see,* for example International Law Association, *supra* note 160.

with, *inter alia*, the Right to Sustainable Development and sovereignty laws.[181] Given that developing countries are responsible for a majority of worldwide carbon emissions, this is especially relevant in the context of climate change. Consequently, Article 3, para. 1 of the UNFCCC states that

> *[t]he Parties should protect the climate system for the benefit of present and future generations of humankind, on the basis of equity and in accordance with their common but differentiated responsibilities and respective capabilities. Accordingly, the developed country Parties should take the lead in combating climate change and the adverse effects thereof.*

Therefore, at least for a certain time frame, increases in GHG-emissions remain allowed for developing countries.[182] Besides the UNFCCC, the idea of common but differentiated responsibilities is referred to in Principle 7 of the Rio Declaration, various UNFCCC CoP decisions, the Johannesburg Plan of Implementation 2002,[183] the outcome of the RUN Conference on Sustainable Development,[184] and most recently, in Article 2, para. 2 of the Paris Agreement.[185] Despite this usage in contractual international law, the idea of common but differentiated responsibilities remains not operational due to a lack of clear substance beyond the Principle of Sustainable Development and is therefore not considered customary international law.[186]

e. The concept of common heritage of mankind

The concept of common heritage of mankind is currently not considered customary international law,[187] but it is nonetheless an important concept in the law of climate change as it relates to the usage of resources in areas outside of national jurisdiction. These areas, such as the high seas, the

181 Frank et al., *supra* note 141.

182 *See* note 181.

183 For example, *cf.* para. 38 of the United Nations' Plan of Implementation of the World Summit on Sustainable Development, https://www.un.org/esa/sustdev/documents/WSSD_POI_PD/English/WSSD_PlanImpl.pdf (last visited January 11, 2020).

184 List taken from International Law Association, Legal Principles Relating to Climate Change, *supra* note 160.

185 UN General Assembly, United Nations Framework Convention on Climate Change: G.A. Res. 48/189 (January 20, 1994).

186 Epiney, *supra* note 124, at 1071.

187 *Cf.* note 186.

sea-bed, Antarctica, outer space and the outer atmosphere (including the ozone layer) are referred to as "global commons."[188]

The concept seeks to find a solution for the dilemma that states without direct access to resources, for example, fisheries in the high seas, face in view of the generally accepted right of capture, which states that whoever captures the resource has the right to it.[189] As of now, the concept is applied to Antarctica, the outer space, the moon and other celestial bodies,[190] and the law of the sea. Regarding the latter, the 1982 UN Law of the Sea Convention[191] (UNCLOS) states in Section 2, Art. 136 that "the [seabed and ocean floor and subsoil thereof, beyond the limits of national jurisdiction] and its resources are the common heritage of mankind." No nation state shall claim or exercise sovereignty or sovereign rights over any part of such areas or its resources, nor shall any nation state or natural or juridical person appropriate any part thereof. No such claim or exercise of sovereignty or sovereign rights nor such appropriation shall be recognized, Art. 137 UNCLOS.[192]

Practically speaking, the applicability of the idea of common heritage of mankind is currently limited to activities in Antarctica,[193] and not currently for activities in outer space etc. The concept is not applied to the atmosphere.

f. The Polluter and User Pays Principle

The "Polluter Pays Principle" is an example of the interaction of economics and law. Developed in the early 1970s by the OECD as an econo-

---

188 Hunter et al., *supra* note 19, at 453.

189 *See* note 188.

190 Treaty on Principles Governing the Activities of States in the Exploration and Use of Outer Space, Including the Moon and Other Celestial Bodies, January 27, 1967, 610 U.N.T.S. 205, reprinted in I.L.M 386 (1967).

191 United Nations Convention on the Law of the Sea (UNCLOS), 1833 U.N.T.S. 3; 21 ILM 1261 (1982), http://www.un.org/depts/los/convention_agreements/texts/unclos/unclos_e.pdf (last visited January 11, 2020).

192 "The United States however, never fully accepted the principle's application to the deep-sea bed, (at least with respect to benefit sharing). To get the united states to join the Law of the Sea Convention, the common heritage principle was removed from Part XI addressing the mining of the deep sea bed," Hunter et al., *supra* note 19, at 455.

193 Antarctic Treaty, Dec. 1, 1959, 402 U.N.T.S. 71. 159.

mic principle,[194] the Polluter Pays Principle was supposed to force the internalization of environmental costs as a means to achieve a level economic playing field and promote efficient use of resources.[195] Based on such, the Rio Declaration, formulated in Principle 16, states,

> *National authorities should endeavor to promote the internalization of environmental costs and the use of economic instruments, taking into account the approach that the polluter should, in principle, bear the cost of pollution, with due regard to the public interest and without distorting international trade and investment.*[196]

In this form, the Polluter Pays Principle has mostly indirect effects as it does not directly force polluters to internalize environmental costs, but rather obliges nation states to create a legal framework for such, requiring nation states to force polluters to internalize the costs of their emissions.[197] Emissions trading programs can and are designed to be a tool to achieve this.

Along with other principles discussed here, the Polluter Pays Principle has been codified as a fundamental principle of European Union environmental law. Article 191, para. II of the Treaty on the Function of the European Union (TFEU) states that

> *Union policy on the environment shall aim at a high level of protection taking into account the diversity of situations in the various regions of the Union. It shall be based on the precautionary principle and on the principles that preventive action should be taken, that environmental damage should as a priority be rectified at source and that the polluter should pay.*

Consequently, all secondary European Union environmental law must be interpreted in light of the Polluter Pays Principle.[198] Domestic U.S. law has also implemented the Polluter Pays Principle. Most notable in the context of climate change are respective provisions in the 1970 Clean Air Act (CAA),[199] such as Section 7414, which obliges emitters to undertake certain measuring and abatement measures at their own costs.

---

194 See Sanford Gaines, *Emerging Principles of International Environmental Law*, 26 TEX. INT'L L. J. 463 (1991).

195 *Proelß* in Graf Vitzthum/Proeßl, Völkerrecht, 5. Abschnitt. Rn 113; *Durner* in Landmann/Rohmer, Umweltrecht, Umweltvölkerrecht Rn. 64.

196 *See* note 122.

197 HUNTER ET AL., *supra* note 19, at 484.

198 *Durner* in Landmann/Rohmer, Umweltrecht, Umweltvölkerrecht Rn. 65.

199 42 U.S.C. § 7401 et seq. (1970).

g. The Due Diligence Principle

Under the Due Diligence Principle, nation states are obliged to act with due diligence with respect to all activities that take place under the jurisdiction and control of a nation state.[200] The ICJ states in the Pulp Mills case that due diligence

> *entails not only the adoption of appropriate rules and measures but also a certain level of vigilance in their enforcement and the exercise of administrative control applicable to public and private operators, such as the monitoring of activities undertaken by such operators.*[201]

Both the International Law Commission and the International Law Association also view the Principle of Due Diligence as a fundamental and binding principle of international environmental law.[202]

h. The Principle of Equitable Utilization of Shared Resources

Equitable Utilization, or the Principle of Equitable Use of Shared Resources, is a principle resulting from the international law of waterways and has been accepted as binding customary law regarding the waterways.[203] Emanating from, *inter alia*, the Principle of Sovereignty, equitable utilization of waterways does not mean equal rights to the resource, but "rather that all States in a watercourse share sovereignty over the resource, and their interests must be reasonably balanced according to a range of factors."[204]

This implies both substantive and procedural elements. Procedurally, in order to allow for a "reasonable balancing" of interests, the principle requires shared duties such as mutual consultation and information, particularly relating to the planned usage of the resource. Substantively, "reasonable balancing" demands that the planned use of the resource needs to consider the interests of other potential users of the resource.[205]

---

200 Case concerning Pulp Mills on the River Uruguay, *supra* note 145.
201 *Cf.* note 200.
202 *See* Frank et al., *supra* note 141.
203 Epiney, *supra* note 124, at 1066, 1072.
204 Hunter et al., *supra* note 19, at 881.
205 Epiney, *supra* note 124, at 1066, 1072.

The applicability of the principle to resources other than waterways is subject to scholarly debate. Some scholars point out that the Principle of Equitable Utilization "was not developed with broader considerations of environmental protection in mind, and it has been poorly suited for addressing environmental harms that do not conflict with another riparian party's use of the river." International practice has, however, extended the applicability of the principle. For example, the ICJ has applied the principle to fisheries. In its series of "Fisheries Jurisdiction Cases," the court held that

> *both Parties had the obligation to keep under review the fishery resources in those waters and to examine together, in the light of the information available, the measures required for the conservation and development, and equitable exploitation, of those resources, taking into account any international agreement that might at present be in force or might be reached after negotiation.*[206]

Following this, the United Nations Environment Programme (UNEP) referred to the principle in its Draft "Principles of Conduct [...] in the Conservation and Harmonious Utilization of Natural Resources Shared by Two or More States," stating, *inter alia*, that

> *[i]t is necessary for States to co-operate in the field of the environment concerning the conservation and harmonious utilization of natural resources shared by two or more States. Accordingly, it is necessary that consistent with the concept of equitable utilization of shared natural resources, States co-operate with a view to controlling, preventing, reducing or eliminating adverse environmental effects which may result from the utilization of such resources.*[207]

The Principle of Equitable Utilization is ultimately derived from the Principle of State Sovereignty[208] and the Principle of Prevention. Both principles govern state action without regard to the specific resource affected. The equitable utilization of shared resources is a prerequisite for the effective protection of state sovereignty as non-equitable use of shared resources infringes on the sovereignty of the disadvantaged state. Consequentially,

206 *See* for example, Fisheries Jurisdiction (Federal Republic of Germany v. Iceland), Judgment (Merits), 1974 I.C.J. 175. 29 (July 25).

207 Principle 1 of the UNEP Draft Principles of Conduct (...) in the Conservation and Harmonious Utilization of Natural Resources Shared by Two or More States, *in* ILM, (1978), S. 1091.

208 *Cf.* note 204.

the Principle of Equitable Utilization should be applied to other shared resources as well.

A separate question is whether the principle's substantive and procedural content, which was developed in view of shared waterways, can be applied to all other types of shared resources or whether differences between types of resources can justify a diverging legal relevance. For instance, regarding the former, it has been proposed to apply the Principle of Equitable Utilization to all resources that share similar characteristics with water.[209] Durner proposes the application on shared waterways, liquid and gaseous minerals, and migratory animal herds.[210]

Scholars have so far not proposed that the principle be applied to carbon emissions or usage of the atmosphere, a shared resource.[211] An argument for this application could be seen in the relationship between the Principle of Prevention and the Principle of Equitable Utilization. Both originate from state sovereignty. While the Principle of Prevention is a defensive right allowing states to protect their territory and their resources from outside influence, the Principle of Equitable Utilization ensures states' rights to participate in the usage of a (shared) resource. Therefore, if the Principle of Prevention is allowed to be applied in the context of the usage of the atmosphere and climate change,[212] the Principle of Equitable Utilization must also be applied as "the other side of the coin."

i. The Liability Principle

A question separate but related to the discussion of the above principles is the question of liability in case of non-compliance with any of the binding principles of international environmental law.

Starting in 1960 with the Paris Convention on Third Party Liability in the Field of Nuclear Energy,[213] nation states have mostly used contractual international law to formulate liability rules for specific environmental

---

209 *Cf.* note 205.

210 See *Durner* in Landmann/Rohmer, Umweltrecht, Umweltvölkerrecht Rn. 53.

211 Resources are usually considered "shared resources" when borders do not suffice for the distribution of a resource; *see* Epiney, *supra* note 124; also *see* note 28.

212 *Cf.* Chapter bb. The Principle of Prevention.

213 OECD Convention on Third Party Liability in the Field of Nuclear Energy of 29th July 1960, as amended by the Additional Protocol of 28th January 1964 and by the Protocol of 16th November 1982, https://www.oecd-nea.org/law/nlparis_conv.html (last visited January 11, 2020).

damages.[214] An attempt to formulate general international rules on environmental liability was the "Convention on Civil Liability for Damage Resulting from Activities Dangerous to the Environment" on June 21, 1993. The so-called Lugano Convention found that "emissions released in one country may cause damage in another country and that, therefore, the problems of adequate compensation for such damage are also of an international nature,"[215] and attempted to establish a liability regime for transboundary systems based on the Polluter Pays Principle discussed above. However, the Convention was never ratified in this form and therefore never entered into force. Therefore, decisions on state liability have been reserved to individual court decisions—for example, the arbitration tribunal's decision in the Trail Smelter case discussed above.

3. Conclusion and relevance for the topic

Given the evolution of international cooperation discussed above, the implications following from international law both for international cooperation as well as national policy measures become increasingly important. As one scholar puts it,

> *At the international level, nations seeking to cooperate on climate change have always been forced to navigate a fine line between substance and process, general principles and specific rules, formal obligations and political commitments. Many of the core issues have been so divisive that progress has only been possible at the expense of specific and binding normative outcomes. As the negotiations on a future climate regime unfold, it is becoming increasingly evident that international cooperation itself is undergoing fundamental change.*[216]

As international cooperation shifts away from binding obligations and targets and focuses on "a general political statement that privileges the voluntary actions of states and devalues the role of international law and

214 For oil spillage, *see* for example, the International Maritime Organization on the International Convention on Civil Liability for Oil Pollution Damage (CLC), November 29, 1969. Entry into force: June 19, 1975; replaced by 1992 Protocol and adopted November 27, 1992; Entry into force: 30 May 30, 1996.

215 Convention on Civil Liability for Damage Resulting from Activities Dangerous to the Environment, June 21, 1993, ETS No. 150, https://www.coe.int/en/web/conventions/full-list/-/conventions/treaty/150 (last visited January 11, 2020).

216 Mehling, *supra* note 24, at 12.

global climate governance,"[217] the relevance of the binding principles of international environmental law moves into focus. Can the current political climate relating to global environmental governance indeed, as one scholar puts it, "imply that climate cooperation is ultimately determined only by the interests, at any given time, of the regime participants"?[218] In view of the principles detailed above, it is clear that climate cooperation is not left to full discretion of state actors but is rather, to some degree, mandated by international law. Against the background of the bottom-up vs. top-down paradigm discussed in this thesis, the outcomes of the Kyoto Protocol and the successive Copenhagen discussions raise questions as to what extent stakeholders can rely on the influence of international law in creating a new approach. Simply put, the nature of international cooperation regarding climate change illustrates the core dilemma of international cooperation. Acting states recognize that, particularly in view of the "tragedy of the commons" situation discussed above, the international scale of the problem of pollution requires international binding action, especially contractual action. However, with each (binding) act, states lose sovereignty and may enter into obligations that could go against their (short term) interests.[219] Put differently: if most governments of developed and developing countries, including the U.S. under the Obama Administration,[220] support a binding top-down regime, why has such a regime not yet been enacted? Is it really just a problem of negotiation?

As some scholars argue, a reason why such policies have not yet been implemented might be a shift in, firstly, the role of developing countries and, more importantly, the perception of the role of binding international law by countries.[221]

At its early stage, the UNFCCC set the expectation that the international legal response to climate change would move forward in a "legally

---

217 David Hunter, *Implications of the Copenhagen Accord for Global Climate Governance*, 10 Sustainable Development Law & Policy 4 (Spring 2010).

218 *Cf.* note 216.

219 Epiney, *supra* note 124.

220 *See*, for example, the U.S. post-Copenhagen submission within the context of the *UNFCCC Ad Hoc Working Group on Further Commitments for Annex I Parties Under the Kyoto Protocol* stating that the U.S. supports a legally treaty as long as the legally binding elements apply to all major economies on a symmetrical matter, U.N. Document FCCC/KP/AWG/2010/MISC.1 (March 1, 2010).

221 Jacob Werksman & Kirk Herbertson, *The Aftermath of Copenhagen: Does International Law have a Role to Play in a Global Response to Climate Change?* 25 Md. J. Int'l Law 109 (2010)

binding form, as long as the commitments it contains are highly differentiated between developed and developing countries."[222] Such expectation has successively changed as legally binding targets became less and less attractive, mostly as a result of the U.S. opposition to emission reduction exceptions for emerging economies and the latter's reluctance to accept binding emission targets. A solution to this might be a paradigm shift to "soft targets" and non-binding, bottom-up regulation.

Relevant in this context is not just the United States' perception of binding international law, but that of developing countries as well. Especially legal scholars in these countries have influenced developing countries' perspective on the UNFCCC by analyzing the Western-dominated UNFCCC from a "southern-world" focused point of view. Such scholarly opinions, referred to as "Third World Approaches to International Law" and often abbreviated as TWAIL,[223] focus on the climate justice aspects that have also been raised in the Western world and are even being argued in front of U.S. courts.[224] Based on the argument that emerging countries—which historically have emitted less carbon, but due to their geographical situation, are generally more likely to be affected by climate change—the TWAIL scholars argue that the UNFCCC with its focus on market based instruments inherently benefits the industrialized countries at the expense of the development interests of emerging countries.[225] Consequently, TWAIL scholars place great emphasis on the Principle of Common but Differentiated Responsibilities (as discussed on page 77) and argue that the shift away from the Kyoto Protocol as the "clearest attempt to transform, activate and operationalize [the Principle] from a legal concept to a policy instrument"[226] led to an erosion of the Principle of Common but Differentiated Responsibilities.[227] Policy instrument in

---

222 *Cf.* note 221.

223 *Cf.* Makau Mutua, *What is TWAIL? in* 94 PROCEEDINGS OF THE 94TH ANNUAL MEETING OF THE AMERICAN SOCIETY OF INTERNATIONAL LAW 31 (2000).

224 *Cf.* notes 151 and 154 *infra* Chapter E for a discussion on this from a western-point of view.

225 For example by droughts or heatwaves causing crop failures or by the rising sea levels, *cf.* also Stephen Humphreys, ed., HUMAN RIGHTS AND CLIMATE CHANGE (2009) *passim* for a discussion on the impact of climate change in developing countries.

226 *Cf.* Christopher C. Joyner, *Common but Differentiated Responsibilities*, 96 PROCEEDINGS AM SOC INTL L 358-359 (2002).

227 Julia Dehm, *Carbon Colonialism or Climate Justice? Interrogating the International Climate Regime from a TWAIL Perspective*, 33 WINDSOR YEARBOOK OF ACCESS TO JUSTICE 129 (2017).

this context should not be understood to mean a "political concept" (as it often does), but rather to mean the transformation of the principle from a theoretical legal concept to a tangible legal instrument with "real-world" implications.

Also relevant in this context is the question of whether binding targets even matter if, as detailed above, not even the "binding" Kyoto Protocol provided any enforcement or compliance mechanism. Arguably, such binding targets do matter, not just because of the "name and shame" game discussed above, but also because by establishing institutions or reporting mechanisms, they kick off the process of institutionalizing cooperation in emission reductions that can lay the foundation for effective international cooperation.[228]

228 For the importance of the process of institutionalizing see Kreuter-Kirchhof, Charlotte, Dynamisierung des internationalen Klimaschutzregimes durch Institutionalisierung, Zeitschrift für ausländisches öffentliches Recht und Völkerrecht (ZaöRV) 2015, 967 f.

D. (National) environmental regulation and the theory of emissions trading

I. Basics of environmental regulation

As knowledge and understanding of the environmental challenges created by greenhouse gas emissions grows, legislators and policymakers on a national and international level are seeking legal responses to the issue of climate change. The historic and current attempts at legal responses demonstrate that climate change, a relatively new and diverse phenomenon, poses challenges not only to the natural sciences, but to our understanding of legal responses to environmental issues that traditionally have been as simple as banning substances causing environmental issues or increasing the price of their use, for example, by taxation. However, relating to climate change, the solution might not be as simple. For example, energy production and consumption, as well as mobility, are core causes of climate change, but also so fundamental to the present Western way of life that policymakers struggle with finding feasible balanced approaches to it.[1]

This conflict is likely the reason why untraditional and seemingly innovative legal approaches, such as the reliance on economic instruments like emissions trading, are so heavily utilized. These attempts at finding new and alternative approaches to environmental issues have changed our perception of what regulation needs to achieve and, as some argue, put a bigger focus on the cost and efficiency of policies, ultimately resulting in a variety of flexible market incentives as opposed to traditional planning-based regulation.[2] This makes sense, at least in theory, as a situation defined by imperfect information is best addressed using a system that economizes information, as in a market system where all participating entities theoretically only need to know the market prices, whereas governmental planning-based regulation requires knowledge of utility and production functions.[3] This argument is supported by empirical evidence

---

1 Michael Mehling, *Implementing Climate Governance: Instrument Choice and Interaction* in CLIMATE CHANGE AND THE LAW 11 (Erkki Holler, Kati Kulovesi & Michael Mehling, eds., 2013).

2 *Id.*

3 FRIEDRICH A. HAYEK, INDIVIDUALISM AND ECONOMIC ORDER (1948).

of the performance of planning regulation as a solution to environmental issues, such as in the Soviet Union or in China, which were a failure in large scale environmental planning.[4]

However, in order to further evaluate such trends towards economic instruments, one must first understand the basics of legal response to climate change. Attempts at a legal response can be systematically grouped into two general and contrasting classes with respective subclasses.

Legal responses can be "*sectoral*" or "*general*" and aimed at "*mitigation*" or "*adaption*."[5]

In this context, *sectoral* approaches focus on a specific economic sector, such as the automotive industry. For example, the not very successful[6] subsidy provided by the German government for the purchase of electronic and hybrid cars[7] can be classified as a sectoral approach targeting the automotive industry using a subsidy, a classic regulatory tool. This attempt can be grouped under the *mitigation* class as well, as it is meant to "reduce the sources of greenhouse gases or enhance the sinks."[8] On the other hand, general approaches have an economy-wide target and often apply to a whole jurisdiction or at least a certain defined region. An

---

4 Dieter Helm, *Economic Instruments and Environmental Policy*, 36 ECON. & SOC. REV. 210 (Winter 2005).

5 *See* also Peters, Heinz-Joachim, Verwaltungsrechtliche Verfahren zur Anpassung von Vorhaben an den Klimawandel, Zeitschrift Kommunaljurist 2017, 41 for a discussion regarding „climateproofing" under German law.

6 According to the latest publicly known information at the time of writing, only 9000 applications were received as of 2017, *cf.* Handelsblatt, January 2, 2017, "Prämie für Elektroautos floppt - Nur 9000 Anträge für E-Auto-Kaufprämie", available online under http://www.handelsblatt.com/unternehmen/industrie/praemie-fuer-elektroautos-floppt-nur-9000-antraege-fuer-e-auto-kaufpraemie/19199008.html (last visited January 11, 2020).

7 *Bundesministerium für Wirtschaft und Energie, Richtlinie zur Förderung des Absatzes von elektrisch betriebenen Fahrzeugen* (Umweltbonus) vom 29. Juni 2016, BUNDESANZEIGER AT 01.07.2016 B1.

8 Definition of mitigation used by the UNFCCC: "In the context of climate change, a human intervention to reduce the sources or enhance the sinks of greenhouse gases. Examples include using fossil fuels more efficiently for industrial processes or electricity generation, switching to solar energy or wind power, improving the insulation of buildings, and expanding forests and other "sinks" to remove greater amounts of carbon dioxide from the atmosphere." *Cf.* UNFCCC glossary of climate change acronyms and terms, https://unfccc.int/process-and-meetings/the-convention/glossary-of-climate-change-acronyms-and-terms (last visited January 11, 2020). In that context, carbon sink is a generalizing term for certain natural or artificial reservoirs, such as forests or the ocean, which, by a process called carbon sequestration, store carbon., thus removing it from the atmosphere.

example can be seen in the adjustments made by German federal states in their State Water Legislation. For example, the German federal state of North-Rhine Westphalia changed its State Water Act (*Landeswassergesetz*) in late 2016. Expressly referring to challenges posed by climate change, Section 37 § 3 *Landeswassergesetz* requires that municipalities develop urban planning concepts to deal with increased heavy precipitation. This is a *general* approach, as it regulates not a specific industry, but rather the way urban planning is conducted in a state. It is also an *adaption* concept, as it does not intend to prevent climate change by reducing the emissions causing it but instead attempts to make "adjustments in natural or human systems in response to actual or expected climate stimuli or their effects, which moderates harm or exploits beneficial opportunities."[9] Most, but not all, enacted emissions trading systems aim at *non-sectoral* emission reductions and can therefore be classified as *general mitigation* regulations. As information becomes increasingly less perfect with a greater field of application, this suggests that when tasked with enacting *general* regulation, regulators tend to use economic instruments. This points to the relationship between imperfect information and the use of economic instruments discussed above and will be evaluated further in this thesis.

Or in other words: is emissions trading the tool of choice when regulators have no better idea? While acknowledging the limitations of legal perspectives in answering this question, the analysis in this thesis allows some conclusions on factors that influence the political decision-making process related to the enactment of emissions trading schemes.[10]

An interesting question in the context of the evaluation of legal regulation is the criteria against which environmental regulation has to be measured. As many emissions trading systems examined herein are essentially compliance tools allowed by regulators to achieve a desired reduction in emissions, the main criteria is easily found: the respective systems must achieve the desired reduction in emissions (often referred to as "environmental integrity" or "environmental efficiency)." Environmental efficiency can be defined as the efficient use of any natural resources. This can be viewed from an economic and an ecological perspective: economically, efficient usage of natural resources ensures the long-term supply and availability of any nationally needed resources. Germany, for example, a country without large supplies of natural resources, imported energy

9 *Id*. Definition of Adaption.

10 See the discussion on emissions trading decision making *infra* Chapter F.IV in this text.

resources with a total net value of approx. 60 billion euro in 2016,[11] which shows the importance of these natural resources. In contrast, ecological use of resources means a minimization of the harmful impact of resource usage on (i) the environment and (ii) the resource itself.[12] Accepted criteria for evaluating the ecological usage of resources is the internalization of externalities[13] resulting from the use of these resources. In theory, a user who internalizes all costs resulting from its use of the resource will minimize said use as much as possible, thus achieving what can be defined as "resource efficiency."

When evaluating and comparing different regulatory regimes, however, the choice of criteria is a less obvious one. Confronted with that question, the IPCC developed four criteria that are generally accepted by scholars as appropriate criteria for reviewing environmental regulation.[14] The IPPC uses the following four criteria: environmental effectiveness, cost effectiveness, distributional effects (including equity), and institutional feasibility.[15]

These criteria are just as helpful when evaluating emissions trading systems and will, along with the principles of international environmental law discussed later, be used in this thesis to compare the enacted systems in the U.S. According to that criteria and the IPCC findings, the success of emissions trading systems requires the following key components: The environmental effectiveness of a given emissions trading program depends on the emissions cap, participation in the program, and compliance. The cost-effectiveness "decreases with limited participation and fewer sectors;" distributional effects depend on initial allocations and finally, the institu-

---

11 Account balance between exports and imports, *cf.* World Energy Council - Deutschland e.V. Energie für Deutschland 2016; Fakten, Perspektiven und Positionen im globalen Kontext, p. 86.; http://www.weltenergierat.de/wp-content/uploads/2014/02/61524_DNK_Energie16_D_final_72dpi.pdf (last visited January 11, 2020). Historically, Germanys net import balance amounts to roughly 100 billion euro; the reduction in 2016 is based on the general price erosion on international energy markets.

12 Apart from this academic point of view, economic and ecological efficiency is of course overlapping: as natural resources are finite, the long-term supply is dependent on the economical use of the existing resources.

13 *Cf. infra* page 98.

14 *Cf.*, for example, DAVID HUNTER, JAMES SALZMAN & DURWOOD ZAELKE, INT'L ENVNTL L. & POL'Y 387 (4th ed. 2011) or Mehling, *supra* note 1, at 16.

15 IPCC, 2007: *Climate Change 2007: Mitigation. Contribution of Working Group III to the Fourth Assessment Report of the Inter- governmental Panel on Climate Change* 19 (B. Metz, O.R. Davidson, P.R. Bosch, R. Dave & L.A. Meyer, eds. 2007).

tional feasibility "requires well-functioning markets and complementary institutions."[16]

II. The tool case: Available instruments

As this thesis is focused on emissions trading, other types of environmental regulations are mentioned only briefly and only insofar as they relate to emissions trading and with a focus on mitigation regulation (as opposed to adaption, *cf.* page 88 f.). The following types of mitigation regulations can be identified: Regulations and standards (or command and control regulation), taxes and charges, tradable permits, voluntary agreements, subsidies and other incentives, research and development, and information policies. [17]

Relating to the objective of emissions trading, i.e., designated and measurable emissions reduction, command and control regulation, and taxes are most relevant and will be analyzed in the following pages along with cap-and-trade regulation, under which emissions trading usually falls.

1. Command and control

Command-and-control policy refers to environmental policy that relies on regulation (permission, prohibition, standard setting, and enforcement) as opposed to financial incentives—that is, economic instruments of cost internalization.[18]

Command-and-control (C&C) regulation can be defined as the exercise of influence by imposing standards backed by criminal or other sanctions. The force of law is used to prohibit certain forms of conduct, to demand certain positive actions or to lay down conditions for entry into an economic sector.[19] In the context of pollution and emissions control, C&C regulation would, for example, target emitters and impose a set limit of

---

16 *Id.* at 767.

17 List taken from the Fourth IPCC Report, *see* note 15.

18 United Nations Department for Economic and Social Information and Policy Analysis, Glossary of Environment Statistics, Studies in Methods, Series F, No. 67, United Nations, New York, 1997, https://unstats.un.org/unsd/publication/SeriesF/SeriesF_67E.pdf (last visited April 3, 2020).

19 Robert Baldwin, Martin Cave & Martin Lodge, Understanding Regulation: Theory, Strategy, and Practice 106 (2nd Edition 2011).

pollution that they may emit. C&C regulation can therefore be aimed at both mitigation as well as adaption. C&C regulation is not an "economic instrument" within the meaning defined in this thesis as it is based on governmental planning, not on the force of the market.

In past and present rulemaking, this approach has often been perceived as problematic by proponents of economic instruments. For example, scholars have argued that many pollution targets promulgated[20] in C&C rulemaking are arbitrary and mostly oriented by what is deemed to be politically achievable.[21] In addition, especially European scholars produced empirical studies suggesting issues with the enforcement of compliance obligations in C&C regulations. According to such studies, regulators often did not enforce obligations to their full extent,[22] and compliance became a question of bargaining power.[23]

C&C control has also been criticized for targeting pollution as an environmental risk and seldom addressing the economic implications of pollution as an externality.[24] This is, of course, more of an academic point, but nonetheless worth noting. The IPCC has identified the following key factors to the success of a C&C environmental regulation: Relating to their environmental integrity, C&C regulation features a set emissions level. Assuming that emission reductions are set correctly (*cf.* the argument made relating to that above), environmental integrity depends on compliance with the cap or deferrals granted. Cost effectiveness depends on individual design. Generally, the broader the application, the higher the compliance costs as the regulation is less tailored towards the regulated subjects. In economic theory, whether a C&C regulation meets distributional considerations depends on a "level playing field," i.e., on whether all market participants share the same characteristic. Small or new market participants in particular may be in a disadvantageous position in relation to larger actors that can, due to a higher profit margin or a dominating market position, burden consumers with compliance costs or in relation to already

---

20 Called "standard setting" in legal literature.

21 Helm, *supra* note 4, at 210.

22 Mayntz, Renate, Vollzugsprobleme im Umweltrecht, Stuttgart, 1978; Übersohn, Gerhard, Effektive Umweltpolitik: Folgerungen aus der Implementations- und Evaluationsforschung, 1990.

23 Bohne, Eberhard, Der informale Rechtsstaat, Eine empirische und rechtliche Untersuchung zum Gesetzesvollzug unter besonderer Berücksichtigung des Immissionsschutzes, 1981.

24 For a general discussion of issues with C & C rulemaking *see* Baldwin et al., *supra* note 19, at 107 ff.

established market participants who have already implemented costs of compliance into their cost structure. According to the IPCC, institutional feasibility "depends on technical capacity; [it is therefore] popular with regulators in countries with weakly functioning markets."[25]

2. Pigouvian taxes

Pigouvian taxes are another model that aims to reduce emissions by affecting behavioral changes by raising the costs of pollution as a result of internalizing social costs caused by such emissions.

In economic terms, such Pigouvian taxes are defined as taxes designed to correct for negative external effects.[26] Under the Pigouvian model, regulation will ensure that an emitter internalizes the social cost caused by pollution by putting a tax on the emissions that are causing such damages. To achieve such an objective, the tax on each unit of emission has to be equal to the social damage caused.[27] According to Pigou, this is more efficient than traditional C&C regulation because C&C is not cost effective in situations where abatement costs differ across emission sources.[28] This reasoning is also advanced by proponents of emissions trading in favor of the latter.

Whether or not Pigouvian taxation is an efficient model for dealing with pollution externalities has been extensively discussed in economic literature.[29] It has been argued that environmental taxes, such as Pigouvian taxes, provide a "double dividend"[30] as they raise revenue while correcting the externality problem. Such revenue can be used to correct more (in economic terms) invasive and distorting taxes, such as labor taxes. It has, however, also been called into question whether the identification and measurement of an externality is a reliable guide to the proper level of a Pigouvian tax.[31] As put by Helm,

---

25 *See* note 15.

26 Agnar Sandmo, *Pigouvian Taxes* in THE NEW PALGRAVE DICTIONARY OF ECONOMICS (Steven N. Durlauf & Lawrence E. Blume, eds., 2008)

27 *Id.*

28 ARTHUR C. PIGOU, THE ECONOMICS OF WELFARE (1920).

29 *See*, for example, Ian W.H. Parry & Kenneth A. Small, *Does Britain or the United States Have the Right Gasoline Tax?* 95 AM. ECON. REV. 1276-1289 (2005).

30 S. Smith, *Environmental and Public Finance Aspects of the Taxation of Energy*, 14 OXFORD REV. OF ECON. POL'Y 64–83 (1998).

31 John V. Nye, *The Pigou Problem*, 31 REGULATION 32-37 (Summer 2008).

> *In the Pigou framework, the choice between price and quantity mechanisms (and regulation) is not determined, because information is perfect. The location of the benefits and damages functions is known. But the science and the policy process is about uncertainty. In practice, policymakers have only the haziest idea about where the functions lie, have limited resources to estimate them, and know that they will be subject to wide ranges of outcomes for small changes in assumption. And if taxes are used, we cannot be sure of the effect on quantities; and vice versa.*[32]

It will be discussed later in this thesis how this argument made in favor of emissions trading holds up against the experiences with enacted trading systems. In addition, it is noteworthy that theories have been developed to deal with the uncertainty problem in establishing a Pigouvian tax.[33] Modern scholarship has argued extensively in favor of taxes over cap-and-trade. Shapiro, for example, argues that a carbon tax "produces no price volatility, because it raises the cost of energy by the constant amount regardless of how fast a company, industry or nation's emissions are growing."[34] While it is true that price volatility is a concern in most cap-and-trade programs reviewed in this thesis, this does not solve the main issue with taxes: correctly pricing the emissions. Shapiro furthermore argues that taxes have a generally comparable effect from country to country, while a global cap-and-trade program would not.[35] This argument is based on the premise that countries implementing a cap-and-trade program will use different baselines for their allotment of allowances. Experiences with multi-jurisdictional cap-and-trade programs do, however, show that multiple jurisdictions can link their allotment under an aggregate cap to achieve a common allowance price. In this situation, it does not matter whether emissions in one jurisdiction do not decline due to trading as the aggregate emissions decline due to linking in the desired amount, at least in theory. Lastly, Shapiro argues that cap-and-trade programs are more difficult to administer and are more vulnerable to evasion, corruption, and

32 Helm, *supra* note 4, at 210.

33 *See* Martin Weitzman, *Prices vs. Quantities,* 41 Rev. Econ. Stud. 477-491 (1974) wherein Weitzman argues that uncertainty is essentially a problem of instrument selection, *cf.* at 490.

34 Robert J. Shapiro, *Addressing the Risks of Climate Change: The Environmental Effectiveness and Economic Efficiency of Emissions Caps and Tradable Permits, Compared to Carbon Taxes* (February 2007), http://www.sonecon.com/docs/studies/climate_021407.pdf.

35 *Cf.* note 34.

manipulation.[36] However, they share this characteristic with taxation: the determination of the tax is just as susceptible to lobbying and industry influence as is the allocation of emissions allowances.

3. Cap-and-trade

Cap-and-trade systems are often referred to as "economic instruments." In practice and in theory, many different trading systems exist. Regardless of their regulatory differences, all cap-and-trade systems share certain regulatory characteristics.[37]

a. What is cap-and-trade

Following the Coasian Theorem displayed below, cap-and-trade systems aim at utilizing market forces to achieve cost-efficient emissions reduction. To do this, a central authority, such as the legislative or administrative branch, or a designated agency, defines a cap on the emission of certain pollutants. This cap is divided and spread out over multiple permits that, in the *Coasian* context, are property rights allowing the emission of a certain volume of pollutants. Participants are required to hold permits equivalent to the amount of their emissions after a defined timeframe. Such emissions are tradable amongst participants of the cap-and-trade system. This allows participants with high emissions abatement costs to buy permits from participants with low emissions abatement costs, leading to a reduction in the total cost of abating relative to a system where the reduction levels are strictly assigned.[38] Such a transaction is referred to as "trade."

To date, the majority of enacted cap-and-trade systems are mandatory for pollution sources within the program's coverage. However, voluntary systems (such as the Chicago Climate Exchange) have been implemented as well.

---

36 Shapiro, *supra* note 34, at 8.

37 *See* Chapter V. Emissions trading theory in detail: Design" *infra* at page 114.

38 Ted Gayer, *Pollution Permits in* THE NEW PALGRAVE DICTIONARY OF ECONOMICS (Steven N. Durlauf & Lawrence E. Blume, eds., 2008).

b. Emission Reduction Credits vs. Allowances

Emissions trading systems can operate via two different ways: emission reduction credits (ERCs) or cap-and-trade regulation using allowances. The difference between the two systems lies in the baseline that serves as a basis for trading. While the baseline in cap-and-trade systems defines the aggregate desired emissions, the employed baseline in systems using ERCs is oriented by existing regulations. ERCs are created if sources reduce their actual emissions below the regulated amount, leading to an initial, activity-based distribution of permits that can be traded after their initial distribution. "The crucial difference is that with allowances the total allowed pollution emissions for the industry cannot increase with economic activity in the industry while with ERCs emissions may increase in proportion to industrial activity."[39] Because of its relative nature, ERC regulation naturally results in an uncertainty about any emission reductions achieved in the future, as it is impossible to calculate the incentive participants will have to reduce their emissions to create ERCs. From a regulator's perspective, this is not a major issue, as due to the C&C-based nature of ERCs, the minimum desired threshold of emission reduction is achieved independent of the creation of ERCs. However, ERC systems are imperfect. Economic studies have shown that usage of ERCs does not always lead to an internalization of social cost. Furthermore, scholars argue that "an ERC system provides no incentive to reduce activity level temporarily, despite the harm caused by emissions, while an allowance system provides continuing incentive to reduce emissions by any efficient means, including reducing activity level."[40] While ERC programs have been utilized in the past—for example the Pilot Emission Reduction Trading (PERT) in Canada—there has been a shift towards the usage of allowances and cap-and-trade regulations.

---

39 Donald N. Dewees, *Emissions Trading: ERCs or Allowances?* 77 LAND ECONOMICS 514 (Nov. 2001).

40 Dewees, *supra* note 29, at 525.

III. Theoretical ideas behind emissions trading

1. Pollution as externality

The idea of emissions trading is based on the economic perception of pollution. In traditional economics, pollution is a problem within the "externalities" class. Externalities are defined as indirect effects of consumption or a production activity—that is, effects on agents other than the originator of such activity, which do not work through the price system.[41] The class of externalities can further be divided into "negative" and "positive" externalities. Consider the following examples: If a house owner hires a private security guard, her neighbor will benefit from the additional security as well, without bearing the costs for the guard. This is a positive externality. However, if a factory owner emits charcoal dust (i.e., pollution) this dust might cause damage to the neighbor's house. This is a negative externality. The problem with such negative externality is that the party that produces the externality is not the party that incurs the resulting costs. The factory owner who emits pollution is not the party incurring the resulting costs, as those are born by the neighbor whose property is damaged.

Apart from the ethical "fairness" considerations involved in such a problem, this also poses a legitimate economic problem, as such negative externalities upset the balance of the market. Economists consider a market to be optimal when it is in the state of "equilibrium." Such market equilibrium is defined as a state in which the forces of supply and demand are in balance with no net pressure for the price and output level to change.[42]

a. Externalities and social costs

Market equilibrium is harmed by the presence of externalities. In a very simplified way, the presence of externalities leads the producer of goods to produce more goods than they otherwise would have produced according to demand in the absence of externalities, as not all costs are reflected in the price of the goods. Consequently, the producer overproduces the

---

41 JJ. Laffont, *Externalities in* The New Palgrave Dictionary of Economics (Steven N. Durlauf & Lawrence E. Blume, eds., 2008).

42 Richard B. McKenzie & Dwight R. Lee, Microeconomics for MBAs: The Economic Way of Thinking for Managers 93 (2nd ed. 2010).

goods compared to demand for such goods. The margin between actual costs (including costs imposed by externalities) and the costs not accounting for externalities are called "social costs," as these are neither born by the producer, nor by the consumer as they are not factored into the price. Economists consider this a "market failure" leading to inefficient allocation of goods. [43] The market itself is not able to force producers of externalities to internalize social costs. This is believed to be a result of the presence of transaction costs. Transaction costs are costs that a party involuntarily incurs while concluding a market transaction.[44] If it weren't for such costs, an economically acting, self-interested consumer would force the producer to internalize the social costs according to this theory. In the presence of transaction costs, however, the cost of carrying out such bargaining is greater than the expected benefit.[45] Consider the following example: If a consumer of steel products would want to bargain with the steel producer to force the latter to internalize social costs imposed by pollution emitted in the steel production, such a consumer would need to analyze and calculate the social costs, its respective share, and bargain correspondingly with the producer. Even if the producer would be willing to bargain, it would be costly to effectively calculate the social costs. As the market itself is not able to solve this paradigm, the remaining inefficiency resulting from the presence of externalities (in addition to the environmental effects) can be used as a justification for regulatory action by regulators that forces producers to internalize the imposed social costs.[46]

Under economic theory, the need for governmental action also arises from another issue present in this paradigm. If producers were forced to internalize the social costs of their product as proposed by said theory, product prices would rise as the environment is continuously degraded, ultimately resulting in a balance between the product's price and society's demand for environmental protection.[47] However, can we wait until this equilibrium is achieved? Not all natural resources are renewable. Are we willing to accept the depletion of irretrievable resources to ultimately

---

43 John O. Ledyard, *Market Failure in* The New Palgrave Dictionary of Economics (Steven N. Durlauf & Lawrence E. Blume, eds., 2008).

44 M. Klaes, *History of Transaction Costs in* The New Palgrave Dictionary of Economics (Steven N. Durlauf & Lawrence E. Blume, eds., 2008).

45 Carl J. Dahlman, *The Problem of Externality*, 22 J. L. & Econ. 142 (1979).

46 *Id.* at 141.

47 Hunter et al., *supra* note 14, at 120.

achieve a balanced market? As most people would not be willing to take that chance, the political process is needed to solve this dilemma.

b. Social costs in institutional economics

While the paradigm of social costs explained above reflects the predominant understanding of economic scholarship, the school of "institutional economics" offers another interesting definition of social costs, mainly developed by Karl William Kapp, arguably as an answer to the perceived "neo-liberal" thought on social costs and the importance of the market.[48] Kapp was influenced by his colleague J. M. Clark, who developed the idea of "overhead costs," i.e., costs that "cannot be traced home and attributed to particular units of business."[49] Taking the idea of these overhead costs, Kapp defines social costs as "all direct and indirect losses sustained by third persons or the general public as a result of unrestrained economic activities."[50] Kapp thus developed an idea of social costs that affect society and future generations as a whole as a result of unrestrained profit maximizing behavior. He criticized that social costs are shifted towards economically and politically weaker sections of society, which are not compensated for bearing these costs.[51] Most memorably and very controversial, he states, "Capitalism must be regarded as an economy of unpaid costs, 'unpaid' in so far as a substantial portion of the actual costs of production remains unaccounted for in entrepreneurial outlays; instead they are shifted to, and ultimately borne by, third persons or by the community as a whole."[52]

To solve this issue, Kapp proposes regulations that today would be understood as "command-and-control" regulations.

---

48 Sebastian Berger, *The Making of the Institutional Theory of Social Costs: Discovering the K.W. Kapp and J.M. Clark Correspondence*, 72 AM. J. ECON. & SOC. 1107 (November 2013).

49 *Cf.* note 48.

50 WILLIAM K. KAPP, THE SOCIAL COSTS OF PRIVATE ENTERPRISE 12 (1964).

51 *Id. at* xiii.

52 *Cf.* note 50.

c. Tragedy of the commons: The prisoner's dilemma in international pollution policy

In the context of global pollution control, nation states face a problem known to behavioral economics as the "tragedy of the commons." This is related to the free-rider problem discussed in Chapter C. The "tragedy of the commons," a theory developed by Garret Hardin,[53] arises when it is difficult and costly to exclude potential users from common-pool resources that yield finite flows of benefits, such as clean air or the environment as a whole, as a result of which those resources will be exhausted by rational, utility-maximizing individuals rather than conserved for the benefit of all.[54] A classic example is that of fishermen who share a lake. The lake only contains a finite supply of fish. If the fishermen were able to establish fishing quotas that allow for the recovery of the population, all fishermen would be able to make a living fishing the lake without exhausting the fish population. As they are not in a position to establish such quotas,[55] they will exploit the natural resource to its exhaustion and ultimately harm their own interest.

While this theory is often criticized, it provides an interesting point of view on the behavior of international actors in pollution control. They essentially face a Prisoner's Dilemma, a situation in which even though they are assumed to be rational actors, they fail to cooperate for their own mutual benefit.[56] International regulation could be an instrument to break the "lock-up," especially a "Coasian solution,"[57] which forces states to form "clubs" whose members internalize the public good and then fix the quantity of the internalized good. International treaties and agreements such as the Kyoto Protocol can be seen as attempts to form such clubs.[58]

---

53 Garrett Hardin, *The Tragedy of the Commons*, 162 SCIENCE 1243–1248 (1968).

54 Elinor Ostrom, *Tragedy of the Commons in* THE NEW PALGRAVE DICTIONARY OF ECONOMICS (Steven N. Durlauf & Lawrence E. Blume, eds., 2008).

55 The absence of possibilities to exclude other users was presumed by Hardin.

56 R. J. Aumann, *Game Theory in* THE NEW PALGRAVE DICTIONARY OF ECONOMICS (Steven N. Durlauf & Lawrence E. Blume, eds., 2008).

57 *Cf.* below for a discussion on the Coasian theorem.

58 Helm, *supra* note 4, at 210.

2. Coase and the problem of social costs

a. Understanding Coasian Bargaining

Before the first cap-and-trade system was promulgated, Ronald Coase developed the groundbreaking theory of social costs and bargaining,[59] which can be understood as the theoretical foundation for cap-and-trade systems today. Coase argued that, provided clearly defined property rights and absent transaction costs, the bargaining outcome of any situation involving property rights will always be the same efficient outcome.

To simplify, this "Coase Theorem" concerns a situation of conflicting property rights, e.g., a situation in which actions of a single person or entity have a harmful action on others, such as pollution from a factory that has a harmful effect on its neighbors in the above example. Such pollution can be considered an externality in this situation. Before Coase, economists considered such a situation as justification for regulatory actions regarding the factory's emissions—for example, a tax on pollution or liability for damages incurred from the pollution, which would ultimately convince the factory to leave the area and move to an area where pollution will not lead to regulatory action. Coase introduced a new perspective on this case by suggesting that this situation is a reciprocal problem instead of a unilateral situation in which the factory infringes on its neighbors' property rights. Indeed, any regulatory action benefitting the neighbor would harm the factory's property rights. The question, therefore, should not be how the factory can be deterred from harming its neighbors, but rather how both interests can be mended without causing harm to either the factory or the neighbor. Coase argues that absent transaction costs, the outcome of bargaining between the parties will always be the same efficient outcome, regardless of which party is awarded the reigning property rights. Applied to the above factory example, Coasean bargaining would lead to the following outcome:

Due to the factory's pollution, its three neighbors incur damages of $500 each. To remedy such damages, the neighbors could either install new airtight windows for $100 each, or the factory could install a new smokestack for $225. The operation of the factory is efficient as long as its profits are higher than the damages from emissions imposed on its neighbor, as the factory is liable for such. If profits are lower than damages, it is more efficient to shut the factory down and save on damages. Even if property

59 Ronald H. Coase, *The Problem of Social Cost*, 3 J. L. & Econ. 1-44 (1960).

rights are introduced into this example, the outcome according to Coase will not differ.

Suppose property rights are awarded to the neighbor. In this situation, the factory will install a new smokestack for $225, as this is cheaper than either paying each of the three neighbors to install airtight windows for a total of $300 or paying $1,500 damages to the neighbors.

Now, suppose property rights are awarded to the factory, i.e., the neighbors may not prohibit the factory from polluting. In this situation, the neighbors will pay the factory to install a new smokestack for $225, i.e., $75 each, as this is a more efficient outcome than each of them installing an airtight window for $100 each.

Consequently, the outcome is the same: a new smokestack will be installed. The allocation of property rights is merely responsible for which party internalizes the externality costs, i.e., who spends the $225 to purchase the smokestack.

This "equilibrium" depends on the absence of transaction costs. Suppose instead that in order to reach an agreement on how to proceed, the neighbors would incur transaction costs, for example attorney fees, of $50 each. The total transaction costs thus amount to $150. If property rights are awarded to the neighbors, the same efficient outcome as above will occur: the factory will install a new smokestack for $225. If property rights are awarded to the factory, the outcome differs. Each of the three neighbors will install new airtight windows for $100, as this is cheaper than reaching an agreement with the other neighbors ($50) and then paying for a share of the smokestack ($75) for a total of $125 per neighbor.

To sum up the Coase Theorem, pollution as an externality only exists in the absence of property rights. If everything is owned, the social costs imposed by pollution will be internalized, either by the polluter or the polluted citizen(s).

Of course, this is an academic economic theory and addresses neither the harmful environmental effects of pollution nor the underlying ethical considerations.[60]

60 *Cf.* Junker, *supra* note 18 in Chapter A.

b. Coase and cap-and-trade: The importance of the market and independent permit allocation

Cap-and-trade programs are understood to implement the Coasean Theorem. By setting a cap and allocating allowances, i.e., "rights to emit," cap-and-trade systems construct a market of tradable property rights, thus allowing the emission sources to allocate the use of such capped property rights in a cost-effective way. Under the Coasean-Model, the initial allocation of these property rights has no effect on the scheme's outcome as allowances will be eventually allotted to the participants that value them the most. In theory, this allows a low-cost allocation of emissions abatement as the market will distribute the abatement instead of a government authority.[61] However, as stated above, Coasean bargaining can only happen in the absence of transaction costs. Correspondingly, the efficiency of allowance allocation depends on various factors as well. These factors should be reviewed as an ideal cap-and-trade system would allow for optimal market performance in order to achieve efficient allocation of allowances.

Not considering potential impacts from offset credits, Hahn and Stavis identify six conditions that can inhibit allowance market efficiency.[62] In reviewing this research, however, it is important to remember that it only concerns the allocation of property rights independent of the initial allocation, not whether the outcome of the allocation is efficient or not.

aa. Transaction costs

The significance of transaction costs, colloquially defined in economics as a "cost incurred in making an economic exchange," has been demonstrated in the example above. In the context of cap-and-trade systems, numerous transaction costs can occur, such as costs for usage of the market to identify and acquire emission allowances or costs resulting from brokerage. Generally, economists identify three major types of transaction cost sources: (a) search and information, (b) bargaining and reaching a

61 This has been defined as "independence property" and was shown, *inter alia*, by Montgomery in his groundbreaking work, *cf.* David W. Montgomery, *Markets in Licenses and Efficient Pollution Control Programs*, 5 J. Econ. Theory 395-418 (1972). See also Robert W. Hahn & Robert N. Stavins, *The Effect of Allowance Allocations on Cap-and-Trade System Performance*, 54 J. L. & Econ. 2 (2011).

62 Hahn & Stavins, *id.* at 3 f.

decision, and (c) monitoring and enforcement, with all three types ultimately resulting from lack of information in a market.[63] As shown in the factory example above, transaction costs can influence efficient bargaining outcomes based on the distribution of property rights. The initial allocation of property rights, the subject of this chapter, is therefore likely not to be affected by bargaining costs.

More important regarding cap-and-trade systems is therefore the question of whether transaction costs can influence the allocation of property rights in a situation where the initial allocation of such property rights is not of concern, but rather the quantity of such an allocation to the participating sources, as overallocation is one of the major concerns in emissions trading.[64] Hahn and Stavins, for example, argue that the effect of transaction costs on the independence of the final allocation compared to the initial permit allocation depends on the nature of the transaction costs present. They therefore argue that steady marginal transaction costs will have no impact, while increasing marginal transaction costs may adversely affect the independence of distribution.[65] Interestingly, other economic research suggests that independent allocations will also not hold under decreasing marginal transaction costs. The cause for this lies in large-scale trading opportunities, which are enabled by the decreasing costs. For example a quantitative discount offered by a broker will incentivize participants to acquire a greater quantitative allotment of property rights, thus distorting the effective allocation.[66]

bb. Market power

Economic research suggests that the market power of individual participants may affect the allocative independence with different outcomes depending on whether the dominating participant is a seller or a buyer of allowances. If the participant is likely a seller of allowances, it will have an incentive to hold more permits than it needs in order to drive up prices of allowances, which will lead to a greater number of allowances

63 Dahlman, *supra* note 45, at 143 ff.

64 Hahn & Stavins, *supra* note 61, at 4.

65 *Cf.* note 64

66 Robert N. Stavins, *Transaction Costs and Tradeable Permits*, 29 J. ENVTL. ECON. & MGMT. 133-148 (1995).

being retired as they may not be used in the given trading period. [67] If the participant is a buyer, it has an incentive to buy only a minimal amount of its required permits in order to utilize its dominant market position to keep allowance prices low.[68]

The interaction of the allowance market and the product market adds another layer to this finding. As proven by Misiolek and Elder,[69] participants with dominating market power can use their dominant position over the allowance market to drive up the allowance price, as explained above, with the aim of increasing production costs for competitors.

cc. Uncertainty regarding future prices

Badlursson and von der Fehr show that with the presence of risk aversion concerning sources and transaction costs, the quantity of initial allocations may affect the utilization of allowances and thus the independence of its allocation.[70] The research suggests that entities with a larger initial allocation of allowances may have an incentive to under-invest in abatement technology in order to hedge against future price decreases, whereas a smaller initial allocation of allowances may incentivize sources to over-invest in their emissions abatement technology to protect themselves against expected price increases. This is, however, only another detrimental effect of transaction costs, for if they were absent, the market would reach an appropriate price for the allowances and achieve an allocation of allowances that is independent of the initial allocation,[71] which again highlights the significant detrimental effect of transaction costs.

---

67 Arun Malik, *Further Results on Permit Markets with Market Power and Cheating*, 44 J. Envtl. Econ. & Mgmt. 371-390 (2002).

68 Robert W. Hahn, *Market Power and Transferable Property Rights*, 99 Q. J. Econ. 753-765 (1984).

69 Walter S. Misiolek & Harold W. Elder, *Exclusionary Manipulation of Markets for Pollution Rights*, 16 J. Envtl Econ. & Mgmt. 156-166 (1989).

70 Fridrik M. Baldursson & Nils-Hendrik von der Fehr, *Price Volatility and Risk Exposure in Market-Based Environmental Policy Instruments*, 48 J. Envtl. Econ. & Mgmt. 682-704 (2004).

71 Hahn & Stavins, *supra* note 61, at 8.

dd. Conditional allowance allocations

Conditional allowance allocations (as used by the EUTS, for example) can have a considerable effect on the independence of allocation and market equilibrium. The allocation of allowances based on emissions output during previous emissions management seasons or based on production choices, etc., essentially serve as a production subsidy for the affected source as it allows sources to increase profits via increasing production to acquire more allowances in the following periods. Sources are essentially provided a product subsidy for emissions-intensive products as the expectation to receive additional allowances offsets costs from the production of emission intensive products. "Output-based allocation therefore means that emissions-intensive products have lower marginal costs than under ordinary free allocations, in which the full value of the embodied emissions would be embedded in the firm's marginal costs."[72] This creates a perverse incentive for sources to increase emissions rather than minimize them. If a device such as conditional allocations should be employed in a cap-and-trade system, often with the motivation to protect certain industries, allowance prices must rise to bring about additional reductions in emissions intensity and shift emissions abatement to other covered sectors.[73]

ee. Non-minimizing behavior by firms

In contrast to the other issues discussed so far, the effect of non-minimizing behavior on the independence of allocation is a question of behavioral economics rather than microeconomics. Hahn and Stavis define non-minimizing behavior as "not equating a sources' marginal abatement costs with the prevailing allowance price," and identify multiple potential reasons for such non-minimizing behavior, as well as how it can affect the final allocation of allowances. [74]

For the purpose of this thesis, the classification of allocation effects following from sources' initial perception of the cap-and-trade as "just" or "unjust," or as "justified" or "unjustified," are interesting. The school of "responsive regulation" argues that managerial decisions on whether to comply or not to comply with the regulations set out in a cap-and-trade

72 *Cf.* note 71
73 Hahn & Stavins, *supra* note 61, at 9.
74 *Id.*.

program are not entirely based on a benefit-cost analysis, but rather may be aimed towards avoiding non-compliance fees for sources' imminent judgment of behaving in a "wrong" way. Thus, whether or not a source will comply with the regulatory rules, which might affect the distribution of allowances, depends on whether or not the regulatory system itself and the initial distribution of allowances is perceived as "just."[75] To illustrate this issue: if a source perceives its initial allocation of allowances as too low, it may opt against compliance with the program and not acquire all required allowances, thus affecting allocation. This shows the importance of the perceived fairness of initial allowance allocations.

ff. Differential regulatory treatment of entities

It comes as no surprise that differences in the regulatory treatment of market participants may have an effect on allocation. Early economic research[76] illustrates this conundrum regarding state level regulation (especially rate-of-return regulation) of electricity producers. Rate-of-return regulation is a type of regulation developed for pricing monopolies that permits utilities to extract only those revenues that are linked with certain costs determined by the regulator to be recoverable in a theoretical, competitive market. As a result of this, allowances may be given to utilities for free rather than being sold, thus meaning that the utility will not incorporate the value of the allowance in its rate base. As a result, utilities will effectively be taxed 100 percent on any revenue from the sale of permits, giving utilities incentives to spend money on other abatement techniques.[77] In a multistate cap-and-trade system where some states have adopted rate-of-return regulation and others follow a ratemaking approach, product prices in rate-of-return states would be cheaper, and independent allocation will not take place.

This is an especially important takeaway for most larger, multistate or multijurisdictional cap-and-trade systems where participants may face

---

75 Hahn & Stavins, *supra* note 61, at 10.

76 For example Robert W. Hahn & Roger G. Noll, *Barriers to Implementing Tradable Air Pollution Permits: Problems of Regulatory Interactions*, 1 YALE J. ON REG. 63-69 (1983); John T. Tschirhart, *Transferable Discharge Permits and Profit-Maximizing Behavior*, *in* ECONOMIC PERSPECTIVES ON ACID DEPOSITION CONTROL (Thomas D. Crocker, ed., 1984); Wallace E. Oates & Diana L. Strassmann, *Effluent Fees and Market Structure*, 24 J. PUB. ECON. 29-46 (1984).

77 Hahn & Stavins, *supra* note 61, at 11.

different regulatory rules depending on their registered office. To avoid market impacts and any detriment to independent allocation, an ideal system would have identical regulatory treatment of all participants regardless of their jurisdiction.

gg. Conclusion

This discussion proves the importance of the market design for the independent allocation of allowances and reveals factors that contribute to an effective allowance market and thus should be present in an idealized cap-and-trade system. While independent allocation, as mentioned above, does not always mean that the most efficient outcome in allocation is reached, it is one of the biggest contributors to the efficient distribution of allowances. To reach such an independent allocation, cap-and-trade systems will need to refrain from regulatory mechanisms that have the potential to disturb the market. Transaction costs in particular are shown to be detrimental to the effective allocation of allowances and should thus be avoided. Regarding the initial allocation of allowances, above research shows that the quantitative allocation may influence the independent allocation and thus, to a certain degree, the most effective allocation, under the presence of the factors discussed above.

c. Takeaways from Pigou vs. Coase

Both instruments are based on the same theoretic economic rational. By forcing participants to internalize the social costs imposed by pollution, both frameworks create a price for emitting pollution.

Thus, in theory, the main difference between the two systems can be found in the way that the instrument arrives at such price.[78] This is relevant as the empirical proof discussed in this thesis supports that cap-and-trade systems are not capable of pricing emissions correctly.

78 Helm, *supra* note 4, at 210.

IV. Emissions trading vs. other types of regulation

1. Cost-benefit analysis and pollution

Regardless of the academic discussions above, some form of regulation is required to approach climate change. In addition to the ecologic necessity for regulation, it is clear that while such required regulations may have immediate detrimental economic effects resulting from diverting resources and capital away from the production of conventional goods and services and into potential cost intensive abatement measures, the advantages of mitigation and adaption measures promoted by regulation will generate greater benefits than costs in the long term.[79] Any discussion of costs can therefore only have one implication: as costs of environmental regulation cannot be a reason to avoid regulation, they can only be the deciding factor between two equally effective regulations with differing cost implications. For this, a cost-benefit analysis could be useful.

A central tool of regulatory assessment, especially in C&C regulation, is a cost-benefit analysis (CBA) of the regulation. In the U.S., Executive Order 12291 requires executive agencies to submit a CBA for all major regulations and only put forward for presidential approval those regulations predicted to produce a surplus of benefits, thus effectively shifting the burden of proof that demonstrates the cost effectiveness of its proposed regulation towards the agency.[80] In contrast, German agencies generally do not conduct a CBA before enacting regulation.[81]

In economic terms, CBA is defined as a collection of methods and rules used for assessing the social costs and benefits of alternative public policies. It promotes regulatory efficiency by identifying the set of feasible projects that would yield the largest positive net benefit to society.[82] Interestingly enough, the concept of using a CBA as the economic instrument of choice to assess regulation is mostly absent from environmental regulations. For

79 Mehling, *supra* note 1, at 15.

80 Baldwin et al., *supra* note 19, at 316.

81 While a CBA is generally not required for legislative action in Germany, Section 7 of the Federal Budget Code (*Bundeshaushaltsordnung*) requires a CBA before any disbursement.

82 David L. Weimer, *Cost-benefit Analysis in* The New Palgrave Dictionary of Economics (Steven N. Durlauf & Lawrence E. Blume, eds., 2008).

example, CBA has been absent from the process of EU Directive setting and establishing CO_2 and greenhouse gas targets.[83]

Indeed, the usefulness of CBA in the context of environmental law is subject to much dispute. While economics has developed a theoretical framework that allows CBA application to environmental issues,[84] others have argued that environmental goods are impossible to assess in a CBA.[85] While it is not overly complicated to assess the costs of environmental regulations, much of the controversy revolves around measuring the benefits of such regulations. Upon first sight it seems impossible to monetize environmental benefits, partly because that would be unethical,[86] but even more so because it is an impossible task. Compared to the questions in some other ethically questionable applications of CBA, such as in the famous Ford Pinto case,[87] using a CBA for environmental protection is even more complex as environmental goods not only benefit present people, but also even more so future generations. It is therefore very difficult to evaluate the benefits of environmental goods as the future is unknown. We also have to deal with a multitude of different expectations. It is clear that impoverished citizens of a developing country will put a drastically lower price on environmental goods than citizens of a Western country with a high standard of living. Correspondingly, existing studies often feature a highly euro-centric perspective, so the lack of information from other areas must be factored in as well. Valuation of goods depends on the availability of information regarding such goods. If only incomplete information is available—for example, the contribution of environmental factors upon human health, which are not fully understood yet—the valua-

---

83 Helm, *supra* note 4, at 217. A reason might be also that, as stated, CBA is mostly absent from policymaking procedures outside of the U.S.

84 See for example Nick Hanley & Clive L. Spash, Cost-Benefit Analysis and the Environment (1993).

85 Frank Ackerman & Lisa Heinzerling, Priceless: On Knowing the Price of Everything and the Value of Nothing (2004).

86 Frank Ackerman & Lisa Heinzerling, *Pricing the Priceless: Cost-Benefit Analysis of Environmental Protection*, 150 U. Pa. L. Rev. 1544 ff. (May 2002).

87 Grimshaw v. Ford Motor Co., 119 Cal. App. 3d 757 (Cal. Ct. App. 1981), a personal injury tort case regarding the safety of the Ford Pinto, a midsized car that had a tendency to burst into flames when rear ended. Ford conducted a CBA valuing the human life with USD 200.000, upon which it decided that the costs of callbacks and safety improvements outweighed the benefits. The court decided such an application of a CBA was malicious and awarded benefits, *cf.* also David G. Owen, *Problems in Assessing Punitive Damages Against Manufacturers of Defective Products*, 49 U. Chi. L. Rev. 1-60 (Winter 1982).

tion will inherently be flawed. This is, of course, an academic discussion as incomplete information is not foreign to applied science, such as engineering or (perhaps even more so) the medical field. However, if one is to academically review regulation, it seems worthwhile to discuss whether a CBA can reliably assess costs as part of a complete discussion.[88]

Additionally, in defense of CBA we can argue that regardless of the problems in assessing costs, environmental regulations do always impose costs, and it is useful to know them. Furthermore, the use of CBA as a factor in the rulemaking process does not automatically mean it is a decision-making rule. "In other words, CBA is an input, not a determinant of the level of economic instruments."[89] A further distinction must be made regarding small scale and local environmental regulation like the ERMS, which will be discussed in a later chapter. In such restricted programs, the CBA is a useful tool that should not be easily discarded. Therefore, CBA of environmental factors should not be generally disregarded in the context of environmental regulation.

2. Other economic and regulatory considerations

Scholars have advanced various arguments in favor of the efficiency of cap-and-trade regulations compared to C&C regulation and Pigouvian taxes.

If done correctly, the C&C regulatory approach requires measurement and emission control for each pollution source within the regulation's coverage. This is a very costly procedure, as regulators need to treat each emission source individually on a case-by-case basis. As this could be considered too expensive and complicated, C&C regulation is usually promulgated as a generalized across-the-board rule. The result is a very broad and economically inefficient regulatory scheme, "with some enterprises finding it hugely expensive to meet the standard and others able to go better than standard at very little cost but given no incentive to."[90] Consequently, emissions abatement might occur, but not necessarily in a cost efficient way. Aside from such criticism, a quick view on the political

---

88 For a similar discussion regarding the application of a CBA to financial regulations see John C. Coates IV, *Cost-Benefit Analysis of Financial Regulation: Case Studies and Implications*, 124 Yale L.J. 882-1345 (2015). Financial regulation faces similar issues in the feasibility of a CBA, as it has the same informational issues as environmental regulation.

89 Helm, *supra* note 4, at 210.

90 Baldwin et al., *supra* note 19, at 110.

implications of C&C regulation shows why most political actors avoid large scale environmental C&C rules: "In political terms, the regulator or government is seen to be acting forcefully and to be taking a clear stand: by designing some forms of behavior as unacceptable (…) and establishing penalties for those engaging in offensive conduct."[91] Political actors tend to avoid such clear decisions for fear of angering their constituency.

Cap-and-trade systems are, however, not free from criticism either. For example, Coase's theorem does not distinguish between polluter and polluted citizen and thus excludes ethical considerations and international law such as the polluter-pays principle discussed on page 79. On the contrary, it has been argued that in practice, cap-and-trade tends towards the polluted citizen paying.[92] This argument is not entirely convincing: thinking in purely ethical categories that would require the polluter to pay costs of pollution, C&C regulation, and Pigouvian taxes can be criticized with the same reasoning. If the price of producing a certain good would increase due to costs associated with a newly promulgated C&C regulation or a Pigouvian tax, the producer would likely increase the price of the product to pass the increased production cost on to the consumer. The question is therefore not who will pay the price, but in what way a producer can be forced to internalize the social costs associated with pollution in order to achieve a price in which pollution is reflected. Helm is, however, correct when he identifies the lack of ethical considerations in regards to "who picks up the check" as an obstacle to the success of international agreements.[93]

Pigouvian taxes are based on the assumption that the social costs from pollution are low enough to be internalized via taxation. Pollution nowadays, however, has proven itself to be a large-scale international problem. For such a problem, emissions trading might be the better tool as it can provide incentives for other jurisdictions to join the trading regime.

In summation, many scholars and policymakers consider cap-and-trade programs to be the most economically efficient regulatory tool to reduce emissions. The Acid Rain Program is widely considered the breakthrough of cap-and-trade as it is generally thought to have succeeded in reducing pollution at a lower price than classic C&C regulation would have imposed.[94]

---

91 Baldwin et al., *supra* note 19, at 106.

92 Helm, *supra* note 4, at 210.

93 *Cf.* also Chapter C.II ff.

94 *See also* page 150 in this text.

V. Emissions trading theory in detail: Design

After the above discussion of the economic ideas behind emissions trading, the following is a brief introduction into the translation of such economic theory into workable law by presenting general legal features of emissions trading systems and their underlying theory.

1. Cap

Capping is used to determine the maximum amount of emissions that participants in the cap-and-trade system may emit. Correspondingly, the cap also defines the allotment of emission permits and is the basis for the allocation of allowances.

a. Absolute and relative targets

Multiple types of cap-and-trade systems are possible, for example, with absolute or relative cap targets and with strict or moving targets. Systems using an absolute target approach aim to reduce emissions to a fixed amount.

Contrary to absolute targets, relative targets (also known as intensity-based targets) are targets that are not based on a combined, generally applicable level but are assessed by pollution levels in individual pollution sources or geographic regions. This can, for example, be either a relative reduction based on previous output or a cap targeted towards just one specific participating region where a different target is set than in another region. This does not allow for trading between participants with different targets and is thus less frequently employed.

Additionally, economic research suggests that the use of relative targets can result in reduced uncertainties regarding abatement costs.[95] Furthermore, the use of relative targets may be easier to implement from a public policy standpoint, as certain industries or regions may be protected from reductions.

---

95 Ian Sue Wing, Denny A. Ellerman & Jaemin Song, *Absolute vs. Intensity-based Emissions Caps*, 3 (Supplement 2) CLIMATE POLICY 24 (2003).

b. Strict or moving targets

Some cap-and-trade systems feature moving targets, according to which emissions are reduced by a certain amount after every trading period. This can be called a "moving" or "declining" target in contrast to strict targets, which stay the same after any given trading period.

c. Coverage

Another question regarding the cap's setting concerns the coverage of participants, i.e., which sources of emissions under which criteria have to participate in the cap-and-trade system. Economic studies suggest that full coverage, i.e., coverage of all sources in a geographical field regardless of, for example, their industry sector, is superior to partial coverage as this increases market size and thus allows for a more efficient allocation of abatement costs between participants.[96] However, studies regarding the European Union emissions trading system have shown that measuring the emission output of certain industries is unreliable. As a consequence, coverage of such industries—for example, agriculture—by the cap-and-trade system may negatively affect the preciseness of the measurement of total achieved emission reduction and thus might interfere with the reduction goals.[97] Consequently, regulators face a dilemma regarding the extent of coverage in their cap-and-trade system. Ultimately, whether or not an industry sector should be covered depends on the reliability with which its emissions can be measured. If no accurate measurement is possible, regulators must include separate measures.

d. Upstream vs. downstream caps

Caps can be designed as an "upstream" or a "downstream" cap. The design difference between these options relates to where the cap is placed. To

---

96 Christoph Bohringer & Andreas Löschel, *Climate Policy Beyond Kyoto: Quo Vadis? A Computable General Equilibrium Analysis Based on Expert Judgments*, 58 KYKLOS 467-493 (November 2005).

97 Martin Herold, *The Significance of Monitoring Capabilities to Decide about the Scope of a Carbon Market,* Presentation at 1st Global Carbon Market Forum on Monitoring, Reporting, Verification, Compliance and Enforcement Session II, May 19, 2008.

use a regulation of fossil fuels as an example: in an upstream cap, the point of regulation is closer to the entry of fossil fuel into the industry—i.e., the point of extraction, processing, or distribution. In a downstream cap, the point of regulation is the end user of the fossil fuel—i.e., where the combustion occurs, or the end user of energy derived from fossil fuel.[98] Since allowance prices are (at least in theory, as explained above) independent of their initial allocation, whether a cap-and-trade system employs an upstream or a downstream cap theoretically has no effect on the economics of the system.

While the European Union Emissions Trading system focuses on downstream coverage, most economists prefer an upstream approach, arguing that "the dispersed nature of CO_2 emissions throughout the economy makes regulation at the point of production/import both most complete and least cumbersome administratively. They emphasize that downstream approaches entail some incompleteness of coverage, which is economically inefficient. The most cost-effective emission reduction exploits abatement opportunities among as many sources as possible, while downstream approaches facilitate leakage."[99]

e. Offset credits

Many cap-and-trade systems feature offset credits, *inter alia.* with the intention of increasing the potential for cost-efficient emission reductions. Generally, offset credits can be understood as allowances that are generated by emissions reductions outside of the cap-and-trade system's specific coverage. This might mean that a participant or a third party creates credits by reducing emissions in another sector that is not covered or by reducing a certain pollutant that is not regulated by the respective system. This creates an incentive for participants to reduce emissions in areas where abatement costs are lower than in the coverage of the respective system, as it allows participants to create allowances at a lower cost compared to reducing their emissions in the covered area or trading for additional allowances:

---

98 Michael Hanemann, *The Role of Emission Trading in Domestic Climate Policy*, 30 The Energy Journal, Special Issue 2: Climate Change Policies After 2012 83 (October, 2009).

99 *Cf. id.* at 104.

> *Offsets play a key role in reducing the overall cost of GHG regulations and achieving reductions in uncapped sectors. The cost containment aspects work in two ways. First, offsets projects, especially those involving land use activities, are often less expensive to implement than emissions reductions by regulated entities. Second, in a market-based program with a strict cap on emissions, offset credits from uncapped sectors create an option for increasing the supply of compliance instruments.*[100]

An obvious problem with this approach is that it might endanger the emission reduction levels targeted by the cap-and-trade system. If, for example, a cap-and-trade system aims to reduce greenhouse gas emissions in a geographic area below the amount of X but allows for offsetting by reducing lead pollution, participants may have an incentive to reduce their lead pollution up to an amount where the created permits would fully cover the participant's greenhouse gas emissions. This will result in a reduction of lead emissions, but not of greenhouse gas emissions, and the system will fail to meet its environmental objective. This issue does not present itself when offset credits are created by reduction of the same pollutants that are covered in the system, but in industry sectors that are not covered. The Illinois Emission Reduction Market System, which is reviewed in a later chapter, follows such an approach.

When creating a regulatory framework for offset credits, regulators face two options regarding the implementation of offset credit trade into the market: offsets can be traded with buyer or with seller liability. The difference between the two approaches describes the burden of liability in case an offset credit, which was traded in the market, is declared invalid by the administration after the completion of the trade. In such cases, the offset credit has to be replaced with a valid allowance. If the framework provides for buyer liability, the buyer of the offset credit is responsible for the replacement, while the seller of the offset credit is liable under seller liability provisions. Buyer liability, which burdens the buyer with the risk of invalidity, has the theoretical possibility of seriously inhibiting offset trading, especially in early phases of a program, as it increases uncertainty and the cost of buying offset credits.

Offset projects have often been criticized for their problems regarding environmental efficiency as they run the imminent risk of allowing en-

---

100 David M. Cooley & Jonas J. Monast, *Carbon Offsets and Environmental Impacts: NEPA, The Endangered Species Act, and Federal Climate Policy*, 28 Pace Envtl. L. Rev. 378 f. (Winter 2011).

tities to "cop-out" of actual emissions reductions, especially if offset allowances do not accurately reflect the emissions reduction. Another common point of criticism relates to the civil rights impact ("environmental justice") of offset credits. Scholars and interest groups argue that the possibility of creating offset credits transfers emission sources into low-income areas. For example, a source could generate offset projects by undertaking forestry projects in a state forest. As a consequence, this source does not have to decrease emissions, resulting in increased pollution in its neighborhood. As most pollution sources are located in industrial and low-income neighborhoods, this mechanism results in disadvantages for marginalized groups.

2. Allocation

The question of allowance allocation concerns the procedure by which allowances are distributed to the system's participants. To establish a functioning system, the total amount of distributed allowances must equal the established cap. To illustrate this with an oversimplified example: In the covered area, greenhouse gas emissions amount to 100,000 tons per year. Those emissions are produced by 100 covered sources. If an emissions reduction of 10 percent is desired, the cap will be established at 90,000 tons. For the 100 covered sources, nine allowances permitting emissions of 100 tons of greenhouse gases (one ton per allowance) are available.

This simple example displays most of the challenges regulators face in the allocation process.

a. Allocation method

Currently enacted cap-and-trade systems utilize two basic methods of determining the baseline for the allocation of allowances: grandfathering and benchmarking.

"Grandfathering refers to free allocation of allowances to enterprises based on their historical emissions, whereas benchmarking refers to free allocation of allowances to enterprises based on 'clean' production standards."[101] It has been argued that the choice between grandfathering and

101 Stefan Weishaar, Emissions Trading Design: A Critical Overview 193 (2014).

benchmarking has no impact on the environmental effectiveness of the emissions trading scheme, but that it constitutes a distributional choice that can be made to enhance political acceptance.[102] However, studies of enacted emissions trading systems show that grandfathering might reduce incentives to invest in abatement technologies: For example, in the context of the implementation of the EUTS in Germany, sources commissioned prior to December 31, 2002 in principle received permits according to 97.09 percent of their historical emissions from 2000 to 2002, which equates a compliance factor of 0.9709, whereas sources commissioned or modernized from 1994 onwards received 100 percent of their historical emissions for a period of 12 years, leading to a compliance factor of 1. This rewards early actions, such as a modernization prior to the cut-off date, and did not result in a significant reduction in emissions. "Due to these allocation rules, only minor differences between allocated and actual emissions are expected. As a consequence, there is little pressure to invest in pollution prevention and reduction."[103] As shown in later chapters E and F, grandfathering provided incentives for sources to manipulate—or at least inflate—their emissions. This supports the superiority of benchmarking as the better allocation method.[104]

However, the following discussion of enacted emissions trading systems will reveal a systematic issue with benchmarking procedures in relation to the Polluter Pays principle. Any regulation that does not, as defined above, use "clean" production standards as an allocation base, but instead just allocates a "significant majority of emissions allowances for free to operators under emissions trading rules" is at odds with this principle, as sources are rewarded for using dirty technology.[105]

---

102 *Compare with id.*

103 Heinrich Tschochohei & Jan Zöckler, *Business and Emissions Trading from a Public Choice Perspective – Waiting for a New Paradigm to Emerge, in* EMISSIONS TRADING, INSTITUTIONAL DESIGN, DECISION MAKING AND CORPORATE STRATEGIES 48 (Ralf Antes, Bernd Hansjürgens & Peter Letmathe, eds. 2008).

104 *See also*, James Salzman & J.B. Ruhl, *Gaming the Past: The Theory and Practice of Historic Baselines in the Administrative State*, 64 VAND. L. REV. 1-57 (2010). Also, in MARK SAGOFF, THE ECONOMY OF EARTH: PHILOSOPHY, LAW AND THE ENVIRONMENT (2d ed., 2008) where p. 90 states:
So far, experience with attempts to "cap" carbon and trade "allowances" have been fraught with corruption as each player has insisted on having a supersized initial endowment. It would be one thing if carbon "allowances" were sold to the highest bidders and the money invested in clean technologies. It is another thing that the "allowances" are constructed from political whole cloth and allocated accordingly.

105 Mehling, *supra* note 1, at 20.

b. Free allocation vs. selling

In contrast to the above-mentioned methods of free allocation, allowances may also be sold or auctioned. Economic literature widely recognizes auctioning of allowances as superior to free allocation. For one, free allocation is considered to distort incentives for reducing emissions, as displayed above. Even worse, this thesis shows that free allocation may create perverse incentives to increase emissions or use "dirty technology" to benefit from maximum allowance allocation. Furthermore, most enacted cap-and-trade systems feature free allocation only for participants of the first trading period. Participants entering the market at a later stage are usually required to trade for the required allowances. This benefits the initial participants and may even create barriers for market entrance.

Weishaar summarizes the advantages of allowance auctioning as follows:

> *1. Auctions lead to self-revelation of the bidder's private values. An auction mechanism can yield higher revenues than simply quoting a price or repeated negotiations with potential buyers, although bidders are generally reluctant to reveal their preferences because they fear that competitors could take advantage of it.*
> *2. Auctions can be designed in such a way as to ensure "allocative efficiency:" auctions award the allowances to the bidder with the highest valuation for them (assuming that bidders have sufficient financial resources). However, auctions are capable of demonstrating their superior allocative efficiency properties only if they are tailor-made towards the respective bidders.*
> *3. Prior knowledge of the auction rules provides bidders with a transparent framework of how their bids will be assessed.*
> *4. Compared with the time-consuming negotiations that may occur with an administrative allocation, auctions are relatively fast allocation mechanisms. Nevertheless, the development of an auction mechanism can be a time-consuming process. Also the time and expense required for companies to gather information and to design an optimal bidding strategy can be substantial.*
> *5. What is particularly attractive is that allowance auction revenue can be spent on lowering distortionary taxes, such as labour taxes, for the industry, which economists usually refer to as the "double dividend hypothesis."*[106]

Especially the last point is noteworthy. Indeed, some scholars have suggested that the use of auctioning proceeds for improvements in low energy

---

106 Weishaar, *supra* note 101, at 113 ff.; *cf.* also Bruce R. Huber, *How Did RGGI Do It? Political Economy and Emissions Auctions*, 40 Ecol. L. Q. 77 ff. (2013).

and emissions technology may be more helpful for reducing pollution than the actual cap itself.[107] Additionally, using auctioning proceeds to provide monetary incentives for investment in low emissions technology can be a valuable asset in fighting emissions leakage as it reduces cost pressure faced by market participants.

In addition to these concerns, grandfathering is thought to lead to windfall profits for covered entities. This was the case for the EUTS in Phase I, which relied heavily on grandfathering for the allocation of allowances. "Having received emissions allowances for free, many electricity generators nonetheless raised their bid prices for wholesale electricity on the expectation of eventual increases in regulatory compliance costs. These cost increases turned out to be much smaller than anticipated, but generators pocketed the surplus, leading to claims that billions of dollars were transferred from electricity ratepayers to generating firms."[108] Environmental groups, traditionally skeptics of cap-and-trade systems, increasingly support allowance auctioning in an attempt to "make the polluter pay."[109]

3. Overallocation

a. Overallocation

A cap-and-trade system is overallocated if annual caps are set at levels beyond "business-as-usual" (BAU) emissions,[110] i.e., if the allowed emissions are not a significant reduction compared to usual emission levels in prior years. An overallocation of allowances will result in sub-optimal or non-performance of the cap-and-trade system. Experience with the enacted systems shows that overallocation is one of the most prolific problems in modern cap-and-trade systems. Two types of overallocation can be differentiated: Absolute and early overallocation.

---

107 *Id. at.* 79.

108 *Id.at* 73.

109 *Cf.*, for example, Greenpeace in David Sassoon, *Business as Usual: A Report to the President on Pending Federal Climate Legislation*, (Greenpeace Report 2009), at page 16 f.

110 *Cf.* Danny A. Ellerman & Barbara Buchner, *Over-Allocation or Abatement? A Preliminary Analysis of the EU Emissions Trading Scheme Based on the 2005-06 Emissions Data*, 41 ENVTL. & RESOURCE ECON. 272 f. (2008), for an attempt to define over-allocation.

Absolute overallocation results when covered emissions are lower than the cap and are expected to be lower than the cap in the future.[111] This can also be classified as a lack of scarcity of allowances. In contrast, early allocation occurs when program caps were above BAU emissions only in their early allotment periods.[112]

Overallocation results in various issues that adversely affect a program's efficiency. The most obvious effect is a low allowance price, as the overallocation results in low demand for allowances. As participants have more allowances available than needed for their BAU allowances or can buy allowances at a low price, they have no incentive to reduce their emissions. As a consequence, no investment in abatement technology will occur. The environmental objective of the trading program will not be reached, as no emission reduction on investment in emission abatement technology occurs. In the situation of such an overallocation, the price of allowances will merely reflect the transaction costs,[113] as the allowances no longer contain any inherent value.

To avoid overallocation, two approaches are available. Regulators may set the cap from the outset to avoid overallocation or an initial overallocation may be corrected by subsequent acts.

aa. Avoiding overallocation—The Feasibility Principle

Avoiding overallocation from the outset is preferable as this allows the cap-and-trade program to work efficiently from its initiation. To assure a stringent initial allocation of allowances, scholars propose to use the "feasibility principle." Such a feasibility principle is regularly used in standard setting procedures under conventional environmental law[114] and can be seen as a competing approach to a CBA. The U.S. Supreme Court recognized the feasibility principle, *inter alia,* in its *American Textile Mfrs Inst. v. Donovan* case, also referred to as the "Cotton Dust case."[115] In this case, the U.S. Occupational Safety and Health Administration (OSHA) had to decide

111 Lesley K. McAllister, *The Overallocation Problem in Cap-and-Trade: Moving Toward Stringency*, 43 Colum. J. Envtl. L. 411 (2009).

112 *Id.* at 412.

113 *Id.* at 416.

114 *See* David M. Driesen, *Distributing the Costs of Environmental, Health, and Safety Protection: The Feasibility Principle, Cost-Benefit Analysis, and Regulatory Reform*, 32 Bc Envtl. Aff. Law Rev. 7-25 (2005).

115 American Textile Mfrs. Inst., Inc. v. Donovan, 452 U.S. 490 (1981).

on an exposure limit after evidence revealed that the inhalation of cotton dust by textile workers resulted in byssonisis, a chronic and irreversible lung ailment colloquially known as "brown lung disease." The court was confronted with proposed cotton exposure limits for yarn production between 100 micrograms per cubic meter of air (ug/m^3) as proposed by labor unions and 500 ug/m^3 as proposed by industry groups. OSHA decided on a limit of 200 ug/m^3 for yarn manufacturing with a more relaxed standard for other industry segments. It found that the industry was not technically capable of achieving the standard proposed by the respective unions, but considered 200 ug/m^3 as economically and technically achievable. The petitioners, industry group representatives, argued against such reasoning and asserted that OSHA was mandated to carry out a CBA. The Supreme Court rejected this argument and found that OSHA is only required to "set the standard which most adequately assures, to the extent feasible [...] that no employee will suffer material health issues." It argued that in promulgating the relevant Occupational Safety and Health Act, Congress had already considered the costs imposed by regulation and decided to put the health and safety of workers above all other considerations, except that of feasibility, which the Supreme Court defined as "what one is capable of doing."

Applying such a feasibility method to the process of defining caps in emissions trading, the caps should be sufficiently stringent to motivate emissions reductions at least as great as those that could otherwise be achieved by requiring the use of economically and technologically feasible emissions control technologies.[116] An important implication of such a technology-based principle is that not every reduction from BAU emissions put forward in the cap automatically prevents overallocation. Rather, the cap can be assessed by its relativity to regulations requiring feasible control technology. "Examples of such regulation include standards based on 'lowest achievable emission rate' or 'best available control technology,' under the Clean Air Act, and 'best available demonstrated control technology' or 'best available technology' under the Clean Water Act. 172."[117] This approach avoids the difficulties faced by regulators in determining social costs.[118]

---

116 See Driesen, *supra* note 114; McAllister, *supra* note 111, at 426.

117 McAllister, *supra* note 111, at 427.

118 *Cf.* Chapter D.II.2 "Pigouvian taxes."

bb. Subsequent correction of overallocation

Another approach is the enactment of regulations allowing for subsequent reductions as a solution to overallocation. This is also referred to as "tightening the cap." While this would allow for subsequent correction of the initial allocation, it also delays emission reductions and allows for lobbying and governmental influence on the allocation of allowances. Scholars such as Helm, Hepburn, and Mash have argued for a model in which an external, independent agency is responsible for setting carbon taxes.[119] The same approach could be used for adjustments to the allocation rates in cap-and-trade systems. Helm argues that the retention of flexibility at the government level increases uncertainty for market participants and is likely to result in a lower than necessary cap.[120] This thesis will, however, show that subsequent flexibility is a useful and necessary (albeit not in itself sufficient) instrument to deal with the overallocation of allowances. He makes a strong case for the "independent agency" structure. In practice, this could be an independent commission of experts routinely reassessing the cap. Another approach could be regulations putting a limit on banking of allowances. While banking is generally useful, voiding allowances after either one trading period or multiple trading periods produces subsequent scarcity by expiration of unused allowances. While this appears to be a logical approach, the following chapters will raise doubts as to its efficiency.

4. Emissions management period

Most cap-and-trade systems feature "compliance" or "trading periods." These terms, which often differ from system to system, define the time period after which a participant must hold allowances in an amount sufficient enough to cover its actual emissions.

If a participant does not hold enough allowances at the end of the period, it will face penalties. Therefore, the participant will use the compliance period to trade for allowances if it requires additional allowances, or it will sell back, respectively, any surplus allowances.

---

119 Dieter Helm, Cameron Hepburn & and Richard Mash, *Credible Carbon Policy*, 19 OXFORD REV. ECON. POL'Y 450 (2003).

120 Helm, *supra* note 4, at 220.

5. Banking

Banking provisions allow sources to use allowances beyond the year in which they were allotted. Negative effects of banking in the case of overallocation of allowances have been discussed earlier, but obvious advantages exist as well. For example, banking clearly reduces abatement costs, as participants are allowed to redistribute their abatement across time to achieve abatement whenever it can be achieved at the lowest cost possible.[121] Banking also reduces uncertainty about future prices as it allows participants to use banked allowances to "hedge" against future allowance price increases. Furthermore, economic studies have shown that banking stabilizes allowance prices.[122]

Banking might, however, negatively affect the environmental integrity of a trading scheme in regards to pollutants such as SO_2 emitters, where the amount of the environmental degradation in a given period depends on time-specific emissions.[123]

6. Borrowing

Borrowing can be understood as reverse banking: instead of allowing participants to use allowances in future compliance periods, borrowing provisions allow participants to use allowances from future compliance periods in current periods.[124] They can be thought of as "allowance credits." Borrowing provisions have the same rationale as banking: they allow for cost reductions by adding intertemporal flexibility to the cap-and-trade system. There might be a concern that borrowing is likely to increase the cost of compliance in the following compliance costs inter-temporarily and can therefore not be considered a downside of borrowing.

However, certain policy concerns exist regarding adverse incentives set by borrowing provisions. For example, borrowing provisions might introduce what economists call a "moral hazard" problem. "Moral hazard may be defined as actions of economic agents in maximizing their own utility to the detriment of others, in situations where they do not

121 Weishaar, *supra* note 101, at 61.

122 Harrison Fell, Ian A. MacKenzie & William A. Pizer, *Prices versus Quantities versus Bankable Quantities*, 34 RESOURCE & ENERGY ECON. 623 (2012).

123 Weishaar, *supra* note 101, at 62.

124 Weishaar, *supra* note 101, at 61.

bear the full consequences or, equivalently, do not enjoy the full benefits of their actions *due to uncertainty and incomplete information or restricted contracts* which prevent the assignment of *full* damages (benefits) to the agent responsible."[125] In other words, a moral hazard is a situation that creates an incentive for a market participant to engage in risky behavior, as other participants will incur the costs that occur if the risk materializes. Borrowing provisions increase such an incentive as they incentivize participants to continuously borrow allowances from future compliance periods instead of reducing emissions or investing in abatement technology, and then to exit the cap-and-trade system once they can no longer obtain the required allowances to operate. Furthermore, regulators may face additional lobbying and political pressure to loosen emissions caps if participants are incentivized to borrow allowances and lobby for a looser cap in future periods.

7. Trading and pricing

By definition, all cap-and-trade systems allow for trading of allowances between participants. The individual trading provisions can differ, however, and must therefore be reviewed on a case-by-case basis for each system. While pricing of allowances will occur by the power of the market, some cap-and-trade designs contain provisions on pricing called "price ceilings."

A price ceiling system, as employed in the Australian emissions trading system, for example, is employed to limit allowance prices to guarantee participants low trading costs, thus achieving easy access to more allowances. A ceiling system works by creating more allowances once the market price reaches a certain trigger price.[126] This can be a problem for other cap-and-trade programs that provide for linking with the program containing a price ceiling. If the price ceiling is triggered, new allowances will be created. Absent a prohibition of such a procedure, these can also be used in other systems that provide for linking, thus effectively raising the cap of the linked system by introducing more allowances into the market,

---

125 Y. Kotowitz, *Moral Hazard in* The New Palgrave Dictionary of Economics (Steven N. Durlauf & Lawrence E. Blume, eds., 2008).

126 Erik Haites, *Harmonization between National and International Tradeable Permit Schemes*, OECD Global Forum on Sustainable Development: Emissions Trading, Concerted Action for Tradable Emissions Permits (CATEP) (Synthesis Paper, 2003); Weishaar, *supra* note 101, at 44.

which can endanger the environmental objective of the system. This is an issue that must be covered in the individual linking provisions.

8. Linking

Linking is a highly complicated subject whose implications are not fully studied yet. "'Linking' is generally defined as a mechanism that allows market participants in one trading scheme to use emission rights issued under another trading scheme to meet domestic compliance obligations."[127] This can be achieved via direct linking or indirect linking establishments, such as the Kyoto Protocol's Clean Development Mechanism.

Scholars identify three general obstacles to linking provisions: loss of political autonomy due to a loss of regulatory control over the respective emissions trading scheme, lobbying, and compatibility issues.[128] However, political and policy advantages exist as well. For example, the basic objective of linking between cap-and-trade systems is the creation of a bigger market, which leads to greater flexibility for participants as well as higher market liquidity and more effective allocation of abatement costs. Suppose entity A operates sources in the cap-and-trade systems I and II. The source in cap-and-trade system I would need to invest large sums in abatement technology to comply with its allocated allowances, whereas the source in cap-and-trade system II utilizes cleaner technology and therefore holds more allowances than it requires. Linking allows for the transfer of surplus allowances from system II to the source in system I, which leads to a cheaper and thus more efficient allocation of abatement costs. Those advantages can even be extended. In theory, an international linking system could provide mechanisms "for countries to coordinate and harmonize their emissions caps, price controls, and other design features. By encouraging systems to work together through decentralized negotiations, linkage could, in principle, take the place of a centralized top-down climate agreement."[129]

127 Weishaar, *supra* note 101, at188.

128 Weishaar, *supra* note 101, at 193.

129 Matthew Ranson & Robert N. Stavins, *Linkage of Greenhouse Gas Emissions Trading Systems: Learning from Experience* 2. (Harvard Project on Climate Agreements, Discussion Paper ES 2013-2, November 2013).

This thesis reviews linking provisions in the context of the respective systems and their potential for a paradigm shift in international emissions regulation policy.

a. Linking design in theory

Linking provisions can be classified into four general categories: "one-way and two-way linkages between cap-and-trade systems; one-way linkages between cap-and-trade and credit systems; implicit linkages via national trading such as under Article 17 of the Kyoto Protocol; and various types of non-traditional linkage."[130]

aa. One-way and two-way linkages

One-way and two-way linking can also be defined as "direct" linking: Participants of one cap-and-trade system may purchase allowances created in another program to fulfill their own compliance obligations. Allowances go "down a one-way street" to another program. Two-way linking allows not just participants of one program to purchase allowances, but equal trade between two programs. The implications of such are clear: if allowance prices in one system are lower than in the other program, participants are incentivized to purchase allowances in the program with lower prices. In theory, this will result in decreased demand for the more expensive allowances, thus reducing their price. Ultimately, prices in the two systems will be equalized. Two-way linkages are the most common type of linking provision. Aside from the U.S. systems displayed later in this thesis, the European Union and Australia agreed to link their respective emissions trading systems starting July 1, 2015.[131]

---

130 *Id.* at 3.

131 *Cf.* European Union, Climate Action Policy News on "International Carbon Market," http://ec.europa.eu/clima/policies/ets/linking/index_en.htm (last visited January 11, 2020).

bb. One-way linkages between cap-and-trade and credit systems

Such linking provisions allow participants to purchase emission credits from credit systems instead of allowances as displayed above. Credit systems are programs such as the one established by the Clean Development Mechanism.[132]

As of now, the European Union Emissions Trading system, the RGG, and the programs established by Switzerland, New Zealand, Australia, and Tokyo have established links to the Clean Development Mechanism.[133]

cc. Indirect national trading linkage

Under the Kyoto Protocol, the developed countries that agreed to emissions reductions were issued Assigned Amount Units (AAU) amounting to the agreed emissions target that they accepted for the first commitment period from 2008 to 2012. At the end of each compliance period, countries were obliged to surrender AAUs covering their actual emissions at the end of the compliance period. Under Article 17 of the Kyoto Protocol, nation states that did not reduce their emissions according to their targets and thus had emissions exceeding their AAU allotment were allowed to satisfy their compliance obligations by obtaining AAUs from another developed country or by producing emission credits under the Clean Development Mechanism or the Joint Implementation Mechanism. In practice, AAU transactions have been rather limited[134] despite the surplus of AAUs allotted to some Eastern European countries, likely as a result of low reduction targets that were easy to achieve.

b. Linking provisions in the real world

Many programs contain linking provisions. Following the argument made above on the premise that countries and states are self-interested actors, this suggests that linking provisions are favorable from an economic and

132 *Cf.* Chapter D for a discussion of the Kyoto Protocol and the Clean Development Mechanism.

133 Ranson & Stavins, *supra* note 129, at 22.

134 *Cf.* data displayed by Ranson & Stavins, *supra* note 129, at 23.

policy point of view. However, as shown by some state's decisions not to link, a variety of reasons for the decision not to link exist as well.

Ranson and Stavins conducted a qualitative analysis of factors that play into linking decisions. Enacted linking provisions show that geographical proximity is a key factor in linking decisions. Ranson and Stavins, in drawing a comparison to negotiated trade agreements,[135] attribute this to, *inter alia*, information about markets and similarities in objectives and goals.[136]

An additional explanation might be the regulator's fear of emissions leakage.[137] Leakage occurs when emissions sources move or shift production outside of the cap-and-trade program's geographical coverage. Leakage will generally occur if abatement costs are higher than the costs of moving or shifting production. If geographical coverage is extended due to linking of cap-and-trade programs, the costs of moving and shifting increase. The energy sector is a good example. The infrastructure needed for transporting energy, such as high-voltage cables, is not expensive and generally available everywhere. Thus, the energy sector is most susceptible to emissions leakage as import of energy into a covered area is not costly. If the geographical area is extended by linking cap-and-trade systems, the costs of importing energy increase and leakage becomes less likely. Thus, linking can contribute to the reduction of emissions leakage. However, if allowance prices are significantly different in the linked markets, emissions may be shifted into the market with cheaper prices.

Another factor identified by Ranson and Stavins is the cost effectiveness of linking. Trotignon found that in the first two years of the Phase II (Kyoto) compliance period from 2008–2009, participants in the EUTS saved at least 280 million EUR by purchasing emissions credits from other Kyoto countries instead of investing in higher-cost abatement technology.[138] This advantage might, however, be offset by the political implications of the welfare distribution caused by linking. Not all participants of a cap-and-trade program will benefit equally from linking. If linking causes emissions price to decrease, the participants that are likely "buyers" of allowances will profit over entities that are likely "sellers" of allowances.

---

135 *See also* the so called "Gravity Model of Trade," which describes the factors influencing international trade, *cf.* Jan Tinbergen, Shaping the World Economy: Suggestions for an International Economic Policy (1962).

136 Ranson & Stavins, *supra* note 129, at 8.

137 For a more detailed discussion of emissions leakage, *cf.* in this chapter VI.10.

138 Raphael Trotignon, *Combining Cap-and-Trade with Offsets: Lessons from the EU-ETS*, 12 Climate Policy 280 (2012).

"Buyers" are especially entities with high abatement costs, such as those with large and technologically intensive operations. Benefitting these participants over potential "sellers" of allowances might be politically controversial.

There are various other factors that can influence the decision whether or not to link. Aside from the major factors discussed above, regulators are also likely to be influenced by similarities in market design and allowance price.

Lastly, linking introduces a problem already discussed in the context of offset credits: environmental integrity and uncertainty. As regulators do not have full insight into another program's environmental integrity, compliance standards, and market stability, they reduce certainty in the cap-and-trade program and among its participants.

9. Compliance

All cap-and-trade systems contain provisions ensuring compliance with the regulations promulgated in the system. Compliance provisions generally concern the monitoring and reporting of emissions as well as procedures that ensure every participant holds the required allowances for their emission output at the designated time. The analysis of enacted cap-and-trade systems in the following chapters will support a theory advanced by Tietenberg, who indicates that under a cap-and-trade system, participants always have an incentive to falsify their emissions data, depending on the method of allocation.[139] This underlines the importance of compliance provisions and procedures also in advance of the system's implementation. The importance of this is also shown by the drastic allowance price drop in the EUTS, which is generally considered to be a result of lax monitoring of emission data prior to the enactment.

Compliance rules also concern penalties imposed on participants that do not hold the necessary amount of allowances at the end of the compliance period. Regulators have to choose between setting penalties according to the current trading price of allowances or at an amount over that price. The latter disincentives non-compliance with the cap-and-trade system, but may also lead to financial damage to participants.

---

139 Thomas H. Tietenberg, Emissions Trading: Principles and Practice 170 f. (2nd ed. 2006).

10. Emissions leakage

Emissions leakage can be understood as another variant of the "moral hazard" problem explained above. Pollution control regulations vary on a national or international scale. Within the same industry, not every source of pollutant is covered by a cap-and-trade system or by any environmental regulation. Consequently, only certain economic actors are forced to internalize the social costs associated with their production while others may not face any regulation. Obviously, the latter will be able to produce at a lower price. As a result, a phenomenon called "emissions leakage" can occur in two different ways: participants may choose to relocate emission sources into an area not covered by regulation, or they will reduce their production while their competitors located in areas without coverage will increase theirs. Both situations lead to the same outcome. Emissions will not be reduced but merely relocated outside of the cap-and-trade system's coverage. While studies suggest that this will only happen at high allowance prices,[140] empirical evidence suggests otherwise.

VI. Conclusion – an efficient cap-and-trade program

For a cap-and-trade program to be considered a success, the program must achieve the intended reduction in emissions. This can be defined as "environmental efficiency" or "environmental integrity" and is the ultimate objective of any environmental regulation. It should therefore be the primary standard against which the program has to be measured.

However, in view of the economic implications of pollution, a cap-and-trade system can only be considered ideal if it is able to achieve an internalization of pollution costs. As the calculation of social costs is an almost impossible task,[141] the economic efficiency of a cap-and-trade system can alternatively be assessed by reviewing whether it achieved a market equilibrium and therefore resulted in an efficient price payable on the pollution. If this is the case, it can be assumed that the program resulted in an efficient allocation of abatement costs as well. The selected cap-and-trade

140 Weishaar, *supra* note 101, at 35. This is only logical, as the marginal costs for compliance with the regulation must be higher than the relocation costs, or at least high enough to influence the product prices.

141 *Cf.* the discussion regarding Pigouvian taxes in Chapter C. II.

markets will therefore be reviewed against the backdrop provided in this chapter.

VII. Bottom-up linking vs. top-down cap-and-trade

As discussed, the Kyoto Protocol set out to establish an international approach to emission reductions, with emissions trading being one of the possible regulative compliance tools allowed to achieve the designated emissions reductions. The United Nations Framework Convention in Climate Change considers the Protocol and the CDM a "trailblazer" in international emissions trading. While the idea of a unified international response to pollution, such as an internationally binding emissions trading program, sounds desirable, it is doubtful whether such a program will emerge anytime soon. If anything, it seems like the Paris Agreement has put a brake on the development of a binding international climate change regime. Consequently, an interesting topic is whether a bottom-up system of nationally or sub-nationally linked emissions programs could be more efficient at reducing worldwide emissions.

Regarding regulatory alternatives to the idea of an international emissions trading system, the proposed post-Kyoto policy approaches can be divided into three general categories: "targets and timetables, harmonized national policies and coordinated and unilateral national policies."[142] Targets and timetables follow the general "top-down" approach as stipulated in the Kyoto Protocol: Countries agree on emissions reductions within a certain timeframe. Harmonized national policies rely on individual country regulatory action but establish unifying principles to be followed by the national regulation. An often-cited example is a national tax on carbon with harmonized tax bases.[143] Coordinated and unilateral national regulations utilize a "bottom-up" approach to regulation, such as linkage of national environmental regulations. Prins and Rayne argue for the development of an international emissions market by allowing markets to grow from the "bottom-up."[144] "The 'bottom up' approach relies on voluntary international mitigation pledges, made binding through nation-

142 Joseph E. Aldy & Robert Norman Stavins, eds., Post-Kyoto International Climate Policy: Implementing Architectures for Agreement 37 ff. (2009).

143 Advanced, for example, by Richard N. Cooper, *Alternatives to Kyoto: The Case for a Carbon Tax* (Harvard University Discussion Paper, 2006).

144 Gwyn Prins & Steve Rayner, Time to Ditch Kyoto? 449 Nature 974 (2007).

al legislation and reported internationally (hence, it is also known as the pledge-and-review-approach). The rationale of this approach is that '[w]hat really matters is that the pledges reflect measurable, reportable and verifiable actions and that they are embedded in domestic law. From this perspective, the international legal character of a future climate agreement seems less important.'"[145]

Opinions on this regulatory policy are divided along a clear line. "Proponents of a 'top down' approach include most developing countries and the EU, while the U.S. and some other members of the Umbrella Group have advocated a 'bottom up' approach."[146] Even before the Paris Agreement, which utilizes a bottom-up approach much like the proposed pledge-and-review-approach, the international community made attempts at developing such a bottom-up regime of linked cap-and-trade programs. Virtually all of the currently enacted cap-and-trade programs provide for the possibility of linkage to other programs, with various programs being already linked.[147] In theory, as somewhat farsighted rational actors, states will eventually link their respective emissions trading programs.[148] Furthermore, most programs incorporate offset credits, and not all programs require the offset projects to be undertaken in the respective program's jurisdiction.

1. Design factors – requirements of an effective policy regime

Based on research carried out under the Harvard Project on International Climate Agreements, Aldy and Stavins, identify five key design factors for the success of a "post-2012" international agreement: "burden-sharing, technology transfer, CDM reform, addressing deforestation, and making global climate policy compatible with global trade policy."[149]

---

145 Kati Kulovesi, *Exploring the Landscape of Climate Law and Scholarship: Two Emerging Trends* in CLIMATE CHANGE AND THE LAW 46 (Erkki Holler, Kati Kulovesi & Michael Mehling, eds., 2013) citing Werksman and Henderson, "The Aftermath of Copenhagen," at 3.

146 *Id.* at 47.

147 Ranson & Stavins, *supra* note 129, at 28.

148 *Cf.* Heitzig Jobst, *Bottom-Up Strategic Linking of Carbon Markets: Which Climate Coalitions Would Farsighted Players Form?* (FEEM Working Paper No. 48.2013, June 5, 2013), https://ssrn.com/abstract=2274724.

149 ALDY & STAVINS, *supra* note 142, at 40 f.

As states are self-interested actors by nature, burden-sharing, i.e., the allocation of costs amongst actors in a regulatory scheme as a notion of "fair play," is often a key point in multinational negotiations. In a bottom-up approach, burden-sharing plays a less significant role, as each jurisdiction decides on their own emission reductions and the following costs. This also addresses concerns regarding emission reductions undertaken by developing countries, for example, those put forward by the U.S.

Technology transfer regarding low-carbon and energy efficient technology can be an important factor, especially regarding the increasing emissions in developing countries. Some analysts consider international carbon markets a driver for investments in research and development as they increase the price of emissions.[150] Correspondingly, investments in low carbon technology can reduce the operating price. However, simply "putting a price" on emissions will not necessarily facilitate technology transfer into developing countries, as seen in the course of the CDM. "If a country has difficulty attracting capital generally, changing the relative prices of carbon-intensive and carbon-lean capital will not resolve this problem."[151] While international action can facilitate technology transfer by decreasing trade barriers, local regulations can provide an additional incentive to developing countries to develop better policy practices, which in turn could facilitate investment and growth.

Deforestation has, for example, proven to be a difficult subject under the current Kyoto regime. The present regime relies on project-based accounting, as discussed above. In practice however, such an approach has not been successful. Problems with the regime included the measurement of the baseline and the so called "additionality" of projects.[152] Consequently, it has been proposed to separate deforestation and the CDM;[153] a bottom-up approach could achieve that. Deforestation could be addressed in national regulations as well as in the context of an emissions trading program, for example as a national offset program. While offset programs of-

---

150 *Cf.*, for example, Ralf Martin, Mirabelle Muûls & Ulrich Wagner. *Climate Change, Investment and Carbon Markets and Prices–Evidence from Manager Interviews* (Climate Strategies, Carbon Pricing for Low-Carbon Investment Project, 2011).

151 Aldy & Stavins, *supra* note 142, at 43.

152 Additionality is the property of an activity being additional and is used by literature and courts in the context of project-based offsets, *cf.* Citizen's Climate Lobby v. Cal. Air Res. Bd., No. 12-519554, slip op. at II (Cal. Super Ct. Jan. 25, 2013).

153 Aldy & Stavins, *supra* note 142, at 49.

ten raise environmental justice concerns,[154] they can be highly effective at incentivizing forest protection and reforestation for the reasons discussed above on page 116.

Compatibility between global climate policy and global trade policy relates especially to the problem of carbon leakage as defined above. International trade must find a solution to the problem of emissions leakage due to differentiating national caps on emissions that are inevitable in a global context. This point exemplifies the true strength of a bottom-up approach with some supra-national coordination: in an international agreement, states could address this issue similar to the approach taken in the Montreal Protocol. The trade sanctions regarding countries not participating in the program are widely considered a defining success factor. Of course, trade sanctions in the Montreal Protocol were successful because all parties recognized the dangers of ozone depletion, and the sanctioned trade was relatively limited. This, however, does not automatically disqualify the use of sanctions in the climate change context. While the causes and affected industries are much more diverse than in the case of ozone depletion, limited sanctions can be a valuable tool. For example, "[f]uture national-level policies to address climate change may be expected to include provisions that target carbon-intensive products from countries deemed to be making inadequate efforts."[155]

2. Economic studies on linking as coalition forming

Early economic studies argued against the efficiency of bottom-up linking. For example, the OECD published a study arguing that a "fully voluntary agreement would comprise at most a small number of signatories and,

---

154 Offset projects have often been criticized for their problems regarding environmental justice as they have the imminent danger of allowing entities a "cop-out" of actual emissions, especially if allowances do not accurately reflect the emissions reduction. Another common point of criticism relates to the civil right impacts perpetuated by offset credits. Scholars argue that the possibility of creating offset credits transfers emissions into low-income areas. For example, a source could generate offset projects by undertaking forestry projects in a state forest. As a consequence, such a source does not have to decrease emissions, resulting in increased pollution in its neighborhood. As most pollution sources are located in industrial and low-income neighborhoods, this mechanism results in disadvantages to marginalized groups.

155 *Cf.* note 153.

therefore, be insufficient to stabilize the climate. A main reason for this pessimistic conclusion is the strong incentive for countries to free-ride."[156] Similar to that, Helm concludes that a global market is unlikely to appear as a result of transnational linkage. According to Helm's findings, the process might actually lead to higher emissions as countries are incentivized to over-allocate allowances when faced with the possibility of international emissions trading as a result of linking. Empirical evidence correlates with this finding as almost all enacted emissions trading programs were over-allocated. In his study, however, Helm did not consider a coordinated emissions cap and made certain assumptions. As a result, his study does not, for example, reflect cost-benefit asymmetries.

Newer studies paint a more optimistic picture. In a more recent study, Jobst employed newer theories of coalition-forming models related to game theory focusing more on underlying payoff structure.[157] Jobst formed a model that estimates payoffs to six major emitters[158] of GHG in each imaginable state of the coalition forming process. In this model, he allowed two types of coalitions: linked markets and groups coordinating their caps. Jobst bases his model on a strict "bottom-up" approach—i.e., he assumes players will choose their respective domestic emissions cap in lieu of an international agreement, and market participants will trade permits without governmental trade, as included in the Kyoto Protocol design. Jobst concludes, that "[i]f it is always possible to immediately include a binding agreement on caps into an agreement to link existing carbon markets, then it seems likely that a global carbon market with a first-best cap will emerge eventually, but probably not in one move."[159] In that case, once markets have been linked, it is likely that they stay linked. However, "[i]f it is not possible to immediately agree on caps at the time of market linkage but only later via separate agreements, it is not clear that a global carbon market with a first- best cap will emerge eventually. If players are not sufficiently farsighted, the process might get stuck in a state without global cap coordination, with several disjoint carbon markets in each of which there is full internal cap coordination, but which are unlikely to be linked further."[160] However, the study also stresses high uncertainty

---

156 Organization for Economic Co-Operation and Development (OECD), Action Against Climate Change: The Kyoto Protocol and Beyond 51 (OECD Publications, 1999).

157 *Cf.* Jobst, *supra* note 148.

158 China, Europe, the former Soviet Union, India, Japan, and the U.S.

159 Jobst, *supra* note 148, at 15.

160 Jobst, *supra* note 148, at 15.

and slow progress with linking as issues with coalition forming. While this is certainly true from an economic perspective, slow incremental progress might not even be environmentally problematic as the biggest emitters worldwide already have emissions reductions systems in place that would allow for linking. Indeed, it can be argued that "[i]n case of climate change, the temporal factor should not be a real concern if the 20 major GHG emitters, responsible for around 80 percent of GHGs in 2008, are on board from the beginning. An incremental expansion to the rest of the UNFCCC membership will not really be detrimental to the global warming effect, as the rest of the UNFCCC membership is only responsible for around 20 percent of global emissions."[161] This, of course, assumes working and sufficient national policies.

The study ultimately shows that self-interested and farsighted players will ultimately link markets, but also highlights the importance of immediate emissions cap coordination. As displayed later in this thesis, empirical evidence from enacted emissions trading systems refutes some of these findings, such as that linked systems will remain linked.

Other theories regarding potential linkage are based on international trade agreements. Leal-Arcas, for example, argues that while trade agreements and environmental agreements have different purposes—trade agreements are essentially commercially motivated while environmental agreements are often intended to protect public goods—trade agreements can be a model for environmental agreements if the incentives are similar.[162] Despite the differentiating objectives, incentives can be aligned. One of the incentives for concluding trade agreements is the search for bigger markets. The same incentives can exist in market-based environmental agreements, (*cf.* to the benefits of linking markets discussed above). However, empirical evidence discussed later shows that environmental agreements alone are not able to develop the same "pull factors" as trade agreements.

161 Leal-Arcas, *Top-Down Versus Bottom-Up Approaches for Climate Change Negotiations: An Analysis, 6 The IUP Journal of Governance and Public Policy 8 (December 2011)* at 24 f.

162 Leal-Arcas, *supra* note 162, at 32.

VIII. Bottom-up and top-down as used in this thesis

This thesis aims to review enacted U.S. emissions trading systems and their lessons for a future (international) approach against climate change. As pointed out by Bodansky, both bottom-up and top-down approaches were present as early as the adoption of the UNFCCC. Article 4, para. 1 of the UNFCCC relates more to a bottom-up approach whereas Article 4, para. 2 refers more to a top-down model. "In essence, the history of the U.N. climate change regime ever since has consisted of variations on these two themes."[163] Given the general policy shift from binding international agreements towards individual approaches many countries have displayed following the Copenhagen negotiations, special attention is given to the bottom-up and top-down paradigm. The objective of this analysis is to review to what extent the multiple U.S. emissions trading systems can be used as an example for bottom-up approaches and what lessons regulators can learn from these systems. For the purpose of this review, a "top-down" approach is characterized mostly by binding targets established by a higher conceptual level, such as the Appendix I targets in the Kyoto Protocol, but also a lack of regulative discretion in how to achieve such target.[164]

To be more detailed, the established scholarship characterizes "strong" top-down approaches by strong global coordination with a focus on a common pursuit, such as a common emissions reductions target, and an implementation by targets and timetables based on "commonly agreed rules, which would be progressively broadened and strengthened over time and would be legally binding, with a strong measuring, reporting and verification (MRV) system and compliance mechanism."[165] Systematically, a strong top-down approach can therefore be defined by five components:

> *(i) it prescribes, in a top-down way, generally applicable policies that are based on commonly understood principles; (ii) it strives to develop targets and instruments of climate governance (regarding mitigation measures, carbon sinks, adaptation efforts) in a comprehensive manner; (iii) it is intended to be universal in its application, applying to all countries according to*

---

163 *Cf.* Daniel Bodansky, *A Tale of Two Architectures*, 43 Ariz. St. L.J. 16 (2011).

164 The latter, of course, was not present in the Kyoto Protocol, which gave its signatory states some discretion over their choice of compliance tools, albeit with the goal of establishing an international emissions market.

165 William Hare, Claire Stockwell, Christian Flachsland & Sebastian Oberthür, *The Architecture of the Global Climate Regime: A Top-down Perspective*, 10 Climate Policy 601 (2010).

> *agreed principles of burden sharing; (iv) it is universal in its negotiation and decision-making process, being based on the primacy of the UN frame-work; and (v) it seeks to establish legally binding international obligations.*[166]

On the contrary, "bottom-up" approaches, as taken by the Copenhagen Accord and successively, the Paris Agreement, are characterized by allowing each individual party broad discretion over their mitigation pledges and regulatory measures. They are identifiable by

> *little or no global coordination of efforts, with coordination confined to, perhaps, a small group of countries. Countries' emission actions would be based on unilateral pledges, rather than on the outcome of multilateral negotiations with set levels of ambition, for which accountability would be assessed domestically and not at the international level (i.e., no international compliance). There would be little or weak common MRV and accounting rules.*[167]

As implied by the usage of terms such as a "strong" or "weak" approach, the top-down vs. bottom-up paradigm is a spectrum, with systems falling somewhere in between either ends.

---

166 Cited from Robert Falkner, Stephan Hannes & John Vogler, *International Climate Policy after Copenhagen: Towards a "Building Blocks" Approach*, 1 Global Policy 258 f. (2010).

167 *Cf.* note 165.

E. Emissions trading in the U.S. and its lessons for international climate change regulation

The U.S., with its strong culture of federalism, can serve as an example for the development of bottom-up regulation for a problem of international scale. In this model paradigm, the relationship between state and federal powers can serve as an analogy to national and supranational powers. Additionally, there are strong cultural and industry differences between states, which leads to the necessity of flexible and adaptable approaches. For example, the power sector is extremely important for the northeastern states assembled in the Regional Greenhouse Gas Initiative, whereas the Western Climate Initiative states have another economic focus. This can serve as a model for nation states with different economic interests and policies.

As the world's largest economy and one of the world's largest GHG emitters, the U.S. position on climate change is fundamental for global action not only against climate change, but environmental pollution as a whole. However, for a long period of time, the White House refused to take a position on the issue of climate change.[1] Press reports even suggest that scientific reports discussing climate change were "systematically changed and suppressed" under the Bush Administration.[2] A few years later, *inter alia,* after drastic natural catastrophes such as Hurricane "Katrina" in 2005, which had devastating effects especially on the U.S. Gulf Coast, the Bush Administration's view on climate change shifted. Additionally, the Supreme Court issued its important 2007 decision, *Massachusetts v. EPA*, which allowed the EPA to regulate carbon and other GHG emissions under the federal Clean Air Act.[3] Therefore, while the United States' active stance on climate change can largely be attributed to the Obama Administration, groundwork for a U.S. climate change regime was set by the

---

1 Michael Mehling & David John Frenkil, *Climate Law in the United States: Facing Structural and Procedural Limitations in* CLIMATE CHANGE AND THE LAW 473 (Erkki Holler, Kati Kulovesi & Michael Mehling, eds. 2013).

2 See for example BBC Report "Climate Chaos: Bush's Climate of Fear," http://news.bbc.co.uk/2/hi/programmes/panorama/5005994.stm (last visited January 11, 2020).

3 Discussed in detail on page 142 ff.

judiciary branch in *Massachusetts v. EPA*, which of course, is rooted in the Clean Air Act.

Enacted by Congress in 1963 and amended from time to time, the Clean Air Act is the fundamental U.S. regulation on pollution from stationary and mobile sources. It differs from the preceding Air Pollution Control Act of 1955 as it allows the regulation of emissions whereas the Air Pollution Control Act generally only allowed the Executive Branch (in this case the Surgeon General) to research and investigate as well as publish information relating to air pollution (*cf.* Section 2 of the Air Pollution Control Act of 1955). Contrary to this, the Clean Air Act vests the Executive with regulative authority. Aimed at, *inter alia*, reducing and preventing air pollution,[4] the Clean Air Act requires the EPA to define "national ambient air quality standard" (NAAQS) for the 190 pollutants defined in the Clean Air Act, amongst them sulfur and carbon.[5] Such standards are classified as either primary standards, aimed to protect public health, and secondary standards, aimed at protecting matters other than public health, such as soil, water, crops, and buildings, CAA Sec. 108(a)(1) and CAA Sec. 109(b)(2) 42 U.S.C. § 7401. Every five years, the standard is reviewed and revised as necessary. Any area meeting such standards is designated as an "attainment area;" areas not meeting the standard are "non-attainment areas," CAA Sec. 107 42 U.S.C. § 7401.[6] States are responsible for implementing regulations achieving the desired standards, CAA Sec. 110(a) and (b), 42 U.S.C. § 7401. In terms of the top-down vs. bottom-up paradigm discussed above, this could be characterized as a harmonized bottom-up approach, as the regulative discretion given to the states is supplemented by binding federal rules. Consequently, the EPA is authorized to review state regulations and issue federal regulations if state regulation in non-attainment areas should fail, CAA Sec. 110(c) 42 U.S.C. § 7401. In order to allow the EPA to do this, states must submit so-called state implementation plans (SIPs) detailing, *inter alia*, emission limits and compliance plans, CAA Sec. 110 42 U.S.C. § 7401. If a state fails to adopt or to implement such a state compliance plan, the EPA has the authority

---

4 The Clean Air Act of 1963 § 101 (a)(3) 42 U.S.C. § 7401.

5 See, *inter alia*, Review of National Ambient Air Quality Standards for Carbon Monoxide, 76. Fed. Reg., 54294 (August 31, 2011) (amending 40 CFR Parts 50, 53, and 58). The EPA is also authorized to add additional pollutants, *cf.* sections 108 and 109 42 U.S.C. § 7401.

6 Areas without appropriate usable data are classified as "unclassifiable" and are treated like attainment areas.

to implement a federal implementation plan, CAA Sec. 110(c) 42 U.S.C. § 7401.

Additionally, non-attainment areas must submit plans no later than three years after being classified a non-attainment area, CAA Sec. 172(b) 42 U.S.C. § 7401. Such plans must designate a strategy to comply with the respective pollutant standards as "expeditiously as practicable," CAA Sec. 172(c)(1) 42 U.S.C. § 7401, *inter alia,* by putting quantifiable incremental limits on the specific pollutants in question, which represent "further reasonable progress," CAA Sec. 172(c)(2) 42 U.S.C. § 7401. For new sources that emit controlled pollutants, the CAA requires a permit. This, *inter alia,* only allows new sources if their added emissions are offset by emissions reductions from old sources, CAA Sec. 173 42 U.S.C. § 7401. This can be achieved by purchasing offset emission credits from old sources—thus, the CAA provides for basic emissions trading rules that were introduced by the 1990 Clean Air Act Amendments in order to encourage "market-based principles" as compliance tools.

In addition to the rules discussed above, the CAA's Section 202(a)(1) 42 U.S.C. § 7521 requires the EPA to set emission standards for any air pollutant from motor vehicles or motor vehicle engines that the EPA considers to cause or contribute to air pollution that may reasonably be anticipated to endanger public health or welfare. In view of this language, environmental groups, scholars, and the EPA itself have argued over the EPA's authority to regulate emissions that cause or contribute to climate change. After a rulemaking petition started in 2003 by the International Center for Technology Assessment and various environmental and citizen organizations, the EPA denied its authority to regulate GHG emissions, stating that

> *Congress has not granted EPA authority under the Clean Air Act to regulate CO_2 and other greenhouse gases for climate change purposes.*
> *EPA has determined that setting GHG emission standards for motor vehicles is not appropriate at this time.*[7]

The EPA furthermore argued that even if it had the authority to regulate GHG emissions, doing so would be unwise as a causal link between GHG and the increase in global surface air temperatures was not unequivocally established.[8]

7 Press release, EPA Office of Public Affairs (August 28, 2003).
8 Massachusetts v EPA 549 U.S. 497 (2007).

Following this statement, a number of states led by Massachusetts[9] brought a suit against the EPA[10] in front of the District of Columbia Circuit Court and ultimately the Supreme Court to challenge EPA's denial of the rulemaking petition. In a 5-4 decision, the Court affirmed that the petitioners had standing to sue the EPA. The dissenting vote by Chief Justice Roberts, who was joined by Justice Scalia, Justice Thomas, and Justice Alito, negated standing with some of the arguments often advanced against the justiciability of the climate change phenomenon. Roberts, *inter alia*, argued that the petitioners were not able to show a particular injury, as climate change threatens "humanity at large" and is not limited to adverse effects on the petitioners. He argues, therefore, that it must be addressed by the legislative branch, not the judiciary.

Not following this dissenting vote, the majority opinion affirmed Massachusetts's standing. Circumventing the often controversial issue of climate change's widespread effects cited by the dissent, Massachusetts was able to demonstrate an injury by arguing that it's quasi-sovereign state rights would be injured by the loss of coastal state property as a result of rising sea levels, thus establishing standing under the doctrine of *parens patriae*.

The majority opinion cites *Georgia v. Tennessee Copper Co.*, 206 U.S. 230, 237 (1907) in which "quasi-sovereign" state rights were established as a base to establish individual injury—i.e., standing was established under the doctrine of *parens patriae*. As the Court put it in *Georgia v. Tennessee Copper Co.*:

> *This is a suit by a State for an injury to it in its capacity of quasi-sovereign. In that capacity the State has an interest independent of and behind the titles of its citizens, in all the earth and air within its domain. It has the last word as to whether its mountains shall be stripped of their forests and its inhabitants shall breathe pure air.*

In his dissent, Chief Justice Roberts disagreed with the applicability of *Georgia v. Tennessee Copper Co.* He argued that in this case, no question about an injury sufficient to establish standing under Article III of the

9 The record shows as petitioners the states of California, Connecticut, Illinois, Maine, Massachusetts, New Jersey, New Mexico, New York, Oregon, Rhode Island, Vermont, and Washington, the Governments of the District of Columbia, American Samoa, New York City, and Baltimore, and various private organizations, Massachusetts v EPA 549 U.S. 497 (2007).

10 The EPA was supported by the states of Alaska, Idaho, Kansas, Michigan, Nebraska, North Dakota, Ohio, South Dakota, Texas, and Utah as well as various trade organizations representing the automotive industry.

Constitution was discussed. Therefore, Chief Justice Roberts argues *parens patriae* is not applicable in Article III cases and that the three-prong test established in *Lujan v. Defenders of Wildlife* must be applied here, i.e., plaintiffs must establish (i) injury in fact, a (ii) causal connection, and (iii) redressability.[11] This argument is too apodictic: nothing in the Court's decision history suggests that *parens patriae* cannot be an additional means to establish standing especially in environmental cases such as the present. And indeed, the facts in *Georgia v. Tennessee Copper Co.* read much like a historic precursor to the modern issue of climate change,[12] which shows a general need for a doctrine that establishes state standing in such cases. Similar to state standing in criminal prosecutions, the *parens patriae* doctrine "provides states with a basis for standing wholly apart from the three-prong test."[13] The majority opinion in *Massachusetts v. EPA* seems to subscribe to this understanding as only after establishing Massachusetts's standing based on *parens patriae*, it does follow with a discussion of Massachusetts's standing based on the three-prong test established in *Lujan v. Defenders of Wildlife*, under which a litigant must show a concrete and particularized injury that is either actual or imminent, that the injury is fairly traceable to the defendant, and that a favorable decision will likely redress that injury.[14] Such a three-prong test is the standard test for Article III review cases. Commentators have interpreted such decisions as a general establishment of state standing in *parens patriae* cases, i.e., cases in which states act on behalf of their citizen's interests.[15] The majority opinion in *Massachusetts v. EPA* applied the three-prong test as follows:

Regarding (i) the injury in fact, the majority opinion argued that the U.S. Federal Government, in which the sovereign power to address climate change as it pertains to the U.S. is vested, has instructed EPA in the CAA to protect states from adverse effects resulting from pollution. EPA's denial to do such caused an injury to Massachusetts. In its argument against this

---

11 Lujan v. Defenders of Wildlife, 504 U.S. 555, 560-561 (1992).

12 In *Georgia v. Tennessee Copper Co*, the State of Georgia sought a judicial enjoinment to stop copper companies located in the neighboring State of Tennessee from emitting noxious gases from their facilities that was believed to damage forests and crops on Georgia's territory.

13 Sara Zdeb, *From Georgia v. Tennessee Copper to Massachusetts v. EPA: Parens Patriae Standing for State Global Warming Plaintiffs*, 96 Geo. L. J. 1074 (2007-2008).

14 Citing Lujan v. Defenders of Wildlife, 504 U.S. 555, 560-561 (1992).

15 See Verheyen, Roda, Lührs, Michael, Klimaschutz durch Gerichte in den USA - 1. Teil: Öffentliches Recht, Zeitschrift für Umweltrecht (ZUR) 2009, Heft 2, 73 with further citations.

reasoning, the dissent, despite stating earlier that it made no statement on whether or not climate change exists, relied on arguing that Massachusetts was not able to establish a fair connection between climate change and a rise in sea level.[16] Considering the clear causation between melting polar caps and rising sea levels, this is surprising. Furthermore, the dissent argued that even if such a connection could be established, the rising sea levels' impact would be too distant to establish an "imminent" injury.

As the EPA did not argue against a connection between GHG and climate change, the Court considered EPA's decision not to regulate as (ii) causal for the injury. The Court did not find EPA's argument that GHG from new motor vehicles contributed only insignificantly to climate change as persuasive. The Court did not consider GHG emissions from the U.S. transportation sector as insignificant and argued that even if they were, small incremental steps towards a goal can be demanded in a court of law. The dissent, on the other hand, evokes the "complex web" concept regarding the causes of climate change and argues that the connection between climate change resulting from atmospheric GHG loading and the local GHG emissions from U.S. domestic new motor vehicles is too "speculative to establish causation."[17] (iii) Redressability of the injury was shown as well. As the Court held, the fact that regulating emissions from U.S. motor vehicles alone cannot reverse global warming by itself, as advanced by the dissent against Redressability, did not mean that EPA may refuse to slow or reduce it.

On the merits, the Court relied on CAA Sec. 307 42 U.S.C § 7607(b)(1). This rule in the CAA expressly allows judicial review of EPA's decision not to regulate new vehicle emissions based on its finding that carbon dioxide is not an "air pollutant" under CAA Sec. 302 42 U.S.C § 7602(g). As dictated in CAA Sec. 307 42 U.S.C § 7607(d)(9), the Court "may reverse any such action found to be arbitrary, capricious, an abuse of discretion, or otherwise not in accordance with law." Such was the case here. The Court found that "because greenhouse gases fit well within the Act's capacious definition of 'air pollutant,' EPA has statutory authority to regulate emission of such gases from new motor vehicles." CAA Sec. 302 42 U.S.C § 7602(g) defines air pollutant as

16 "[T]he Court observes that 'global sea levels rose somewhere between 10 and 20 centimeters over the 20th century as a result of global warming' and that '[t]hese rising seas have already begun to swallow Massachusetts' coastal lands. [...] But none of petitioners' declarations supports that connection." 549 U.S. 497 (2007).

17 *Id.*

> *any air pollution agent or combination of such agents, including any physical, chemical, biological, radioactive (including source material, special nuclear material, and byproduct material) substance or matter which is emitted into or otherwise enters the ambient air. Such term includes any precursors to the formation of any air pollutant, to the extent the Administrator has identified such precursor or precursors for the particular purpose for which the term "air pollutant" is used.*

According to the Court, this definition includes airborne compounds of "any stripe."[18] As GHG are physical and chemical substances, they fall under such a definition. Since EPA did not establish that Congress meant to curtail EPA's power to regulate GHG, the Court established EPA's authority to regulate GHG and therefore new motor vehicles. The Court furthermore did not follow EPA's alternative argument that even if the Court found EPA has authority to regulate GHG, doing so would be unwise at the given time. As EPA found that GHG contributes to climate change and climate change does endanger public health and welfare, the Court found EPA obliged to act. EPA's reference to voluntary programs and the President's ability to negotiate with developing nations did not sway the Court's opinion.

While attempts at shaping U.S. climate policy did not stop here, *Massachusetts v. EPA* remains the most significant step in U.S. climate policy. In May 2010, Senators John Kerry (D-MA) and Joe Lieberman (I-CT)[19] presented a senate climate policy bill titled "American Power Act" (APA). The APA was "designed to be a comprehensive sector-based approach to enhance energy security, spurring the development and deployment of clean energy technologies and reducing greenhouse gas emissions."[20] The bill contained seven titles: domestic clean energy development, global warming pollution reduction, consumer protection, job protection and growth, international climate change activities, community protection from global warming impacts, and budgetary effects,[21] and it would have established a multi-sector cap-and-trade program.[22] The bill did not gain the necessary

18 Cf. *Id.*

19 John Kerry is a member of the Democratic Party. Joe Lieberman is a former member of the Democratic Party who ran for Senate on an independent ticket.

20 PEW Center for Global Climate Change, Summary of the American Power Act, (May 2010).

21 *Cf.* note 20.

22 David Hunter, James Salzman & Durwood Zaelke, International Environmental Law and Policy 724 (4th ed. 2011).

votes with the democratic majority in the 111th Congress during the Obama Administration, but it did inspire further legislative action on the topic of climate change. Notably, the "American Clean Energy and Security Act" of 2009 (ACES)[23] introduced by Henry A. Waxman (D-CA) and Edward J. Markey (D-MA) passed the House of Representatives by a narrow margin of 219-212.[24] The bill aimed at reducing CO_2 emission reductions from major sources to 17 percent by the year 2020, 42 percent by the year 2030, and 83 percent by the year 2050 compared to a 2005 emission level benchmark. Electric utilities would have been obligated to meet 20 percent of their electricity demand from renewables by the year 2020. To achieve those desired reductions, the bill would have established an economy-wide (i.e., non-sectoral) binding emissions trading system.[25] The bill, however, did not gain the necessary votes and was never introduced in the Senate.

Ultimately, the Executive Branch during the Obama Administration stepped up and, *inter alia,* relying on the outcome of *Massachusetts v. EPA*, "issued a comprehensive array of regulations through the EPA aimed at mitigating GHG emissions from stationary sources such as electric power plants and increasing fuel efficiency standards for the automotive sector."[26] As a response to its mandate as a result of the Court's decision in *Massachusetts v. EPA*, EPA issued an "Endangerment Finding" under Section 202(a) 42 U.S.C. § 7521 in May 2009, stating that "greenhouse gases in the atmosphere may reasonably be anticipated both to endanger public health and to endanger public welfare."[27] EPA furthermore stated that "the combined emissions of these greenhouse gases from new motor vehicles and new motor vehicle engines contribute to the greenhouse gas air pollution that endangers public health and welfare under CAA section 202(a)."[28] Subsequently, EPA used the resulting mandate established under the CAA to issue GHG regulations for motor vehicles, power plants, and

23 H.R.2454, *American Clean Energy and Security Act of 2009*, 111th Cong., (1st Sess., June 26, 2009), available at https://www.congress.gov/bill/111th-congress/house-bill/2454.

24 111 Cong. Rec. 155, 9, at H7471-H7686 (daily ed. June 26, 2009).

25 *Cf. supra* note 23.

26 Mehling & Frenkil, *supra* note 1, at 473.

27 Specifically, the EPA found the following six GHGs to endanger both the public health and the public welfare of current and future generations: carbon dioxide (CO_2), methane (CH_4), nitrous oxide (N_2O), hydrofluorocarbons (HFCs), perfluorocarbons (PFCs), sulfur hexafluoride (SF_6).

28 U.S. Environmental Protection Agency, *Endangerment and Cause or Contribute Findings for Greenhouse Gases Under Section 202(a) of the Clean Air Act, Final Rule*, 74 Fed. Reg. 66496 (December 15, 2009).

fuel. For example, EPA issued the "Clean Power Plan" of 2014, which established emissions reduction guidelines for existing power plants, as opposed to new plants, for which EPA had already issued national "new source performance standards" under Section 111(b) 42 U.S.C § 7411. Furthermore, EPA obligated states to achieve individual "statewide rate-based CO_2 emission performance goals." States have discretion regarding their policy approach but must submit emissions reduction plans. If they don't or the plan fails, the EPA may issue one instead. By establishing such standards, the Clean Power Plan aims at reducing national GHG emissions to 32 percent below 2005 emission levels by the year 2030.[29] After the 2016 general election, President Trump issued an Executive Order "on Promoting Energy Independence and Economic Growth" on March 28, 2017 that mandated the EPA to review the plan.[30]

Another example of EPA using its executive power under the CAA is the Renewable Fuels Standard program under Section 211 42. U.S.C § 7545. The statutory provisions in the CAA were subsequently modified and extended by the Energy Independence and Security Act of 2007. The Renewable Fuels Standard aims at reducing GHG emissions and increasing energy security[31] by prescribing an annual "volume standard" of renewable fuel content in U.S. transportation fuel, 40 CFR Part 80.[32] Renewable fuel includes cellulosic biofuel and various other fuels derived from renewable sources.

Summarized, the U.S. federal climate policy approach remains in an unconsolidated and fragmented state. Consequently, the U.S. response to climate change draws on "federal, regional and local efforts to achieve the official U.S. target of a 17 percent GHG reduction below 2005 levels by 2020,"[33] as pledged in the Copenhagen Accord. For the purpose of this thesis, this fragmented state is an interesting opportunity as it allows for a review of individual regulations on a (bottom-up) state level within one overlaying narrative, which is the reduction of GHG emissions and

---

29 *Carbon Pollution Emission Guidelines for Existing Stationary Sources: Electric Utility Generating Units*; 80 Fed. Reg. 64,661 (October 23, 2015).

30 Available at https://www.whitehouse.gov/the-press-office/2017/03/28/presidential-executive-order-promoting-energy-independence-and-economi-1 (last visited January 11, 2020).

31 I.e., to reduce the United States' dependence on imported fuel sources.

32 Environmental Protection Agency, *Renewable Fuel Standard Program: Standards for 2017 and Biomass Based Diesel Volume for 2018*, 81 Fed. Reg. 89,746 (December 12, 2016).

33 Mehling & Frenkil, *supra* note 1, at 487.

the development of a legal response to pollution and climate change. In the bottom-up vs. top-down context, it allows for the analysis of sub-federal state action and cooperation ("coalition forming") in lieu of federal action. Specifically, the following discussion will review individual state legislation relating to emissions trading as a means to achieve reductions in GHG emissions and how states have used this as a tool to link regulations. Pertaining to the research objective discussed on page 17, this review ultimately intends to establish whether and to what extent current experiences in U.S. climate change approach can serve as a model for an international approach.

The following review focuses on the Acid Rain Program, the Illinois Emissions Reduction Market System, the Regional Greenhouse Gas Initiative, and the Western Climate Initiative and California's Cap-and-Trade Program, respectively.

I. The Acid Rain Program

In the late 1980s, the U.S. experienced rising public concern about the concentration of sulphur dioxide (SO_2) in the atmosphere. SO_2 was mainly emitted by coal-powered power plants and, along with (and to a lesser degree) nitrogen oxides, was believed to react in the earth's atmosphere and to form sulfuric und nitric acids ultimately resulting in so-called acid rain, which was harmful to forests and aquatic systems.[34] In response to this, the U.S. Congress passed the 1990 CCA Amendments and established an emissions reduction program aimed at reducing annual domestic SO_2 emissions to 10 million tons below the 1980 level. Part of this emissions reduction program is the Acid Rain Program (ARP), a cap-and-trade program for SO_2.

The ARP is particularly interesting for two main reasons: as mentioned previously, it was the first actually enacted emissions reduction program utilizing cap-and-trade as the main tool to achieve desired emissions reductions. This allows a review of a cap-and-trade program that was enacted against a "clean slate," i.e., without any prior experiences in emissions trading. The ARP therefore is often called an "experiment in public policy."[35] Additionally, it was successful enough to be considered the "break-

34 Richard Schmalensee & Robert N. Stavins, *The SO_2 Allowance Trading System: The Ironic History of a Grand Policy Experiment*, 27 J. Econ. Persp. 103 (Winter 2013).

35 *Cf.* note 34

through" for emissions trading and is thus at least partially responsible for some of the perception of emissions trading we have today.

1. History

a. Background

The Acid Rain Program was enacted against the background of growing concerns about environmental and economic damages caused by so-called "acid rain." Acid rain is a form of acidic precipitation that is caused by emissions of certain atmospheric gases such as carbon dioxide, sulfur dioxide, and nitrogen oxides. When these gases combine with water in the earth's atmosphere or elsewhere, they form acidic substances.[36] Acid rain has several harmful effects: It is responsible for acidifying lakes, streams, and ground water in sensitive watersheds, resulting in damage to fish and other aquatic life. It also affects human health via the contamination of drinking water and food supplies from toxic metals leaking from soils, pipes, and other metal-bearing substances and contributes to the deterioration of man-made structures.[37] Researchers identified electricity plants powered by coal as the main source of the pollutants responsible for the formation of acid rain. Ironically, this can be traced to compliance with EPA's national ambient air quality standards as defined in the 1970s. To comply with the standards for SO_2, utilities aimed to reduce local concentration of certain gases by erecting more than 400 tall stacks, some over 500 feet tall. This did spread out the stack gases as intended but released them high enough into the atmosphere to contribute to the formation of acid rain.[38] Environmental regulations were enacted to cap emissions levels for those pollutants, which led to the enactment of the Acid Rain Program by Title IV of the Clean Air Act Amendments of 1990.

---

36 U.S. Dept. of Interior, Geological Survey Water Fact Sheet, *Acid Rain*, (Open-file report, 1987), https://pubs.usgs.gov/of/1987/0399/report.pdf (last visited April 3, 2020).

37 *Cf.* note 36

38 Schmalensee & Stavins, *supra* note 34.

b. Regulatory history

From the outset, the ARP was designed to be implemented in two phases, which is a key point in reviewing the system. Phase I from 1995 to 2000 affected 263 emission sources in twenty-one states and aimed to reduce SO_2 emissions by 7.5 million tons. These sources were hand selected by regulators as the dirtiest, largest generating units in the country. An additional 182 units joined the program in Phase I as "substitution or compensating" units, bringing the total number of Phase I affected units to 445.[39] The subsequent Phase II began in 2000 and affected approximately 2000 sources.[40] Units that were included for the first time in Phase II included smaller units fired by coal, oil, and gas. The program affects utility units serving generators with an output capacity of greater than 25 megawatts as well as all new utility units.[41]

2. Regulatory structure in phase II

As mentioned above, the ARP's legal framework is contained in Title IV of the 1990 Amendments to the Clean Air Act. The individual regulations are promulgated in 40 CFR Parts 72 through 78. The legal structure of the promulgated regulations is not very complicated: 40 CFR Part 72 contains provisions on emission allowances (called "permits"), 40 CFR Part 73 describes the allowance system, 40 CFR Part 74 provides opt-in rules for interested sources, and 40 CFR Part 75 promulgates rules for compliance and emissions monitoring, which have undergone several revisions since the ARP's initial enactment. Further, 40 CFR Part 76 provides regulations on NO_x, whereas 40 CFR Part 77 deals with excess emissions, and 40 CFR Part 78 concerns appeal procedures.

a. Coverage

In reviewing the ARP's coverage, geographical coverage and the covered sources may be differentiated.

---

39 Data provided by the Environmental Protection Agency, *Acid Rain Program*, https://www.epa.gov/airmarkets/acid-rain-program (last visited January 11, 2020).
40 Stefan Weishaar, Emissions Trading Design: A Critical Overview 74 (2014).
41 *Cf.* note 39

aa. Geographical

The hand-selected sources with Phase I coverage were located in the states of Alabama, Florida, Georgia, Illinois, Indiana, Kansas, Kentucky, Maryland, Michigan, Minnesota, Mississippi, Missouri, New Hampshire, New Jersey, New York, Ohio, Pennsylvania, Tennessee, West Virginia, and Wisconsin. The ARP was from its outset designed to be a multi-state program. Phase II brought a considerable expansion of the geographic coverage, as the program moved from coverage of pre-selected sources to a general applicability for all sources that met the relevant criteria.

bb. Covered sources

The ARP utilizes a so-called "bubble" structure to characterize covered sources: Each unit that is subject to the regulations in the CAA is a covered unit. If a source includes one or more affected units, it is an affected source. Thus, sources with more than one unit are counted as one source, which was intended to minimize compliance costs.

The covered sources are defined in 40 CFR § 72.6 as "affected units," *inter alia,* with reference to tables identifying individual units in 40 CFR 73.10. Furthermore, 40 CFR § 72.6 provides for coverage of utility units that are not mentioned in the tables. This relates to "new units," i.e., units that commenced commercial operation on or after November 15, 1990, including units that serve a generator with a nameplate capacity of 25 MWe or less or that is a simple combustion turbine, 40 CFR § 72.1. Simple combustion turbine means a unit that is a rotary engine driven by a gas under pressure, which is created by the combustion of any fuel. This term includes combined cycle units without auxiliary firing, but excludes combined cycle units with auxiliary firing, unless the unit did not use the auxiliary firing from 1985 through 1987 and has not used auxiliary firing at any time after November 15, 1990. Sources may also become covered sources if they increase their emissions or install certain technical facilities, such as auxiliary firing. The regulatory framework specifically exempts certain sources from coverage under the ARP. This, *inter alia,* concerns certain types of combustion turbines that commenced operations before November 15, 1990 or non-utility units. Retired sources are exempt as well, 40 CFR § 72.8(a).

In Phase II, the ARP's coverage was extended to include new units as defined above and all new utility plants and plants with an output capacity exceeding 25 megawatts (MW), 40 CFR § 72.6 and 42 USC § 7651d. In 2012, a total of 3,652 units were covered under the ARP.[42]

Under 40 CFR § 72.2, entities other than sources may choose to participate in the ARP if they purchase, hold, or transfer allowances. Additionally, ARP provides for numerous opt-in provisions for certain technical facilities, such as the opt-in provision for industrial boilers in 42 USC § 7651i.

b. Cap

In Phase I, the ARP aimed at an emission reduction of 5.7 million tons per year. This cap was tightened in Phase II to an aggregate national emissions cap of 8.95 million tons per year,[43] which reflects a reduction of approximately 50 percent from the 1980 levels, when power-sector emissions were about 17.5 million tons.[44]

The cap of 5.7 million tons placed on allowances in Phase I was calculated by taking the emission rate of 2.5 lb. SO_2/ millions of British Thermal Units (mm Btu) and multiplying it by fuel input per year for the years 1985–87. In Phase II, the cap of 8.95 million tons SO_2 per year was calculated by multiplying the federal NSP standard of 1.2 lb. SO_2/mm Btu by fuel use for the years 1985–87.[45]

c. Allocation of allowances

Pursuant to the cap defined above, sources were allotted allowances based on their baseline emissions. Generally, baseline emissions were determined by the average quantity of fossil fuel, measured in mm Btu, consumed dur-

42 Data retrieved from U.S. EPA Progress Reports, 1999–2012, Acid Rain Program, https://www.epa.gov/airmarkets/acid-rain-program-historical-report (last visited January 11, 2020).

43 Even though the total emission caps are higher, the aggregate cap is lower as coverage was extended significantly.

44 Gabriel Chan, Robert Stavins, Robert Stowe & Richard Sweeney, *The SO2 Allowance Trading System and the Clean Air Act Amendments of 1990: Reflections on Twenty Years of Policy Innovation*, 65 Nat. Tax J. 419, 422 (2012).

45 Ger Klassen & Andries Nentjes, *Sulfur Trading under the 1990 CAAA in the US: An Assessment of First Experiences*, 153 Journal of Institutional and Theoretical Economics (JITE) 384, 391 (June 1997).

ing the calendar years 1985, 1986, and 1987. This method of allocation was described as "grandfathering" in chapter C.V.2.a. p.37. The regulation contains numerous ways in which sources can affect their baseline or obtain additional allowances. 42 USC § 7651c provides for so called "substitution provisions," which allow sources to substitute units of their choice in lieu of the units specified in the regulations; this allows sources to make use of those unit's historic emissions to receive more allowances (by inflating their baseline). In addition to this, sources in Phase I could obtain additional allowances for the installation of emissions reduction equipment[46] or other voluntary measures, 42 USC § 7651c(d) ff.

In Phase II, the basic formula used to generate allocations involved multiplying the unit's baseline utilization by an emissions rate of 1.2 pounds of SO_2 per mm BTU. However, the program contains over thirty individual allocation rules deviating from the standard formula, mainly due to compromises made in the political process. [47] The calculated amount is reduced to not exceed 8.9 million tons, the cap for Phase II, 42 USC § 7651b(a)(1), so-called "ratched." This amounted to a 10 percent reduction pro rata.[48]

Pursuant to 40 CFR § 72.9, each source must, at the end of the compliance period, hold allowances at least equal to its total annual emissions of SO_2 for the previous calendar year. An allowance is a limited authorization to emit SO_2 in accordance with the ARP, 40 CFR § 72.9(c)(5), but does not constitute a property right. Each allowance permits emission of one ton of SO_2. At the beginning of the ARP, most allowances were freely allocated. However, some allowances were also auctioned. The EPA is required to hold back approximately 2.8 percent of allowances and auction them every year (*cf.*, for example, 40 CFR § 73.70). The auction proceeds are redistributed to affected entities. Beginning in 2000, up to 530,000 allowances (reflecting one ton each) per year were deposited as "bonus allowances." From the ARP's beginning, such bonus allowances were deposited mainly for policy reasons, as states were affected differently by the allocation of allowances based on their baseline. A majority of the dirty plants were located in the Midwest, specifically along the Mississippi river, while other states had less dirty plants located within their jurisdictions. Bonus allowances are furthermore required to supply new sources that are

---

46 Such as so-called "Scrubbers."

47 Lesley K. McAllister, *The Overallocation Problem in Cap-and-Trade: Moving Toward Stringency*, 43 COLUM. J. ENVTL. L. 400 (2009).

48 *Id.* at 401.

entering the ARP without allowances. These sources will not receive free allowances but must participate in a yearly auction held at the Chicago Board of Trade.[49] Direct sales are available as well at a fixed price of $ 1,500, indexed to inflation.[50]

In Phase I, sources emitted less SO_2 than they would have been allowed to. In the years 1995 to 1999, the cap amounted to between 6.9 and 8.7 tons of SO_2 while emissions from Phase I sources remained around 5.5 million tons approximately. Correspondingly, Phase I sources used only about 77 percent of their allocated allowances. The surplus amount was banked. At the end of 1999, allowances for 11,607,955 tons of SO_2 were banked. With Phase II starting in 2000, sources consistently used more allowances than they were provided. With an average cap of 9.5 million tons of SO_2, sources emitted roughly 11.2 million tons of SO_2 in 2000. This amount remained somewhat consistent with yearly emissions of roughly 10.5 million tons, which declined slightly to 9.3 million tons in 2006 and 3.2 million tons in 2013. The increase in emissions through 2006 relative to Phase I indicates a heavy use of banked allowances, which is also suggested by the size of the allowance bank, which declined from allowances equal to 11.6 million tons to 6.2 million tons of SO_2, a reduction of about 53 percent.[51]

d. Banking and trading

aa. Rules

42 USC § 7651g(b) allows for the unlimited transfer of allowances between sources or other participants. The related regulation is promulgated in 40 CFR § 73.50 ff., which also defines procedures for transfers of allowances. Such procedures are extensive. For example, for a transfer to be valid, a written certification signed by the responsible official of each party is required and must be received and recorded by the administration. Allowance credits may not be sold, 40 USC § 7651b(b). That means that

49 Klassen & Nentjes, *supra* note 45, at 392.
50 Klassen & Nentjes, *supra* note 45, at 393.
51 Data retrieved from U.S. EPA Progress Reports, 1999–2012, Acid Rain Program, https://www.epa.gov/airmarkets/acid-rain-program-historical-reports (last visited January 11, 2020) and data retrieved from EPA Air Markets Program Data, available at http://ampd.epa.gov/ampd/ (last visited January 11, 2020).

allowances cannot be transferred before the day they are issued. For the purpose of receiving and recording the transfer, the EPA administers an official allowance tracking system.

Borrowing is not permitted under the ARP. 40 CFR 72.9(c)(5) states that an allowance shall not be deducted for compliance purposes prior to the year in which the allowance was allocated. However, the APR does not contain any regulations limiting banking. Allowances can be kept for an indefinite amount of time, *cf.* 40 CFR 73.36(a), which states that any allowance not deducted will remain in the compliance subaccount.

bb. Allowance market

The ARP established a stable market environment. The year 2012 was the third year in which prices for ARP allowances remained below $3 per ton of SO_2. In 2012, 1,947 transactions for a total amount of 8,446,197 allowances were conducted.[52] However, the enactment of the Cross-State Air Pollution Rule by the EPA in 2011 severely changed the regulatory environment of allowance trading under ARP by, *inter alia*, restricting banking and trading.

In analyzing the allowance trade volume in the years 1995 and 1999 (Phase I) and 2000-2009 (Phase II), certain trends emerge.[53]

In 1994, the year prior to the program's enactment, only 9.2 million allowances were traded between entities. This is in stark contrast to the average trading volume of 16.9 million trades across all of the program's compliance periods. In particular, only 0.9 million of such 9.2 million trades were made between separate entities. On average, 7.6 million trades between separate entities were made across all of the program's compliance periods.

In the following year (1995), 16.7 trades were made, an increase in trades of approximately 81 percent. Another sharp increase in trading volume can be noted in 2000, the first year of the Phase II implementation. In

52 Data retrieved from U.S. EPA Progress Reports, 1999–2012, Acid Rain Program, https://www.epa.gov/airmarkets/acid-rain-program-historical-reports (last accessed January 11, 2020) and data retrieved from EPA Air Markets Program Data, http://ampd.epa.gov/ampd/ (last visited January 11, 2020).

53 Data retrieved from Douglas A. Burns, Jason A. Lynch, Bernhard J. Cosby, Mark E. Fenn, & Jill S. Baron, *National Acid Precipitation Assessment Program Report to Congress 2011: An Integrated Assessment*. (Report to Executive Office of the President of the United States, 2011).

2000, 25 million allowances were traded, a high in the 1995–2009 period and an increase of 59 percent compared with the previous year, 1999. Of the 25 million trades, 12.7 million trades were made with separate entities. Following this year, the trading volume remained somewhat consistent around 20 million trades per year and eventually started decreasing in 2007 after a high of 22.4 million trades in that year.

Interestingly, the monthly trading price remained fairly consistent in ARP's first decade. Nominal prices ranged between 100 and 200 USD, with a dramatic price increase starting in 2004. At their height in 2006, prices were up to 1,600 USD. Ultimately, prices dropped to 450 in 2007, and decreased further from there. EPA officials estimated the allowance price to be between 250 USD and 500 USD in Phase I and 500 USD to 1,000 USD in Phase II.[54]

cc. Banking data

Due to ARP's two-phase implementation, scholars expected massive banking of allowances. And indeed, the emissions data discussed above shows that banking allowed participating sources to emit more SO_2 in Phase II than they would have been allowed to pursuant to the allocated allowances in that Phase. The year 2000 had the highest actual emissions with 11.2 million tons of SO_2 emitted, while the allocated allowances would have allowed for emissions amounting to 10 million tons only. In total, sources had banked so many allowances that they would have been allowed to emit a total of 21.6 million tons, roughly double the allocated amount. Sources continued to emit more SO_2 than allocated until 2005.[55]

e. Offset credits and projects

The ARP does not provide for the integration of offset credits and is thus a "true" cap-and-trade program as opposed to programs implementing offsets (which have been characterized as "hybrid" cap-and-trade programs). This has been pointed out in subsequent discussions regarding new trad-

---

54 *Id.* at 11.
55 *Id.* at 8.

ing programs and was mentioned as a contributing factor to the ARP's success in reducing emissions.[56]

f. Compliance

Each source has to name a designated representative for compliance purposes, 40 CFR § 72.30(b), for example a person working for the company that operates the source. Covered units must comply with the monitoring requirements promulgated in 40 CFR § 75. Rules on recordkeeping and reporting requirements are provided in 40 CFR § 72.9(f).

Each participant is required to operate continuous emissions monitoring equipment. This ensures continuous measurement and reporting of actual SO_2 emissions. In the event that a source should emit more SO_2 than is allowed based on its allowances, the source must pay an "excess emissions penalty." Pursuant to 42 USC § 7561j(a), such a penalty is calculated on the basis of the number of tons emitted in excess of the unit's emissions limitation requirement or, in the case of sulfur dioxide, of the allowances the operator holds for use for the unit for that year, multiplied by $2,000. It is thus fairly substantial, which creates a strong incentive to comply with the allowance requirements. This is demonstrated by a lack of penalty allowance deduction, i.e., an advanced deduction of allowances from subsequent periods, in most years.[57] Additionally, the owner or operator of any affected source that emits sulfur dioxide during any calendar year in excess of the unit's emissions limitation requirement or of the allowances held for the unit for the calendar year shall be liable to offset the excess emissions by an equal tonnage amount in the following calendar year, or such longer period as the Administrator may prescribe, 42 USC § 7561j(b).

3. Analysis

The ARP was a successful program, as shown by multiple factors. The ARP succeeded in achieving emission reductions. As displayed above, par-

---

56 The Market Advisory Committee to the California Air Resources Board, *Recommendations for Designing a Greenhouse Gas Cap-and-trade System for California* 98 (2009).

57 EPA, *supra* note 51

ticipating sources had reduced annual SO_2 emissions by 64 percent in 2009 compared to 1990 levels. In 2006, the ARP achieved its goal of reducing emissions to the intended long-term goal, i.e., an emissions reduction of 10 million tons below 1980 levels.

This was achieved at a relatively low cost. The cost of ARP's implementation in Phase I has been estimated to total 12,170 to 19,979 million USD, of which 9,500 to 17,000 million USD was designated for pollution control and the rest for implementation. This was substantially cheaper than traditional C&C regulation, whose costs have been estimated between 19,100 to 30,900 million USD.[58] As the EPA data suggests,[59] compliance was almost at 100 percent, likely due to the rather high fine for each missing allowance (compared to a price of 1,500 USD for allowances from ARP's reserve). Studies have also found evidence that the ARP brought down abatement costs by incentivizing participating sources to invest in innovative technology. "Utilities learned how to burn cost-effective mixtures of different types of coal, how to take allowance prices into account in operating decisions, and how to build more cost-effective flue gas desulfurization devices, called "scrubbers."[60] This was supported by de-regulation of the railroad industry, which allowed sources access to coal with less sulfur content. It has also been pointed out that due to technical advances in emission abatement technology, marginal abatement costs for SO_2 are much lower today than they were estimated to be in 1990, which is argued to have lowered the cost of achieving the emissions reduction under traditional C&C regulation as well. Under this premise, the cost savings achieved with allowance trading compared to a C&C regulation amounts to 250 million USD p.a. in Phase I and 748 million USD p.a. in Phase II, with about 43 percent of costs arising from compliance with C&C control.[61]

The ARP's allowance market is generally considered to be very efficient.[62] This is, for example, suggested by the large amount of trade between unrelated entities. The amount of trade, however, does not necessar-

58 Klassen & Nentjes, *supra* note 45, at 394.

59 *Cf.* EPA, note 51.

60 Schmalensee & Stavins, *supra* note 34, at 107.

61 Curtis Carlson, Dallas Burtraw, Maureen Cropper & Karen L. Palmer, *Sulfur Dioxide Control by Electric Utilities: What Are the Gains from Trade?* 108 J. Pol. Econ. 4 (December 2000).

62 *Cf.* Danny A. Ellerman, Paul L. Joskow, Richard Schmalensee, Juan-Pablo Montero & Elizabeth M. Baily, Markets for Clean Air: The U.S. Acid Rain Program 195 ff. (2000).

ily implicate an effective market, as the efficient volume of trade depends on the initial allocation of allowances and the efficient distribution of emissions among regulated entities. Consequently, very low volumes of allowance trading can also be consistent with overall cost minimization.[63] Unfortunately, the allowance prices only allow for limited opportunities to study the market's effectiveness, as regulatory action outside of the ARP's framework had significant impact on the market price. While the allowance price stayed rather consistent in the 100 to 200 USD range throughout Phase I and II from 1994 to 2002, the EPA's implementation and subsequent vacation of the Clean Air Interstate Rule, the Clean Air Transport Rule, and the Cross-State Air Pollution Rule had drastic effects on the allowance price. For example, the finalization of the Clean Air Interstate Rule led to a price increase from the 100 to 200 USD range in 2003 to 703 USD in the 2005 auction. This sharp increase of roughly 250 percent can be attributed to the more stringent cap in the Clean Air Interstate Rule. As such, the program also allowed for banking, and sources attained allowances to "hedge" against future price increases. In 2006, the allowance price reached its absolute high of 1,600 USD. Following this point, the EPA, under the pressure from various litigation against the Clean Air Interstate Rule, announced that it would reconsider the Clean Air Interstate Rule. As a consequence, allowance prices dropped sharply. It can, however, be noted that, aside from such impacts, market prices stayed rather consistent. This can be considered an implication of a stable market environment. However, Klassen and Nentjes suggest a market failure arising as a consequence of the "retirement gap." As shut down sources continue to receive allowances under the ARP and new sources have to comply with stricter emission standards under non-ARP related regulatory rules, the replacement of an old source can increase supply and depress demand for allowances.[64] Due to banking possibilities, this expected future excess supply was reflected in the allowance price since the ARP's initial stages. This shows the detrimental effects of non-related regulation on the cap-and-trade market.

Considering the data displayed above, the efficiency of allowance banking under ARP is controversial. Studies suggest evidence that the intertemporal allocation of abatement costs with the help of banking was efficient, with "greater-than-required emissions reductions in Phase I used (via bank-

---

63 Schmalensee & Stavins, *supra* note 34, at 108.

64 Klassen & Nentjes, *supra* note 45, at 401.

ing) to delay more expensive reductions by Phase II units."[65] Interestingly, this contradicts the effect of marginal abatement cost reductions discussed above. As abatement technology became cheaper, one would expect higher emission rates in Phase I and lower rates in Phase II. This phenomenon can be explained with the uncertainty market participants faced regarding future regulatory rules and allowance prices. This is a strong indicator that independent allocation was not achieved as such uncertainty incentivized participants to bank allowances to "hedge" against potential future developments. It follows that the market may not have achieved optimal performance. Furthermore, the unlimited banking was in combination with the additional reserve of more than 10 percent of allowances for sources reducing their emissions by installing scrubbers, suspected to have provided a strong incentive to invest in abatement technology instead of trading for allowances.[66] While the above-mentioned decreases in abatement technology prices may have distorted the effect, the high volume of trade between entities proves that such a (desirable) incentive was not strong enough to discourage trading entirely.

For a discussion of various other positive and yet unintended effects of ARP as well as factors not related to ARP's regulatory framework that may have contributed to ARPs success, see Schmalensee and Stavins.[67]

4. Conclusion

The above analysis shows that the ARP can generally be considered a success. Compliance rates were 100 percent and emissions were reduced to the intended levels. Deciding factors were the establishment of a functioning market. However, the ARP exemplifies issues arising from unlimited banking as it allowed sources to emit more emissions in Phase II than they were allowed to based on their allocated allowances. While this had no long-term detrimental environmental effect relating to Acid Rain in the area, it may have had hazardous effects on cap-and-trade systems dealing with other emissions. The high amount of banking also provides reason to doubt the effectiveness of the ratchet-provisions contained in the ARP. One reason for that might have been that the ratchet required the EPA to reduce allowances if the allocation resulted in allowances that exceeded

65 Schmalensee & Stavins, *supra* note 34, at 108.
66 Klassen & Nentjes, *supra* note 45, at 402.
67 Schmalensee & Stavins, *supra* note 34.

the cap. This formula, however, did not consider banked allowances, thus reducing the efficiency of the ratchet and endangering the cap.

The ARP also shows that a functioning allowance market can considerably limit compliance costs.

The effects of outside regulation on established cap-and-trade systems can be seen in the interaction between the allowance price and the legislative and judicial history of the Clean Air Interstate Rule, the Clean Air Transport rule, and the Cross-State Air Pollution Rule. This provides a valuable lesson for cap-and-trade frameworks as it exemplifies the need for flexibility in the framework.

5. The Acid Rain Program after 2010

Following the changes in the regulatory environment discussed above and the vacation of the Clean Air Interstate Rule in 2008, the Obama administration pushed for a replacement to the Clean Air Interstate Rule. The EPA finalized this replacement in 2011 with the Cross-State Air Pollution Rule, imposing reductions on SO_2 and NO_X in twenty-seven states. The EPA estimated that by 2014, this rule and other federal regulations will have reduced annual emissions by 6.4 million tons of SO_2 p.a. compared to 8.8 million tons in 2005 and 1.4 million tons p.a. of NO_X compared to 2.6 million tons in 2005. To achieve this goal, the Cross-State Air Pollution Rule contained state-specific emission caps, thus effectively ending interstate allowance trading in connection with the EPA Transport Rule promulgated in 2010.

6. The Acid Rain Program as an example for bottom-up regulation

The ARP was not only the first emissions trading program, but was (so far) also the only federally implemented emissions trading program in the U.S. In the "top-down" vs. "bottom-up" paradigm discussed above, it would be considered a top-down regulation from the perspective of the federal to state relationship. Its value as an example of bottom-up regulation is limited, especially since other than climate change, acid rain can be effectively approached on a local level as it is caused by local concentrations of certain atmospheric gases.

If anything, the ARP displays how the interaction of different regulative regimes can affect the effectiveness of a specific regulation. This is an important point, relating to bottom-up regulation, as a local bottom-up approach can be easily "overridden" or impaired by a conflicting overlaying regulation from a higher authority. An example could be a national or state bottom-up regulation being affected by international or federal regulation, respectively. This exemplifies a weakness in the idea of bottom-up regulation replacing top-down approaches: as regulation works in a hierarchical way and higher-level regulation often overrides lower-level rules, local bottom-up regulation is significantly more susceptible to conflicting regulation.

7. Lessons learned from the Acid Rain Program for a post-Kyoto world

Upon first sight, it seems that the ARP has no real significance for a post-Kyoto approach. Acid rain is not comparable to climate change as it can be traced to a relatively small class of pollutants originating from the production of only a few products. Solutions to acid rain are well known and relatively easy to implement: reduction of a certain class of pollutants was a sufficient response to the environmental issue at hand. The issue of climate change on the other hand, is more complicated; other than acid rain, our understanding of climate change is severely limited, with new knowledge and scientific data emerging regularly. Thus, regulation aimed towards climate change must be more complex and flexible.

However, the ARP can teach valuable lessons about the efficiency of emissions trading and the impact of certain design factors on the success of such a regime. Also, while the ARP is a top-down regulation in the "federal to state" relationship, it shows that effective environmental regulation does not necessarily need international pressure to be implemented. Of course, one may argue that acid rain, when compared to climate change, has more immediate and local effects, which makes it easier for policymakers *vis-à-vis* their constituency to implement restricting regulation on a local level without international pressure. Furthermore, the implication of the "free-rider" issue discussed above does not exist in local pollution issues. If that were the case, the question of effective local climate change regulation would become one of education as climate change's effects may not be as immediate as acid rain's, but will affect almost any region locally; further, an educated constituency would accept climate change regulation.

In addition to that, one further aspect of the experiences with the ARP should not be underestimated. It seems to have shaped both public and professional opinion of emissions trading, specifically in the U.S. In fact, the qualitative review of legal literature suggests that the positive outcome of the ARP in the late 1990s set the tone for later policy experiments with the emissions trading systems discussed below. For example, commercial interest groups refer to the ARP as a preferable template of environmental regulation.[68]

Regulators have been influenced by this as well. For example, as discussed later, the RGGI was explicitly built on the ARP architecture and theory. Mary D. Nichols, chair of the California Air Resource Board in charge of enacting California's cap-and-trade program reviewed below, has repeatedly cited the Acid Rain Program, which she was also involved in enacting, as a positive blueprint for emissions trading enacted by states,[69] as well as for California's program specifically.[70] The articles of legal scholars citing the ARP as a successful example for climate change regulation encountered in the course of researching this thesis are too numerous to list here.[71]

II. Illinois Emissions Reduction Market System (ERMS)

1. Introduction

The ERMS is a trading program adopted by the Illinois Pollution Control Board in November 1997 in order to reduce organic compounds that were considered responsible for an increase in ozone levels in Illinois.

Prior to adoption, the Greater Chicago Area—comprised of the counties of Cook, DuPage, Kane, Lake, McHenry, Will, and the townships of Aux Sable, Goose, and Kendall—was designated by the EPA as a marginal nonattainment area for the eight-hour ozone National Ambient Air Quali-

---

68 Interview with Charlie Ingram, The U.S. Chamber of Commerce, Washington D.C., January 23, 1995, cited in Gert Tinggaard Svendsen, *U.S. Interest Groups Prefer Emission Trading: A New Perspective*, 101 PUBLIC CHOICE JOURNAL 109-128 (1999).

69 Hearings before Senate Subcommittee on Clean Air, Wetlands, Private Property, and Nuclear Safety, Committee on the Environment and Public Works, 105th Cong. (July 24, 1997)(statement of Mary D. Nichols, Assistant Administrator for Air and Radiation, U.S. Environmental Protection Agency), https://www.epw.senate.gov/105th/epa_7-24.htm.

70 STANDARD CARBON, *Interview with Mary Nichols, Chair of the California Air Resources Board,* https://www.standardcarbon.com/2010/12/qa-with-mary-nichols-chair-of-the-california-air-resources-board/ (last visited January 11, 2020).

71 Instead of the many, *cf.* Chan et al., *supra* note 44.

ty Standard (NAAQS) pursuant to the Clean Air Act (CAA). As discussed above on pages 141 ff., nonattainment areas are defined as areas that do not meet the national primary or secondary ambient air quality standard for a certain pollutant. The standard is defined in L. 91-604, Sec. 109. The CAA obliges nonattainment areas to make reasonable further progress pursuant to 42 USC § 7501(1) to lower the pollution levels to comply with the federally determined ambient concentration standard of 0.125 part per million by 2007 to avoid the risk of losing certain federal funding.[72] Subsequent testing identified volatile organic material (VOM) emissions as a primary cause for ozone depletion and concluded that such emissions would need to be reduced in order to make reasonable further progress. However, at that time, VOM emissions were already subject to broad control by C&C based rules, which led the Illinois Environmental Protection Agency (IEPA) to propose a cap-and-trade program to achieve further reductions in a less costly way.

The ERMS was the first non-voluntary U.S. cap-and-trade program with broad coverage, which makes it interesting as one of the first attempts at voluntary emissions trading and thus a basis for the more recent programs. Furthermore, it is interesting due to a multitude of very unusual provisions. For example, while most cap-and-trade programs have longer trading periods, the ERMS is seasonal and restricts emissions only during May through September, as ozone problems mostly affect the Greater Chicago Area in the summer. Furthermore, while many cap-and-trade-systems limit emissions rates, the ERMS focuses on actual emissions. It also provides for provisions implementing technology-based emissions reductions.[73] Interestingly, the allocation of permits in the ERMS is based on so called baseline emissions that generally do not fluctuate. This leads to a steady (i.e., non-declining) cap on emissions.

The legal framework for the ERMS is based on Title 35, Subtitle B, Chapter I, Subchapter b Part 205 of the Illinois Administrative Code. It was created by the IEPA to implement the Emissions Reduction Market System regulatory program, consistent with the assurances that are specified in Section 9.8 of the Environmental Protection Act.[74]

---

72 *Cf.* South Dakota v. Dole, 483 U.S. 203, regarding this common federal tool. The Supreme Court held that non-coercive financial incentives by Congress are a constitutional exercise of the taxing and spending power.

73 For a list, see Illinois Environmental Protection Agency, *Emissions Reduction Market System, Annual Performance Review Report-2013* (May 2014).

74 Ill. Admin. Code tit 35, § 205, 110.

2. Coverage

a. Geographical coverage

The geographic applicability of the ERMS is strictly limited to the Greater Chicago area, which as defined in Section 205.130, is composed of Cook, DuPage, Kane, Lake, McHenry, and Will counties and Aux Sable Township, as well as Goose Lake Township in Grundy County and Oswego Township in Kendall County.

b. Emissions management period

Under Section 205.150[75] the Emissions Management Period consists of an emissions control period (Seasonal Allotment Period) from May 1 through September 30 as this period sees the most dramatic increase in ozone, and a reconciliation period from October 1 to December 31, in which regulated sources shall compile data of their emissions during the preceding Seasonal Allotment Period and submit a report on their seasonal emissions.

At the conclusion of the reconciliation period, sources must hold the respective permits for their emitted material or compensate for the lack of permits.

c. Regulated sources and participants

The ERMS applies to sources of VOM located in the area defined above and operating prior to May 1, 1999, which either emit 25 tons or more of volatile organic material[76] or have the potential to do so and have baseline emissions of at least 10 tons of seasonal emissions in any Seasonal Allotment Period beginning in 1999 (Section 205.2000). It furthermore

75 All further sections in this chapter refer to the Illinois Administrative Code.

76 Volatile Organic Material (VOM) reacts with nitrogen oxides to form ozone on warm summer days. Prevalent VOMs are benzene, perchloroethylene, toluene, and xylene. Interestingly, it is not defined in the ERMS, but can only be understood to refer to Volatile Organic Compounds (VOCs) pursuant to the Clean Air Act.

applies to sources that are required to obtain a Clean Air Act Permit Program (CAAPP) permit.[77]

Under the ERMS, sources that were not operating prior to May 1, 1999 are sources if they emit more than 25 tons per year of volatile organic material or have the potential to do so and have, or will have, seasonal emissions of at least 10 tons. Such new sources that require a CAAPP permit are considered sources under the CAAPP as well. Section 205.205 provides for exemptions from the EMRS for sources that meet the criteria detailed above.

Non-regulated sources, entitics, or citizens may participate in the ERMS by choice, for example for ideologically motivated reasons. Section 205.610(c) contains the relevant provision for so called "Special Participants." Special Participants are defined as "any person" who "may purchase allowances to retire them for air quality benefit." This allows, *inter alia,* interested citizens or public interest groups to purchase and "retire" allowances, thus effectively limiting the amount of allowances in the market and, consequently, VOM emissions in the Chicago area. It is noteworthy that per the section's wording, Special Participants may only acquire Allotment Trading Units (ATU) for the purpose of retiring them. Investment in or commercial trading with allowances, as conducted in subsequent programs, is therefore not possible for Special Participants.

This has the theoretical potential to artificially increase allowance prices due to increased demand, as the Special Participant can influence the supply of allowances. In theory, this could adversely affect the market equilibrium and thus the efficient allocation of abatement costs. In practice, the small number of Special Participants and their small capitalization makes that unlikely. Furthermore, while Special Participants may acquire allowances from general participants, they may not trade allowances amongst each other (Section 205.630), thus further limiting their influence.

---

77 CAAP is the Illinois version of the federally required operating permit pursuant to Title V of the Clean Air Act.

3. Allocation of allowances

a. Baseline emissions

Baseline emissions play an important role in the ERMS as a basis for the allocation of allowances to each participating source (*cf.* below). Baseline emissions are defined in Section 205.130 to mean a participating source's VOM emissions for the seasonal allotment period based on historical operations as determined by procedural provisions, *inter alia,* in Section 205.320. Under such rules, the baseline emissions are generally calculated by using the average of the two seasonal allotment periods with the highest VOM emissions during 1991, 1995, and 1996. This is defined as grandfathering on the above pages 118 ff. Sources may apply with the agency to use other calendar years for determination of their baseline emissions if they emitted an unrepresentative amount due to abnormal conditions, such as strikes, fires, floods, and market conditions. In other circumstances—for example if a source has seasonal emissions of less than 10 tons and is thus not covered by the ERMS but subsequently increases its emissions and becomes covered by the ERMS—the agency is competent to determine baseline emissions based on a process set out in Section 205.320(b) and (c).

The ERMS contains provisions on subsequent increases or decreases of the baseline emissions value. An increase of the baseline emission value shall occur in case of a source's voluntary over-compliance, which results in an emissions level that is lower than the required level in 1996. Correspondingly, the baseline can be decreased in various situations in which, in a simplified way, the originally determined baseline level proves to be inaccurate.

The allocation of allowances based on baseline emissions leads to a steady cap on emissions, which differs from other cap-and-trade programs that feature declining caps.

b. Allocation basics

Pursuant to Section 205.400, each source as defined above shall receive a number of ATUs allocated to the source by the competent agency as established in the source's CAAPP permit or Federally Enforceable State Operating Permit (FESOP), see Section 205.130. ATUs serve as allowances for the emission of VOM.

The EMRS bases the initial allotment of ATUs for each source on baseline emissions for the respective source as determined by Section 205.320 reduced by 12 percent, unless the source is excluded from further reductions by the ERMS. Such exclusion applies, for example, to direct combustion emission units designed and used for comfort heating purposes, Section 205.405. The allotment can be exemplified as follows: if a non-exempted source A has baseline emissions of 100 tons of VOM, the ATU allotment will generally be good for 88 tons of emissions. "Allotment Trading Unit" (ATU) means a tradable unit that represents 200 lbs. of VOM emissions and is a limited authorization to emit 200 lbs. (90.71 kg.) of VOM emissions during the seasonal allotment period, Section 205.130. Source A in our example will receive 880 ATUs. If the baseline emissions are increased in accordance with provisions set out in the ERMS for this case,[78] the allotment shall be increased. This allows for flexibility of ATU allotment and seeks to avoid industry disadvantages by imposing strict standards.

The respective ATUs shall remain at the initial levels, i.e., according to the baseline emissions reduced by 12 percent, unless the competent agency formally[79] demonstrates that a further reduction is required.

New sources, as defined above (i.e., sources that were not operating prior to May 1, 1999 and fit the emitting criteria,) will not be allotted ATUs under the provisions of the ERMS. Pursuant to Section 205.400 f), such sources shall not be issued ATUs, but are required to hold ATUs as necessary to cover their emissions by the end of the reconciliation period, which means that new sources are forced to acquire ATUs (*cf.* below). If a source stops operating or loses its permit for whatever reason, 80 percent of the allotted ATUs remain with the source's operator, whereas 20 percent are issued to the Alternative Compliance Market (ACMA), Section 205.410(a). Alternatively, the operator may, pursuant to Section 205.410(c), authorize the issuance of future ATUs to the Transaction Account of another participating source, new participating source, or general participant by submitting a transfer agreement authorizing a permanent transfer of all future ATUs.

It is noteworthy that ATUs are allotted on the basis of actual emissions, not emission rates, as is the case in many other cap-and-trade programs. The ERMS thus features an absolute cap rather than a relative cap.

78 *See* Ill. Admin. Code tit 35 § 205.320(f).

79 *See* Ill. Admin. Code tit 35 §§ 9.8, 27, and 28 of the Act [415 ILCS 5/9.8, 27 and 28].

4. Banking and trading of credits

a. General provisions on trading

The ERMS contains provisions regarding market transactions of ATUs. Procedural requirement for this is a transaction account with the agency that must be applied for no later than thirty days before the first seasonal allotment period in which the source is required to participate, Section 205.610(a). An official record of the transaction must be made. Apart from such procedural aspects, the material transaction requirements are rather limited. Expired or retired ATUs may not be subject to a transaction. The parties' transaction account must show the amount to be transferred, and no sale may include partial ATUs or concern less than one ATU, Section 205.630(c).

In the 2013 season, the EMRS generated 28 seasonal trades. Furthermore, there are currently 29 active long-term transfer agreements. These transactions involved a total of 40 sources as sellers and 50 as buyers (including excursion compensation sources). Five general participants and three participating sources both bought and sold ATUs in 2013.[80]

b. Alternative Compliance Market Account (ACMA)

The Alternative Compliance Market Account (ACMA) is operated by the IEPA as a competent agency and allows sources access to a secondary market for ATUs, which as long as they remain "banked" in the ACMA, do not expire but must be used by the source once purchased, Section 205.710.

The agency issues ATUs to the ACMA in an amount equal to one percent of a given year's allotment—i.e., if 1000 ATUs are allotted in a given season, the agency will issue 10 ATUs in the ACMA. In addition to that, ATUs allotted to sources that were shut down during a season will be issued to the ACMA as well. Moreover, the competent authority may try to obtain additional ATUs for the ACMA by accepting voluntary contributions of ATUs from participating sources or other persons for deposit into the ACMA, Section 205.710(c)(1).

The wording relating to "other persons" poses an interesting question related to Special Participants as explained above, as these participants may

80 Illinois Environmental Protection Agency, *supra* note 73, at 10.

only acquire ATUs for the purpose of retiring them. Thus, "other persons" can only relate to general participants in the ERMS, which are persons, other than sources, that obtain a transaction account and are allowed to participate in ATU transactions, Section 205.130. The only difference, as set out in the ERMS, between general participants and Special Participants is that Special Participants do not need an admitted account officer, thus allowing interested citizens to participate without much bureaucracy. General participants may thus be understood as either a "broker" of ATUs or sources that shut down their operations but maintain a transaction account.

Finally, sources may opt out of being regulated by the ERMS by achieving at least 18 percent seasonal emissions reductions pursuant to Section 205.210(b). Following this, ATUs equivalent to any amount of VOM emissions reductions achieved by the source beyond 12 percent (i.e., at least 6 percent) are issued into the ACMA. An example: Source A, which would have emitted 100 tons of VOM, reduces its emissions by 20 percent and opts to be exempt from the ERMS. Eight percent of such will be allotted to the ACMA, i.e., ATUs covering 8 tons of emissions. At 200 lbs. per ATU, this will amount to 80 ATUs.

Such a procedure is to be understood within the context of the ERMS objective to reduce emissions by 12 percent. Any (quasi-) voluntary emissions reductions beyond 12 percent can be reintroduced into the market to allow for more flexibility.

The ERMS grants sources and general participants two different types of access to the ACMA, regular and special. Which type of access is granted largely depends on the availability of ATUs in the ACMA. Regular access to the ACMA is always available for all participants provided that there is a positive balance of ATUs in the ACMA. ATUs deposited in the ACMA are available for the lower price of either 1,000 USD per ATU or 1.5 times the current average market price, if enough transactions have occurred to reliably establish such. Furthermore, participants may have special access to the ACMA pursuant to Section 205.710(e) if there is no sufficient amount of ATUs deposited in the ACMA to accommodate the respective request and provided that the transaction does not exceed ATUs amounting to one percent of the next seasonal allotment—i.e., it does not deplete the ACMA of ATUs. Participants that desire special access to the ACMA must demonstrate that during the reconciliation period, the source has not been able to obtain regular access to the ACMA and was not in the position to obtain ATUs by conducting market transactions during the reconciliation period and that its actual emitted VOMs exceed their ATUs. The purchase price in special access transactions is the lesser of 1,000 USD per ATU or twice the market price, increasing the incentive for sources to secure the necessary permits during the reconciliation period. As with regular access, a special access transaction may not deplete the ACMA.

Technically, the ATUs "deposited" in the ACMA for special access are emission permit credits as, contrary to regular access, there is no fixed deposit of ATUs per season, but rather credits made to the agency with up to one percent of ATUs from the seasonal allotment of the next season. In the subsequent calendar year, the agency must offset that amount by crediting any expired ATUs from the transaction accounts of all ERMS participants to the ACMA after the end of the reconciliation period and seek to achieve an equivalent reduction in the amount of VOM emissions to offset those ATUs or to credit the ACMA with one percent of ATUs as needed from the next seasonal allotment. This procedure was defined as "borrowing" in Chapter C.VI.5 in this text. As argued in Chapter C.VI.5, borrowing may introduce a "moral hazard" issue into the system. However, the ERMS data does not show any signs of the materialization of such a moral hazard. One may therefore argue that the concerns with borrowing only partially apply to smaller emissions trading systems with only local coverage, as the price incentive to engage in risky behavior is smaller compared to systems with larger coverage.

Ultimately, the ACMA increases the amount of available ATUs and thus artificially decreases the market price by adding more available ATUs to the market, which serves an important role in increasing liquidity of the ERMS permit market.

c. Banking

Contrary to the ARP, the ERMS does not provide for express banking provisions but rather implicitly allows limited banking of permits by allowing ATUs to stay valid for use during the seasonal allotment period following issuance, i.e., the period in which the respective ATUs are allotted to the source and the next following seasonal allotment period, Section 205.400.

According to the IEPA, such limited banking was designed to ensure that companies could not accumulate ATUs indefinitely, which the agency thought would have left open the possibility of a source having more emissions than anticipated in a single season.[81] While the lack of solid

81 Illinois Environmental Protection Agency, *supra* note 73, at vii.

long-term banking would normally be a point of criticism, limitations on banking appear reasonable considering the very short emissions management periods, as otherwise sources could accumulate a high amount of ATUs in a short period of time and emit an amount of VOMs that would counteract efforts to keep emissions under a certain threshold to avoid high ozone levels.

d. Market efficiency

The short emissions management terms in the ERMS and limits on banking pose questions regarding the validity of the ERMS permit market. Economic methods of determining market accessibility and efficiency have been discussed in Chapter D. A good understanding of the general market accessibility of the ERMS can be achieved by reviewing the relationship between supply and demand for the ATUs on the market. In 2013, the ERMS market (excluding long-term transfer agreements) contained 4,630 ATUs posted for sale, whereas demand amounted to 66 ATUs requested by a single source. While the Illinois EPA considers this surplus to be a sign of a well-functioning market,[82] it also may very well be understood as a lack of balance between supply and demand levels, endangering the equilibrium of the market. This is usually considered a market inefficiency. While microeconomics often considers this a result of too-high pricing, in this case it is likely a result of an overallocation of ATUs, as shown by the high rate of unused ATUs and the sharp drop of ATU prices following the enactment of the ERMS.

Apart from that, the IEPA considers the following market features a sign of market efficiency. [83]

After an initial stark decline of ATU prices following the first seasonal emissions management periods from 75.87 USD per ATU to 51.93 USD in 2001, 32.85 USD in 2002 and 18.75 USD in 2003, the ATU price subsequently remained in the 19 to 20 USD range, with some sharp drops in 2005 and 2007 (to 13.99 USD and 14.86 USD respectively).

Furthermore, the IEPA cites a lack of interest in the regular access ACMA during the reconciliation period and concludes that the sources that were looking to acquire ATUs found them in the market. Considering the extremely low demand as displayed above, this rather indicates an

82 Illinois Environmental Protection Agency, *supra* note 73, at 14.
83 Illinois Environmental Protection Agency, *supra* note 73, at vii.

overallocation of allowances, which makes a scenario in which sources need to acquire ATUs unlikely. The same applies to the IEPA's argument that only a small number of sources were fined for not having sufficient ATUs to cover their emissions as well as the high number of retired ATUs. After the 2013 season, 62,859 ATUs, which represent 62.8 percent of all ATUs allotted for the 2013 seasonal emissions period, expired.

Such data furthermore shows that only between 30 and 40 sources regularly participate in the market. Given the total number of participating sources, this means that only 35 percent of all sources participate in the ERMS market. This might be a result of high transaction costs due to mandatory account officers under the ERMS and likely means that the market was not able to achieve the competitive equilibrium that cap-and-trade markets should strive for to achieve an effective allocation of allowances.

5. Offset credits and projects

Under the process set out by Section 205.500, sources and/or operators may acquire additional ATUs by facilitating VOM emission reductions by any other source if, *inter alia*, such remission reductions are based on the use of technology and material (i.e., not just a mere drop in production) or the source does drop its production, provided that the curtailed emissions are not just distributed to another source in the Chicago area. For example, if an operator operates source A and source B within the Chicago area and reduces VOM emissions from source B by 400 lbs. (181.2 kg.), source A may receive two additional ATUs upon the operator's valid proposal to the component agency.

6. Linking

Because of its regional character, the ERMS does not provide for linking provisions. However, the above-mentioned provisions regarding transferable emissions reductions reflect linking provisions contained in other cap-and-trade programs on a local level.

7. Criticism

a. Overallocation

aa. Data

For the 2013 season, 144 participating sources in the ERMS program emitted 3,298.8 tons of VOM, which equates to 69.4 percent less VOM than they would have been allowed to emit under their emissions baselines, with the aggregate baseline being 11,056.5 tons. This equals a difference of 66.1 percent between actual emissions and the allotted ATUs. The allotment shows a 9.5 percent reduction from the original baseline.[84] This alone may seem to indicate an overallocation considering the corresponding 12 percent reduction of the baseline as a basis for ATUs, but it takes into account the many sources exempt from reduction whose ATU allotment is based on the baseline without a reduction. However, a total of 62,859 ATUs (including ERG and Intersector ATUs) were retired in 2013. This amounts to 62.8 percent of all ATUs allotted for the 2013. This, in combination with the points discussed above, shows a clear case of overallocation of ATUs.[85] As one scholar put it: "During the design of ERMS, the Illinois EPA had predicted a price of 344 USD per allowance. Instead the allowance prices averaged about 75 USD per allowance in 2000 and steadily declined, reaching an average of 14 USD per allowance in 2005."[86] As discussed earlier, with such an overallocated state allowance, prices merely reflect transaction costs.

The first seasonal emissions management period in 2000 showed that sources emitted 44.1 percent less than their baselines would have allowed them to emit, and 37.9 percent less than their actual ATU allotments for this year.[87] This shows that the initial season saw an overallocation as well, which is supported by the displayed radical drop in ATU prices. Correspondingly, we can infer that the ERMs design, which is based on a steady cap that does not decline (as reviewed above), has aggravated the issue of overallocation, which makes an argument for flexible caps and

---

84 Illinois Environmental Protection Agency, *supra* note 73, at 6.
85 *Cf. also* McAllister, *supra* note 47, at 408.
86 McAllister, *supra* note 47, at 415.
87 Illinois Environmental Protection Agency, *Emissions Reduction Market System, Annual Performance Review Report – 2000 2* (April 2000).

an overall mechanism that allows for flexible midcourse corrections in cap-and-trade programs.

bb. Explanations for the overallocation

Reasons for the overallocation of ATUs are not easily found. It seems logical to seek them in the allotment process discussed above, especially in an inflation of the baseline. As noted, baseline emissions were calculated by averaging the two highest emissions in seasonal emissions management periods between 1994 and 1996, and subsequently reducing them by 12 percent to calculate the base for ATU allotments. Evans and Kruger suggest that some inaccuracies in the data for the initial allotment could be a possible cause of the overallocation.[88] Indeed, the ERMS allocation procedure poses an incentive for sources to calculate their emissions on the higher side in order to achieve a higher baseline and correspondingly receive more ATUs, or at the very least to document emissions more accurately than before and, when possible, to err on the higher side rather than the lower. The same has been observed regarding other cap-and-trade-programs.[89] From this perspective, the establishment of a cap-and-trade-system and the initial allocation provides for a completely opposite incentive than the enactment of regulatory rules: estimate emissions on the higher side rather than on the lower. Evans and Kruger, however, suggest that such an overestimate would be compensated in the following reconciliation period as the sources that have overcalculated their emissions by using a certain measuring method will use the same measuring method in the subsequent periods and will thus have to forfeit more allowances to cover for such emissions.[90] This result is, however, not guaranteed given the flexibility the ERMS allows regarding measurement of emissions. Section 205.330 provides that the owner or operator of each source shall determine VOM emissions from the source during the seasonal allotment period using methods as necessary to demonstrate compliance with this part. Furthermore, the section sets out a list of acceptable methods that may

88 David A. Evans & Joseph A. Kruger, *Where are the Sky's Limits? Lessons from Chicago's Cap-and-Trade Program*, 49 Environment: Science and Policy 24 (2007).

89 *Cf.* for example Juan-Pablo Montero, Jose Miguel Sanchez & Ricardo Katz, *A Market-Based Environmental Policy Experiment in Chile*, 45 J. L. & Econ. 267, 287 (2002) regarding experiences with cap-and-trade and Chile or other trading systems discussed in this thesis.

90 Evans & Kruger, *supra* note 88, at 24.

be employed. This allows the IEPA some leeway in determining the emissions, which could have contributed to an overallocation of ATUs.

It seems likely that the ability of sources to utilize the two years with the highest emissions to calculate their baseline emissions was a contributor to the overallocation. Calculating the baseline on the basis of two years that are potentially significantly higher than the average has potential to distort the baseline.

Evans and Kruger make another highly interesting point in suspecting industry contraction as a contributing factor in the overallocation of ATUs, as under Section 205.410, sources continue to receive 80 percent of their ATUs in the event of a shutdown if they become general participants.[91] Indeed, the 2013 performance report shows that in 2013, only forty-five sources with a total number of 19,783 expired ATUs shut down.[92] This amounts to roughly 51.2 percent of all expired ATUs. This data shows that around half of all ATUs expired due to source shutdowns. The provisions allowing shut down sources to further receive ATUs are therefore not the entire reason for the overallocation of ATUs, but it is at least statistically a significant contributor.

Kosobud, Stokes, Tallarico, and Scott furthermore suggest that participating sources might have reduced their emissions to comply with other federal regulations requiring emissions reductions .[93] This is a possible solution as the ERMS contains provisions regarding compliance with other regulations. Indeed, the federal schedule for the promulgation of hazardous air pollutant rules shows that in the time span from 1997 to 2007, seventy regulations have been promulgated, a majority of which affect VOM emissions.[94] Evans and Kruger point towards a regression analysis supporting that there appears to be a drop in emissions at sources that are required to comply with such hazardous air pollutant rules. It is, however, also pointed out, that such an effect likely only accounts for

---

91 Evans & Kruger mention 100 percent. The rule has been amended at 29 III. Reg. 8848, effective June 13, 2005.

92 Illinois Environmental Protection Agency, *supra* note 73, at 7.

93 Richard F. Kosobud, Houston H. Stokes, Carol D. Tallarico & Brian L. Scott, *The Chicago VOC Trading System: The Consequences of Market Design for Performance* (Massachusetts Institute of Technology Center for Energy and Environmental Policy Research, Working Paper #04-019, 2004), http://ceepr.mit.edu/working-papers-2000-2004/ (last visited January 11, 2020).

94 United States Environmental Protection Agency, *Table of Final MACT Rules*, http://www.epa.gov/ttn/atw/mactfnlalph.html (last visited January 11, 2020).

5 percent of the unused allowances in 2005.[95] This is in stark contrast to the fact that during 2005, sources emitted 61.9 percent less than they would have been allowed to under their baselines, which amounts to 57.9 percent less than their actual ATU allotment for this year.[96] Thus, such additional regulations may not sufficiently explain the overallocation of ATUs as much as provide another valuable lesson on regulative issues that may arise from related regulations (*cf.* the same issue in the ARP).

b. The ERMS in economic scholarship

To date, three economic studies have been conducted on the ERMS. In 1996, the IEPA conducted a feasibility study of the proposed ERMS regulations using a marginal cost approach. Two years later, Evans conducted a more thorough study using a mixed-integer programming model that was never published, but it is routinely cited in secondary literature.[97] In 2002, Liao and Onal conducted a third study also using a mixed integer programming model.[98] The Liao and Onal study was, however, the first review of the ERMS to also consider source's optimizing behavior, i.e., a source's multi-period planning horizon and independent, optimizing behavior. Liao and Onal developed a social planner's model and estimated the total cost of the first five years would be approximately 8.5 million USD with an annual average control cost of 1.7 million USD. Extrapolating these numbers, Liao and Onal concluded that about 3 percent of the ERMS participants would adopt new emission reduction technologies, 7 percent of participants will increase their own control efficiency, while 90 percent would be ATU buyers.[99] Consequently, the ERMS has provided little incentive to invest in new emissions reducing technology. This is

95 Evans & Kruger, *supra* note 88, at 27.

96 Illinois Environmental Protection Agency, *Emissions Reduction Market System, Annual Performance Review Report – 2005* (April 2006), http://www.epa.state.il.us/air/erms/apr/2005/cover.pdf.

97 David A. Evans, *An Analysis of the Emissions Reduction Market System* (1997) (Unpublished Master's Thesis, University of Illinois, Urbana-Champaign).

98 Chao-Ning Liao & Hayri Onal, *An Economic Analysis of the Emission Reduction Market System in Chicago*, Address at the 2002 Annual meeting of the American Agricultural Economics Association (now the Agricultural and Applied Economics Association) (July 28-31, 2002) at 7.

99 *Cf.* note 98.

probably a result of the overallocation of ATUs, which led to a low price and a correspondingly low incentive to reduce emissions.

Another economic criticism concerns the role of Special Participants in the ERMS. The introduction of Special Participants into the market may lead to an artificial decrease in allowance prices, as the Special Participant can influence the supply of allowances. In theory, this could adversely affect the market equilibrium and thus the efficient allocation of abatement costs. Unfortunately, as discussed above, the ERMS is overallocated. As a consequence of this overallocation and because of the small number of Special Participants, serious studies of the allowance price and the effects of special participants cannot be performed in this context.

c. Conclusion

Given the data analyzed in this chapter, we can conclude that the ERMS was successful in reducing emissions to the desired level but failed in establishing an appropriate ATU allotment and a functioning market for allowances. So while it achieved sufficient environmental integrity, the primary objective of the program, it was not successful at achieving its secondary objectives.

It also provides for valuable lessons in efficient cap-and-trade program design. It especially shows the importance of determining an accurate baseline for the allotment of permits and a regulatory approach allowing for flexible adjustments of the baseline. The methods used by the IEPA to determine the baseline did not reflect the theorem discussed as "feasibility theory." As a result, the baseline was simply too high. An interesting aspect of the ERMS is the state of independent allocation of allowances. As discussed in Chapter C.III.2, the quantity of allocation may affect the independent allocation in the presence of certain factors. As the allocation of ATUs in the ERMS is based on previous emissions in past seasons, we face the problem of endogeneity bias[100] in assessing statistically whether allocation was independent. We can therefore only review allocation by indirect

100 John Geweke, *Endogeinity and Exogeinity in* THE NEW PALGRAVE DICTIONARY OF ECONOMICS (Steven N. Durlauf & Lawrence E. Blume, eds., 2008). "Endogeneity and exogeneity are properties of variables in economic or econometric models." Endogeinity exists when there is a correlation between the parameter or variable and the error term.

evidence of possible permit market distortions.[101] In reviewing potential factors responsible for market distortion defined in Chapter C.III.2, we can conclude that multiple factors are present in the ERMS. As discussed above, transaction costs are present in the ERMS. With the obligation to have an Account Officer and other procedural requirements for trading, we can estimate such costs at the higher end of the spectrum. Furthermore, the data shows evidence of non-cost maximizing behavior from sources. The presence of such factors provides indirect evidence of possible permit market distortions and provides evidence that the independent allocation of allowances was not achieved.

8. The ERMS as an example for bottom-up regulation

It is debatable whether the ERMS can serve as an example for bottom-up regulation. While it was enacted by the IEPA, a state authority, to deal with a local pollution problem, it was established as a reaction to the designation of the Greater Chicago Metropolitan Area as a non-attainment area in the CAA Amendments of 1990, which obliged Illinois to reduce ozone depleting emissions by 9 percent every three years from 1996 until the area reached attainment. It is therefore more of a local compliance tool within a top-down regulation, similar to the European Union's emissions trading system as a compliance tool within the Kyoto Protocol. It also does not provide for any linking possibilities that would allow for the study of linking between systems. But again, just like the ARP, the ERMS shows that international cooperation is not necessarily a *conditio sine qua non* for local environmental regulation.

Unfortunately, just like the ARP, the significance of the ERMS in terms of climate change approaches is limited to its design factors: Ozone depletion, just like acid rain, is a well understood environmental problem and can be grouped into the "tame" problem paradigm, which limits its value as an example for climate change regulation.

9. Lessons learned from the ERMS for a post-Kyoto world

The ERMS shows that emissions trading can be environmentally effective in limiting a specific pollutant. It is, however, debatable whether this

101 Employed also by Hahn & Stavins, *supra* note 61 in Chapter D.

very small-scale experiment can be extrapolated to emissions trading as a response to climate change since the coverage and the area of applicability for climate change is exponentially greater and the ERMS shows signs of overallocation.

However, an interesting point relating to a bottom-up approach as an alternative approach to the Kyoto Protocol is the lack of signs indicating the presence of the above-mentioned moral hazard issue resulting from borrowing possibilities. As suggested above, one may argue that the concerns with borrowing only partially apply to smaller emissions trading systems with local coverage as the price incentive to engage in risky behavior is smaller compared to systems with larger coverage, *inter alia*, due to higher possibilities of leaving the system. This is a valuable insight as it can also relate to bottom-up programs, which are inherently smaller and more confined than international regimes.

As discussed above, studies suggest that around 3 percent of the ERMS participants would adopt new emission reduction technologies, 7 percent of participants would increase their own control efficiency, while 90 percent would be ATU buyers. A substantial investment in new abatement technology due to the program is not predicted to occur. This is a problem, given the need for new energy efficient technology discussed above. We can conclude that in the case of the ERMS, emissions trading was not sufficient to provide incentives for R&D. However, the reason for this is likely the low ATU price. From an economic standpoint, this is not surprising and, given the average emissions price of 14 USD per ton and no sign of a subsequent revision of the cap, sources had no incentive to invest. Such investments will only occur if the investments will bring cost reductions that are greater than the cost of emissions.

III. Regional Greenhouse Gas Initiative

The Regional Greenhouse Gas Initiative (RGGI) was the first mandatory, albeit regionally and substantively restricted, multi-pollutant emissions trading program in the U.S.

It stems from a memorandum of understanding (MOU) regarding the reduction of CO_2 emissions in the U.S. northeastern and mid-Atlantic region signed by the governors of Connecticut, Delaware, Maine, New

Hampshire, New Jersey,[102] New York, and Vermont. In 2007, the states Maryland, Massachusetts, and Rhode Island joined the group. In the program, the states' representatives committed to propose for legislative approval a "CO_2 Budget Trading Program" aimed at stabilizing and subsequently reducing CO_2 emissions within the participating states as well as implementing a regional CO_2 emissions budget and allowance trading program that would regulate CO_2 emissions from fossil fuel-fired electricity generating units having a rated capacity equal to or greater than 25 megawatts.[103] The designated launch date for the program, which was initially planned with a regional emissions cap of 121,253,550 tons,[104] was January 1, 2009.[105] The cap was subsequently modified to reflect the entrance of further states into the RGGI.

1. The Memorandum of Understanding

Apart from the provisions displayed above, the RGGI MOU's most prominent feature is a declining cap on carbon emissions, titled "scheduled restrictions." Under part D of the MOU, each state's annual CO_2 emissions budget, as apportioned under the aggregate cap, was designed to decline by 2.5 percent per year beginning in the year 2015. In aggregate, this amounts to a reduction for each state's base annual emissions budget of 10 percent by 2018.

The program's compliance period was agreed to be a minimum of three years. However, the MOU also provides for a "safety valve" mechanism. Under this mechanism, if the 12-month average regional price of CO_2 allowances equals or exceeds a certain value after the first 14 months of each compliance period, the compliance period can be extended by one year, for a maximum compliance period of four years.[106] The value was 10 USD per allowance in 2005. It is to be adjusted by the Consumer Price Index plus 2 percent per year, according to part E (2) of the MOU. This was a

102 New Jersey subsequently withdrew from the program with a declaration dated November 29, 2011.

103 *Cf.* Regional Greenhouse Gas Initiative, Memorandum of Understanding, https://www.rggi.org/program-overview-and-design/design-archive/mou-model-rule (last visited January 11, 2020).

104 *Id.* at 2.B.

105 *Id.* at 2.A

106 *See* 1(a) of the first Amendment to the MOU, https://www.rggi.org/program-overview-and-design/design-archive/mou-model-rule (last visited January 11, 2020).

political compromise intended to protect the program's participants from high allowance prices. The state's representatives assumed that given a longer compliance period, allowance prices would decrease, or participants would have more time to reduce emissions or acquire allowances.

The MOU also provides for a basic design regarding the implementation of offset credits, which can be used as compliance units. For this, the MOU defined key aspects and general requirements for the eligibility of offset certificates. According to the MOU, any offset project must be real, surplus, verifiable, permanent, and enforceable. Offset projects are to be approved by the state. The MOU defines specific projects that can be approved by the state administration, such as landfill gas (methane) capture and combustion, sulfur hexafluoride capture and recycling, and afforestation, the latter of which has proven to be a difficult-to-handle project in other programs and has been repeatedly criticized regarding its environmental justice implications. The MOU also defines limits on the creation and utilization of offsets: projects based inside participating states can create offset certificates for each CO_2 equivalent ton of certified reduction, whereas projects outside the participating states can only create offset certificates for every two CO_2 equivalent ton of certified reduction. A source may only cover up to 3.3 percent of its reported emissions with offset allowances. Furthermore, the MOU sets out highly interesting price adjustment mechanisms for offset credits that will be evaluated in detail below.

By signing the MOU, the participating states agreed to create a "regional organization" intended to fulfill multiple organizational responsibilities, such as the development, implementation, and maintenance of a system to receive and store reported emissions data and to allow for tracking allowance accounts. This regional organization is also charged with the development of the offset implementation.

An interesting clause in the MOU addresses the problem of emissions leakage. The participating states acknowledge that the implementation of the cap-and-trade program may lead to increased electricity imports and associated emissions leakage, 6.A.MOU. To address this problem, the participating states aim to establish a working group mandated, *inter alia,* with finding ways to address leakage and to monitor leakage data. The concern about leakage is valid and shows a structural problem in the regulation of the energy sector: import of energy from non-regulated jurisdictions is often cheap and effective, especially if the respective infrastructure, such as cross-border power lines, already exists. Therefore, leakage will take place if the costs of importing energy are lower than the costs imposed by compliance with the cap-and-trade program—something an effective program must address. Whether the RGGI succeeded in its attempts to avoid leakage is assessed below.

2. From the model rule to state legislature

As agreed in the Memorandum, the first compliance period began in January 1, 2009. Until 2013, the program operated on the basis of the RGGI Model Rules (RGGI MR), which were initially drafted as a blueprint for the promulgation of rules by the participating states. Subsequently, the participating states enacted individual state legislation to promulgate cap-and-trade systems.

Below, the MR are reviewed as RGGI's main legal framework. With regards to specific design questions not regulated in the RGGI MR, Delaware's adoption of the RGGI will be referred to as an example for other frameworks.

3. Model rules: The CO2 budget trading programs

The Model Rules set out a model legal structure for the establishment of a "CO_2 Budget Trading Program" (Program) in the participating states, which according to XX-1.1 RGGI MR, is designed to stabilize and then reduce anthropogenic emissions of CO_2, a greenhouse gas, from CO_2 budget sources in an economically efficient manner.

a. Coverage

The RGGI opted for limited, industry-specific coverage of the electricity sector. It only applies to fossil fuel-fired stationary boilers, combustion turbines, or combined cycle systems that at any time on or after January 1, 2005, served an electricity generator with a nameplate capacity equal to or greater than 25 megawatt electrical (MWe), XX-1.4 RGGI MR. Coverage began on January 1, 2009. According to the reviewed data, 168 facilities region-wide are covered.[107]

107 Regional Greenhouse Gas Initiative Fact Sheet 2015, no longer available online.

The program's first compliance period began on January 1, 2009. Planned are three compliance periods of three years respectively, i.e., January 1, 2009, to December 31, 2011, followed by a second compliance period from January 1, 2012, to December 31, 2014, and a third compliance period from January 1, 2015, to December 31, 2017.

The RGGI MR provides for optional regulations on exemptions of sources. States have the option to exempt sources from coverage at their own discretion; however, the tons attributable to sources in a state's initial inventory shall be removed from the state's emission budget, XX-1.4(a) RGGI MR.

Sources operating based on a state law permit containing a condition restricting the supply of the unit's annual electrical output to the electric grid to less than or equal to 10 percent of the annual gross generation of the unit benefit from a limited exemption from the Program, XX-1.4(b) RGGI MR. Limited exemption means that such sources need only comply with certain requirements, unless states choose to allocate allowances to such sources. In that case, full compliance is mandatory.

Individuals may request to participate in emissions trading by opening a general account for the purpose of holding and transferring CO_2 allowances. *Cf.* for example XX-6.2(b)(1) RGGI MR.

b. Cap

The RGGI initially capped CO_2 emissions at 188.1 million tons per year from 2009 until 2015.[108] Based on this, the RGGI features a declining cap as agreed upon in the MOU regarding the individual participating state's budget, *cf.* D. MOU. Each state's annual CO_2 emissions budget as apportioned under the aggregate cap, will decline by 2.5 percent per year beginning in the year 2015. This amounts to a reduction for each state's base annual emissions budget of 10 percent by 2018.

Delaware's initial emissions cap was set at 7,559,787 short tons of CO_2 for Delaware and further required a minimum of 25 percent of Delaware's allocation of CO_2 allowances under the cap-and-trade program to be used for public benefit purposes, 76 Del. Laws, c. 60 § 6043(a)(9). Correspondingly, Delaware's annual CO_2 budget in 2014 was 4,064,687 tons. In 2015, it was reduced to 3,963,993 tons of CO_2, 7 Del. Admin Code 1147, 5.1.1.

108 Kari Larsen & Vanessa Tanaka, *Emissions Trading Schemes across the U.S.*, article 9-381-2351 PRACTICAL LAW 3 (2008).

As set out in the MOU, the states adjusted the cap in 2012. The updated aggregated CO_2 emissions cap for the year 2014 was 91 million tons and will be reduced by 2.5 percent per year until it reaches approximately 78 million tons in 2020.[109]

c. Allocation of allowances

Participating states are allocated allowances, called CO_2 allowances. A CO_2 allowance under the CO_2 Budget Trading Program is a limited authorization by the regulatory agency or participating state to emit one ton of CO_2 in accordance with the Program, XX-1.5(c)(2) RGGI MR.

The amount of allowances allocated to individual states from the aggregate budget are not defined in the RGGI MR. How participating states allocate their allowance budget is at the state's administrative discretion. However, participating states must dedicate at least 25 percent of the allocations to a consumer benefit or strategic energy purpose account, XX-5.3(a) RGGI MR. The consumer benefit or strategic energy purpose account is a general account from which allowances are

> *sold or distributed in order to provide funds to encourage and foster the following: promotion of energy efficiency measures, direct mitigation of electricity ratepayer impacts attributable to the implementation of the CO_2 Budget Trading Program, promotion of renewable or noncarbon-emitting energy technologies, stimulation or reward of investment in the development of innovative carbon emissions abatement technologies with significant carbon reduction potential, and/or the administration*

of a participating state's component of the CO_2 Budget Trading Program, XX-1.1(am) RGGI MR.

In the first control period, the states chose to auction at least 90 percent of their allowance budget.[110] Indeed, market data shows that 94 percent of all these allowances have entered the market through an auction. The RGGI has conducted twenty-two auctions through the end of 2013, selling

109 *Annual Report on the Market for RGGI CO_2 Allowances: 2013,* Potomac Economics (May 2014), https://www.rggi.org/sites/default/files/Uploads/Market-Monitor/Annual-Reports/MM_2013_Annual_Report.pdf.

110 Regional Greenhouse Gas Initiative, RGGI Fact Sheet 2015, no longer available online.

a total of 651 million CO_2 allowances for 1.6 billion USD. [111] Delaware, for example, has chosen to auction 100 percent of its available allowances, 7 Del. Admin Code 1147, 5.3.1.

Allowance allocations are adjusted after certain periods. This also applies to banked allowances, *cf.* XX-5.3(e) RGGI MR. The administrative agencies administering the program have the discretion to retire undistributed or unsold CO_2 allowances at the end of each control period. This adjustment theoretically allows the administering agency to address common problems occurring from cap-and-trade allocations, such as over-allocation of allowances. It could, however, also theoretically increase costs as it adds a further uncertainty factor.

aa. Price control in the RGGI MR: The Cost Containment Reserve

In addition to CO_2 allowances, the administrative agency distributes "Cost Containment Reserve" (CCR) allowances. Such allowances are allocated to the auctioning account separate from CO_2 allowances and in addition to the state's general CO_2 budget for the purpose of containing the cost of CO_2 allowances, XX-5.3(d) RGGI MR. CCR allowances are allocated and subsequently adjusted under a formula set out in the RGGI MR.

Delaware, for instance, has opted to allocate an initial amount of 228,929 allowances into the CCR reserve, 7 Del. Admin Code 1147, 5.3.4.1. In relation to its overall 2014 budget of 4,064,687, this amounts to roughly 5.6 percent of the overall allowances. In subsequent years, Delaware aims to allocate CO_2 CCR allowances in an amount equal to 457,658, minus the number of CO_2 CCR allowances that remain in the State of Delaware Auction Account at the end of the prior calendar year, 7 Del. Admin Code 1147, 5.3.4.2.

Generally, CCR allowances are to be auctioned under XX-9.1 RGGI MR. Regarding the auctioning process, the administrative agency, *inter alia*, defines a minimum reserve price and the CCR trigger price for the auction. The CCR trigger price is the minimum price at which CCR allowances are offered for sale at an auction. The CCR trigger price is set to 4.00 USD per CO_2 allowance for calendar year 2014, 6.00 USD per CO_2 allowance in calendar year 2015, 8.00 USD per CO_2 allowance in calendar

111 *Annual Report on the Market for RGGI CO^2 Allowances: 2013*, Potomac Economics (May 2014), https://www.rggi.org/sites/default/files/Uploads/Market-Monitor/Annual-Reports/MM_2013_Annual_Report.pdf.

year 2016, and 10.00 USD per CO_2 allowance in calendar year 2017. Each calendar year thereafter, the CCR trigger price will be 1.025 multiplied by the CCR trigger price from the previous calendar year, rounded to the nearest whole cent, XX-1.2(r) RGGI MR. In contrast, the minimum reserve price in calendar year 2014 was 2.00 USD. Each calendar year thereafter, the minimum reserve price was 1.025 multiplied by the minimum reserve price from the previous calendar year, rounded to the nearest whole cent, XX-1.2(bc) RGGI MR.

CCR allowances can only be sold in auctions in which total demand for allowances above the CCR trigger price exceeds the number of regular CO_2 allowances available for purchase at the auction, XX-9.1(b)(1) RGGI MR. Thus, the introduction of CCR allowances increases allowance supply in case of a low supply to reduce costs for market participants.

bb. Voluntary renewable energy market set-aside allocation

The program allows states to implement a set-aside provision for an optional renewable energy market. If states choose to do so, they may allocate a certain number of tons from their aggregate budget to such a renewable energy market.

Allowances are allocated to a voluntary renewable market account based on the estimated MWh of eligible voluntary renewable energy purchases. Such an amount will be multiplied with an "emissions factor" that is defined in the RGGI MR and largely depends on the employed fuel. The product of both values equals the amount of allowances to be set-aside to the voluntary renewable market account. At the end of any given compliance period, the allowances in the voluntary renewable market account will be retired in an amount up to the number of tons of CO_2 represented by actual voluntary renewable energy purchases based on actual MWh purchases and the emissions factor, XX-5.3(j)(3) RGGI MR.

cc. Optional limited exemption set-aside allocation

The Model Rules allow states to opt for a limited industrial exemption set-aside allocation, *cf.* XX-5.3(k) RGGI MR. This applies to covered sources operating on a state law permit that limits the supply of the unit's annual electrical output to the electric grid to less than or equal to 10 percent of the annual gross generation of the unit, XX-1.4(b) RGGI MR.

The administrative agency retires for each subsequent allocation year the number of CO_2 allowances in the limited industrial exemption set-aside account equal to the exempt source's average annual emissions over the most recent three calendar years for which data are available. The retired tons shall be taken from the set-aside account established for such a purpose, XX-5.3k(2). After the retiring of allowances, the administrative agency decides whether any allowances remain in the limited industrial exemption set-aside account based on a formula defined in the RGGI MR.

As of now, Delaware has not chosen to implement a limited exemption set-aside allocation.

d. Trading and banking

aa. Regulatory rules

Trading—i.e., the transfer of CO_2 allowances between participants—is initiated by the submission of a transfer request to the competent regulatory agency that contains certain required information. Upon receipt of such a transfer request, the administrative agency must record the transfer generally within five business days, unless one of few exceptions applies. XX-1.5(c)(7) RGGI MR states that a CO_2 allowance shall not be deducted in order to fulfill the compliance requirements for a control period or interim control period that ends prior to the year for which the CO_2 allowance was allocated. This prohibits the borrowing of allowances from future compliance periods.

In contrast to borrowing, banking is expressly allowed. Under XX-6.6 RGGI MR, allowances held in the participating source's compliance account or general account will remain in the account unless and until the CO_2 allowance is deducted or transferred. Participants made extensive use of banking possibilities: "The number of CO_2 allowances in circulation on December 31, 2013 was 319 million, while cumulative compliance obligations for the second control period were 179 million. Therefore, the surplus number of CO_2 allowances at the end of 2013 was 140 million." [112] Compliance entities held substantially more CO_2 allowances than needed to satisfy compliance obligations for 2012 and 2013: "11 Compliance entities held 244 million allowances at the end of 2013 compared to second control period emissions of 179 million. The surplus CO_2 allowances held

112 *Id.* at 8.

by compliance entities at the end of 2013 (65 million) accounted for 46 percent of the overall private bank of surplus allowances. Thus, investors held 54 percent of the private bank of surplus CO_2 allowances at the end of 2013."[113]

bb. Market data

The market data provided by the RGGI shows a drastic initial decrease in allowance prices, with allowances traded around the reserve price and a subsequent stabilization of prices at a low level.

The primary market for allowances opened with the first auction in September 2008. In the first auction, 2009 vintage allowances, i.e., allowances designated for usage in the year 2009, were sold at the nominal price of 3.07 USD. Subsequently, the price increased to 3.51 USD in March 2009 before decreasing to 2.05 USD in the December 2009 auction. The prices for 2012 vintage allowances had a similar development: 2012 vintage allowances sold for 3.05 USD in the third auction and subsequently fell to 2.06 USD in auction four and 1.87 USD in auction five. In the four auctions with 2009 vintage and 2012 vintage offerings, the 2012 vintage allowances cleared at a significant discount to the 2009 vintage allowances, ranging from 36 percent in auction four to a discount of 9 percent in the sixth auction, indicating participants' uncertainty about the program's future development—a common theme with most programs.

Futures were traded at an initial price of 4.06 USD and drastically declined to 2.26 USD in the last quarter of 2009. After losing 44 percent, the price stabilized between 3.50 USD and 4 USD from October 2008 to May 2009 and then fell from June through the end of 2009.

In total, participants purchased 79 percent of all offered 2009 vintage allowances and 93 percent of all offered 2012 vintage allowances, likely due to lower allowance prices.

Secondary market activity increased during the year 2009, with an average daily volume of 0.5 million traded contracts in the first quarter to 4.8

113 *Id.*

million in the third quarter, before it fell to 2 million contracts in the last quarter.[114]

The primary market saw further price declines in 2010. Auctioning prices for 2010 vintage allowances decreased further from 2009 levels to 2.07 USD in the March 2010 auction to 1.88 USD in June and to the level of the reserve price of 1.86 USD in September and December. Future vintage allowances remained equal to the reserve price of 1.86 USD over all auctions in 2010. Futures decreased further from the 2009 level to 2.03 USD in 2010. "Trading activity in the secondary market for RGGI CO_2 allowances fell in 2010 from the previous year. This is reflected in the average daily volume of trading of CCFE-listed contracts, which fell from 2.7 million in 2009 to 0.21 million in 2010."[115]

The 2011 period is characterized by more stable prices at a low level. In the first control period of 2011, allowances were cleared at the reserve price of 1.89 USD. The volume weighted average auction clearing prices for the first control period fell 2 percent from 1.93 USD in 2010 to 1.89 USD in 2011. In the second control period, the 2011 average clearing prices were 1.89 USD, as the first two auctions of the year both closed at the reserve price. While the volume-weighted average auction-clearing price in the second period increased by 2 percent, this is a result of an increase in the reserve price, not the market-based carbon price. The volume-weighted average price for futures in the first control period decreased by 8 percent from 2.10 USD in 2010 to 1.93 USD in 2011. Allowance prices in the secondary market have remained stable at a low level close to the auctioning reserve price.[116]

Clearing prices in 2012 did not change, but remained at the reserve price, which amounted to 1.93 USD in 2012. The secondary market traded allowances at a slight premium over the auction-clearing price, likely due

---

114 All 2009 data retrieved from *Annual Report on the Market for RGGI CO^2 Allowances: 2009*, Potomac Economics 15-39 (August 2010), https://www.rggi.org/sites/default/files/Uploads/Market-Monitor/Annual-Reports/MM_2009_Annual_Report.pdf.

115 All 2010 data retrieved from *Annual Report on the Market for RGGI CO^2 Allowances: 2010*, Potomac Economics 15-39 (April 2011), https://www.rggi.org/sites/default/files/Uploads/Market-Monitor/Annual-Reports/MM_2010_Annual_Report.pdf.

116 All 2011 data retrieved *Annual Report on the Market for RGGI CO^2 Allowances: 2011*, from Potomac Economics 15-39 (May 2012), https://www.rggi.org/sites/default/files/Uploads/Market-Monitor/Annual-Reports/MM_2011_Annual_Report.pdf.

to the first compliance period deadline in March. Correspondingly, the volume-weighted average price for the first control period CO_2 allowances was 2.00 USD prior to March, 4 percent higher than the March auction clearing price and the average transaction price of second control period allowances. Future prices were consistent with auction clearing prices.[117]

2013 saw an increase in auctioning volume. One hundred percent of the 153 million CO_2 allowances offered for sale in auctions during 2013 were sold, which is an increase of 59 percent compared to 2012. Auction clearing prices increased 51 percent from the 2012 price of 1.93 USD to 2.92 USD in 2013, mostly due to a subsequent update to the RGGI MR published in 2013. This update adjusted the CO_2 emissions cap, as anticipated by market participants. Auction prices reached their high point in the second quarter June auction at 3.21 USD. Secondary market prices were consistent with auctioning prices and with the prices of physical deliveries in the allowance tracking system installed by the RGGI (COATS) throughout the year. The volume-weighted average futures price for all vintage and control periods reached a quarterly high of 3.41 USD during the second quarter. For the 2013 full year, the average futures price increased by 53 percent to 3.03 USD.[118]

e. Offset credits

As agreed by the participating states in the MOU, the RGGI allows participating units to generate offset credits with offset projects that reduce or avoid "atmospheric loading of CO_2, CO_2 equivalents or sequestered carbon." The Model Rules provide for extensive provisions on such offset projects with the general purpose of ensuring that CO_2 offset allowances awarded represent CO_2 equivalent emissions reductions or carbon sequestration that are real, additional, verifiable, enforceable, and permanent within the framework of a standards-based approach, XX-10.1 RGGI MR.

"Additional" in this context means that the offset project may not be a required action under federal law or the relevant law of the state in

117 All 2012 data pulled from *Annual Report on the Market for RGGI CO² Allowances: 2012*, Potomac Economics 15-39 (April 2013), https://www.rggi.org/sites/default/files/Uploads/Market-Monitor/Annual-Reports/MM_2012_Annual_Report.pdf.

118 All 2013 data pulled from *Annual Report on the Market for RGGI CO² Allowances: 2013*, Potomac Economics 15-39 (May 2014), https://www.rggi.org/sites/default/files/Uploads/Market-Monitor/Annual-Reports/MM_2013_Annual_Report.pdf.

which the project is located. A limited exemption applies if a project is recognized as an offset project under the RGGI and later becomes required by federal or state law: in this event, the project remains eligible to produce offset credits until the end of the given compliance period.

The RGGI accepts only certain defined offset projects: landfill methane capture and destruction;
reduction in emissions of sulfur hexafluoride (SF6); sequestration of carbon due to reforestation, improved forest
management, or "avoided conversion;"[119]
reduction or avoidance of CO_2 emissions from natural gas, oil, or propane end-use combustion due to end-use energy efficiency; and
avoided methane emissions from agricultural manure management operations, XX-10.3 (a)(1) RGGI MR. Further restrictions apply, e.g., offset projects may not include an electric generation component. Technical requirements for the eligibility of individual projects, such as the minimum baseline reductions for eligibility, are defined as well. Projects must either be located in a participating state or in a state within the U.S. that has entered into a separate memorandum of understanding regarding certain obligations, such as audits of offset project sites. Projects located (in whole or in part) in one or more participating states are not eligible for CO_2 offset allowances unless a greater amount of the CO_2 equivalent emissions reduction or carbon sequestration achieved by the offset project is projected to occur in one state rather than in any other participating state, XX-10.3(a)(2)(ii) RGGI MR. In that case, the state in which the greater amount occurs is considered the state where the project is located.

If a project is accepted by the administrators, offset credits are awarded for an initial 10-year allocation period. After this period, the offset project sponsor must apply for continuation of eligibility. If this is approved, offset credits are awarded for another 10-year allocation period. Projects more long-term in nature, such as projects involving reforestation, improved forest management, or avoided conversion, have a 25-year initial allocation period.

It is noteworthy that even though coverage of the program only extends to CO_2 emissions, offset credits can be produced with offset projects that reduce other emissions as well, such as CO_2 equivalents.

119 Avoided conversion is defined as action that avoids the deforestation of privately owned forestland.

As of 2013, no offset credits have been awarded,[120] most likely due to low allowance prices that made offset projects economically unfeasible.

f. Compliance

The administrative agency establishes multiple accounts for covered sources. It, *inter alia*, establishes a compliance account and a general account for the purpose of holding and transferring CO_2 allowances. Any deductions or transfers of CO_2 allowances are recorded in this compliance account.

At the end of each compliance period, defined as the allowance transfer deadline, a participant must in its compliance account hold allowances covering its actual amount of emissions in tons for that period. Allowances must be eligible for usage to comply with the Program. Under XX-6.5 RGGI MR, allowances are eligible for usage for compliance purposes if they are from allocation years that fall within a prior control period, the same control period, or the same interim control period for which the allowances will be deducted and are being held in the source's compliance account. As stated in the RGGI MOU, offset allowances can only be used up to a maximum of 3.3 percent of a source's total compliance obligation.

If, after making the regular deductions from allowances recorded in the sources compliance account according to the source's emissions, the source has excess emissions, the administrative agency deducts from the CO_2 budget source's compliance account a number of CO_2 allowances from allocation years that occur after the control period in which the source has excess emissions, i.e., futures, equal to three times the number of the source's excess emissions. In the event that a source has insufficient CO_2 allowances to cover three times the number of its excess emissions, the source is obliged to immediately transfer sufficient allowances into its compliance account. No CO_2 offset allowances can be deducted to account for the source's excess emissions, XX-6.5(d)(1). The RGGI MR allow sources to litigate against the administrative agency's determination of excess emissions. If the procedure finds that the administrative agency deducted too many allowances, it distributes additional allowances to make up for the excess deduction.

The RGGI MR sets out various compliance obligations for participating sources. Sources are required to have operating permits under state law

120 Potomac Economics, *supra* note 118.

as well as under the RGGI MR. Applications for operating permits must, *inter alia*, include a complete CO_2 budget permit application, XX-1.5(a)(1)(i) RGGI MR. Sources must also name an account representative. In contrast to many other programs, only one representative may be selected, XX-2.1(a) RGGI MR. However, the representative may designate one alternate account representative who may act on its behalf, XX-2.2(b) RGGI MR. Representatives may be changed at any time under certain procedures defined in XX-2.3 RGGI MR and can delegate parts of their responsibilities, XX-2.6 RGGI MR.

Owners and operators of covered sources as well their respective account representative for the program's purposes must comply with monitoring requirements defined in the RGGI MR and the federal requirements under 40 CFR 75. The emissions measurements recorded and reported in this manner are used to determine compliance with the allowance holding requirements, XX-1.5(b) RGGI MR. For this purpose, sources are, *inter alia*, obliged to install systems to monitor CO_2 emissions and to record, report, and quality-assure the data from the monitoring systems. Monitoring systems must generally be certified by the administrative agency. Technical requirements and other conditions to be met for certification are defined in the RGGI MR. Generally, the Model Rules provide for very detailed technical rules on emissions monitoring and reporting.

The RGGI MR state in XX-1.5 (f)(3) RGGI MR that any provision of the CO_2 Budget Trading Program that applies to a CO_2 budget unit (including a provision applicable to the CO_2 authorized account representative of a CO_2 budget unit) shall also apply to the owners and operators of the unit. As discussed in earlier chapters, this is suboptimal as it can result in a breach of an entity's limited liability by establishing personal liability.

d. Linking

The RGGI MR do not provide for provisions on linking with other cap-and-trade programs.

4. Analysis

a. Environmental analysis

Judging by the reviewed numbers, the implementation of RGGI appears to have resulted in a substantial reduction of emissions in the participating states. However, it is debatable whether this reduction is a direct result of the RGGI or rather outside factors, especially considering the very low allowance prices displayed above.

Compiled historical emissions data from RGGI sources in the states Connecticut, Delaware, Massachusetts, Maryland, Maine, New Hampshire, New Jersey, New York, Rhode Island, and Vermont show a 2006–2008 annual CO_2 emissions average of 163,000, 379 tons.[121] Compared to this baseline, the 2009 to 2010 average emissions from covered sources decreased by 30 million short tons of CO_2, following the implementation of the program in January 2009. This amounts to a reduction of 18.9 percent compared to the baseline. Correspondingly, the electric generation output of covered sources decreased by 14 million MWh, which is a reduction of 6.9 percent compared to the baseline. Emissions by sources not covered by the program did not increase following the implementation. The electric generation output increased slightly by 0.1 percent. The data does not show an increase of annual CO_2 emissions related to either net electricity imports into the ten-state RGGI region or from small fossil fuel-fired electric generators in the ten-state RGGI region that are not subject to state CO_2 Budget Trading Program regulations in the first two years of the program, 2009 and 2010.[122]

The 2009 to 2011 average emissions data shows further emissions reductions. Compared to the baseline, CO_2 emissions from RGGI electric generation sources decreased by 33.8 million short tons of CO_2, or 21.3 percent. Compared to the previous year, this amounts to a 3.8 ton reduction. The electric output decreased slightly compared to the previous year. The electric generation from covered electric generation sources decreased by 18.5 million MWh, or 9.1 percent compared to the baseline, which

121 Historical Emissions data retrieved FROM REGIONAL GREENHOUSE GAS INITIATIVE, *CO2 Data for RGGI Units 2000-2008*, https://www.rggi.org/allowance-tracking/emissions (last visited January 11, 2020).

122 *CO2 Emissions from Electricity Generation and Imports in the Regional Greenhouse Gas Initiative: 2010 Monitoring Report*, REGIONAL GREENHOUSE GAS INITIATIVE 3, 4 (August 6, 2010), https://www.rggi.org/sites/default/files/Uploads/Electricity-Monitoring-Reports/2010_Elec_Monitoring_Report.pdf.

is a decrease of 2.2 percent. CO_2 emissions from non-covered electric generation did not increase in 2009 to 2011, the first three years after the implementation of the RGGI program, relative to the baseline. However, electric generation by these sources increased slightly by 1.2 percent.[123]

The latest reviewed emissions data concerns the year 2012, which again saw a further, albeit minor, decline of recorded emissions. This year (2012) was also the first year after New Jersey's withdrawal. Compared to the baseline, emissions decreased by 35.1 million short tons of CO_2, which is a reduction of 25.4 percent. Compared to the previous year, this is a further reduction of 1.6 tons or 4.1 percent. Electric generation from covered electric generation sources decreased by 18.8 million MWh, or 10.6 percent, compared to the baseline. Non-covered sources did not increase emissions. The decrease in emissions from non-RGGI in-region electric generation offsets the slight increase in emissions related to electric generation from imports into the RGGI region. This indicates slight emissions leakage. Electric output increased by 4.4 percent.[124]

While this data suggests a successful reduction of emissions, scholars have indicated multiple environmental factors that may have contributed to the emissions reductions displayed by the data.

Citing other researchers, Murry, Maniloff, and Murry identify four possible explanations for the emission reduction:[125] the RGGI might have provided incentives for investments in low-carbon and energy efficient investments, thus reducing emissions. Furthermore, research suggest that the economic crisis in the years 2008 and 2009 might have lowered economic activity within RGGI covered regions, thus lowering energy demand and emissions. Research also indicates that natural gas as alternative energy sources has become more widely available, mostly due to advances in environmentally harmful hydrofracturing technology. Lastly, emission reduc-

---

123 *CO2 Emissions from Electricity Generation and Imports in the Regional Greenhouse Gas Initiative: 2011 Monitoring Report,* Regional Greenhouse Gas Initiative 3, 4 (June 27, 2013), https://www.rggi.org/sites/default/files/Uploads/Electricity-Monitoring-Reports/2011_Elec_Monitoring_Report.pdf.

124 *CO2 Emissions from Electricity Generation and Imports in the Regional Greenhouse Gas Initiative: 2012 Monitoring Report,* Regional Greenhouse Gas Initiative 3,4 (August 11, 2014), https://www.rggi.org/sites/default/files/Uploads/Electricity-Monitoring-Reports/2012_Elec_Monitoring_Report.pdf.

125 Brian C. Murry, Peter T. Maniloff & Evan M. Murry, *Why have Greenhouse Emissions in RGGI States Declined? An Econometric Attribution to Economic, Energy Market, and Policy Factors*, 51 Duke Envtl. & Energy Econ. 581, 586 (September 2015).

tions are associated with the impact of complementary state environmental programs such as renewable portfolio standards.

In their empirical assessment of such factors, Murry, Maniloff, and Murry conclude that the RGGI program is the dominant factor in the emissions reductions and that the economic recession accounted only for about 1 percent of the emissions decline. However, they also find that "[p]ower sector emissions would be more than 60 percent higher by 2011 in RGGI states were it not for the combination of policy, natural gas market, and macroeconomic factors that emerged in the late 2000s."[126] Furthermore, they find that "[n]atural gas markets were responsible for more than one-third of the region's emissions decline. They induced substitution in the generation mix from higher-emitting fossil fuels to natural gas."[127]

This is not necessarily true, as electric output within the RGGI increased slightly. This would argue for increasing investments in energy efficient technology as a dominating factor in the program's success.

b. Market analysis

The market data discussed above shows the familiar phenomenon of drastically falling prices after the initial allowance trades. As RGGI allowances can be banked for future compliance periods, their prices reflect the expected uses of the allowances over many years. Price variations across trading periods indicate uncertainties regarding future developments, something that is common among cap-and-trade programs.

The data indicates that participants banked large amounts of allowances. As mentioned above, the number of CO_2 allowances in circulation on December 31, 2013, was 319 million, while cumulative compliance obligations for the second control period were 179 million. The surplus number of CO_2 allowances of 140 million at the end of 2013 indicates extensive usage of banking. Despite this extensive banking, retired allowances account for one-fifth of the cap in the 1990 to 2010 period. Participants were not able to purchase these allowances due to the price floor under which no bids for allowances could be accepted.

---

126 *Id.* at 605

127 *Cf.* Murry et al., *supra* note 125.

5. Conclusion

a. Environmental effects

The implementation of the RGGI correlates with an emissions decline in the covered region. However, there is uncertainty about the impact of environmental factors outside of emissions trading on this result. Given these effects, the RGGI cannot be considered an environmental success with certainty, despite the generally positive data.

Furthermore, the market data and the initial stark drops in carbon prices indicate an overallocation of allowances, which supports the conclusion that the emissions cap could have been more stringent. The low allowance prices also support the theory that achieved emissions reductions were not a result of trading but of outside influences.

The overallocation and the corresponding low allowance price likely helped to avoid emissions leakage.

It is likely that the two steps of allocation decisions contributed to the overallocation. As shown above, the program designers first had to define the amount of allowances allocated to the states. In a second step, state officials decided on the allocation of allowances to participants. As the allocation process is always susceptible to lobbying, the two allocation steps made the RGGI vulnerable to industry influence.[128]

Early studies were concerned with emissions leakage and suspected substantial increases in power exports from non-covered states, which resulted in emission leakage rates of more than 50 percent in the programs early stages.[129] The data displayed above shows that in the later stages, no significant leakage occurred, most likely due to the comparatively low allowance prices.[130]

---

128 Bruce R. Huber, *How Did RGGI Do It? Political Economy and Emissions Auctions*, 40 Ecol. L. Q. 76 (2013).

129 Ian Sue Wing & Marek Kolodziej, *The Regional Greenhouse Gas Initiative: Emission Leakage and the Effectiveness of Interstate Border Adjustments*, (Mossavar-Rahmani Center for Business and Government, John F. Kennedy School of Government, Regulatory Policy Program Working Paper RPP-2008-03, 2008).

130 *Cf.* Richard G. Newell, William A. Pizer & Daniel Raimi, *Carbon Markets 15 Years after Kyoto: Lessons Learned, New Challenges*, 27 J. Econ. Persp. 134 (Winter 2013).

b. Market design

The RGGI's market design is notable especially for its usage of auctions as the primary allocation mechanism. As discussed in the introductory chapter, auctions are generally considered economically beneficial, but they are not used in most programs due to the political barriers towards using initial auctions. In all other reviewed programs, excepting the small 2.8 percent of allowances in the Acid Rain Program, the implementation of auctioning failed due to strong political opposition. The use of auctioning as a primary allocation mechanism also provides indications for independent allocation of allowances. However, data shows that in 2013, the two biggest sources under the RGGI accounted for 31 percent of the total projected demand for allowances, a moderate increase from 2012. Despite this, the amount of held allowances was generally distributed across firms consistent with their compliance obligations. The top ten compliance entities accounted for 56 percent of total holdings, smaller compliance entities accounted for 21 percent, and seven investors accounted for 23 percent.[131] This supports an independent allocation of allowances.

The RGGI market design is furthermore interesting regarding its usage of price mechanisms such as the floor price for auctions or the Cost Containment Reserve. The price floor clearly reduced cost uncertainty by limiting low-cost outcomes. It also provided an incentive to reduce emissions despite falling allowance prices and functioned like a low carbon tax.[132] Unfortunately for the purpose of this review, the allowance price was never high enough to trigger the "safety valve" as the performance of this unprecedented design feature would have been interesting.

In addition to this, the adjustment of the cap in 2012 took care of overallocation and raised carbon prices. This makes a good case for flexibility provisions regarding emissions caps, despite the obvious risks discussed in the introductory chapters, such as lobbying.

6. The RGGI as an example for a top-down regulation

The RGGI is a mandatory multi-state program. It was enacted by a group of states, but features a binding emissions cap for the entire region, of which participating states take a binding share within their own discre-

131 Potomac Economics, *supra* note 118.
132 Newell et al., *supra* note 130, at 135 ff.

tion. Despite being voluntary shares, their binding design makes the RGGI a (harmonized) top-down program, similar to the Kyoto Protocol.

Similar to the WCI, the RGGI provides for model rules for a joint cap-and-trade system, but such model rules are not binding, and participating states are free to enact different rules. The emissions reduction each state has to achieve is, however, binding. This differs from the "strict" bottom-up approach used in the WCI.

7. Lessons from the RGGI for a post-Kyoto world

The emissions data from sources in the RGGI states show a 2006–2008 average of 163 million tons of CO_2,[133] which after the implementation of the program, subsequently decreased by 30 million short tons. This amounts to a reduction of 18.9 percent compared to the baseline. Correspondingly, the electric generation output of covered sources decreased by 14 million MWh, which is a reduction of 6.9 percent compared to the baseline. Emissions by sources not covered by the program did not increase following the implementation, i.e., no significant leakage occurred. Unfortunately, other environmental effects dilute this outcome to the point that the RGGI cannot be credited with all achieved emission reductions.

However, just like the WCI, the RGGI displays multiple interesting facts with regards to potential bottom-up linkage as Kyoto alternative.

(1) While the RGGI does not contain any linking provisions, officials immediately became engaged in active discussions with WCI and the Midwestern Greenhouse Gas Reduction Accord regarding linking possibilities. This shows that even absent linking provisions, linking incentives remain, i.e., linking design is important, but may not be the sole, or even the most important, factor in the decision to link. In addition to the possibility of linking, the RGGI exemplifies another method by which cap-and-trade systems can grow: other jurisdictions, such as Maryland, Massachusetts, and Rhode Island in the RGGI's case, can join a regulatory regime. This is drastically different from enacted command-and-control regulation or carbon taxes. As discussed above, established emissions markets create incentives to join, especially for neighboring states. Other types of regulation do not exert the same incentives, thus making them less likely to evolve

133 Historical Emissions data retrieved from Regional Greenhouse Gas Initiative, *CO2 Data for RGGI Units 2000-2008* https://www.rggi.org/allowance-tracking/emissions (last accessed January 11, 2020).

into a trans-jurisdictional regulative tool. And indeed, IEPA director Doug Scott stated:

> *We believe in trying to move this ball forward. If there isn't any federal cap-and-trade legislation, the work that we're doing takes on that much more importance. The idea that you've got a market, instead of several markets, existing makes a lot of sense to us.*[134]

Even European scholars have suggested linking the RGGI with the European Emissions Trading System in an effort to keep the U.S. engaged in the international effort against climate change and to build a bottom-up network in lieu of cooperation on a national level.[135]

(2) In addition to this, the RGGI shows the advantages and disadvantages of harmonized emissions caps in the context of bottom-up regulation. Environmental groups favor the harmonized approach as it allows for more certainty and control of the emissions reductions as agreed by the parties. However, it may pose barriers to entry for jurisdictions as they might feel that they are not in the position to agree on binding caps. An interesting conclusion from the RGGI is that in a harmonized approach, parties can agree to exemptions of certain sectors or sources as such exemptions can be accounted for in the total emissions budget of a jurisdiction.

This is a valuable lesson, particularly as it relates to the question of involving developing countries in emissions trading agreements as such exceptions allow them to protect certain industries that they might consider vital for economic development. This can incentivize countries to enact cap-and-trade systems without hindering development.

Lastly, the binding emissions cap not only presents barriers to entry, but may also motivate state actors to leave trading systems. Such was the case for Governor Christie of New Jersey, who withdrew New Jersey's participation in the RGGI. While Christie argued that the withdrawal was

134 Evan Lehmann, *Regional Carbon Regulators Could be Linked if Congress Fails*, ClimateWire (November 10, 2009), http://www.eenews.net/climatewire/2009/11/10/3/.

135 Volmert, Barbara, Roßnagel, Alexander, Hentschel Anja, Rechtliche Möglichkeiten und Grenzen einer Verknüpfung des europäischen Emissionshandelssystems mit der amerikanischen „Regional Greenhouse Gas Initiative", Zeitschrift für Umweltrecht (ZUR) 2012, 666.

based on the malfunction of the program, he also argued that the RGGI had increased energy costs.[136]

IV. California Global Warming Solutions Act of 2006

In addition to federally induced regulations, such as the Acid Rain Program discussed in Chapter I, some state initiatives exist. The Western Climate Initiative (WCI) is another one of them. It was started by the state governments of Arizona, California, New Mexico, Oregon, and Washington, and also involved Montana, Utah, and the Canadian provinces of British Columbia, Manitoba, Ontario, and Quebec. Subsequently, all states but California, Quebec, and Ontario left the WCI. The U.S. American member states initially compromised about 20 percent of the U.S. economy, while the Canadian member provinces compromised 70 percent of the Canadian economy.[137] The WCI conference aims to establish a multistate cap-and-trade system for greenhouse gases on a state level. Observer states, i.e., states interested in joining the system, are currently Alaska, Colorado, Idaho, Kansas, Nevada, and Wyoming, and the Canadian provinces of Nova Scotia, Saskatchewan, and Yukon as well as the Mexican states of Baja California, Chihuahua, Coahuila, Nuevo Leon, Sonora, and Tamaulipas.

As a participant in the WCI, California already has a cap-and-trade system in place: the California Global Warming Solutions Act of 2009, also known as Assembly Bill 32.

---

136 Christopher Baxter, *Gov. Christie Announces NJ Pulling Out of Regional Environmental Initiative*, NJ.COM, (May 26, 2011; updated March 31, 2019), http://www.nj.com/politics/index.ssf/2011/05/gov_christie_to_announce_nj_pu.html (last visited May 1, 2020)

137 ARNAUD BROHÉ, NICK EYRE & NICHOLAS HOWARTH, CARBON MARKETS: AN INTERNATIONAL BUSINESS GUIDE 189 (2009).

1. Western Climate Initiative

The WCI conference produced Design Recommendations for the WCI Regional Cap-and-Trade Program in 2008,[138] and a Design for the WCI Regional Program.[139]

According to sec. 1 of the Design Recommendations for the WCI Regional Cap-and-Trade Program (WCI Recommendations),[140] the cap-and-trade design aims to reduce emissions of global warming pollution at a low cost by using emissions trading, allowance banking, and inclusion of offset components. The specific design details for this framework are provided in the Design for the WCI Regional Program (WCI Design).

a. Coverage

Under Section 1.1, coverage of the program extends to the greenhouse gases carbon dioxide, methane, nitrous oxide, hydrofluorocarbons, perfluorocarbons, and sulfur hexafluoride, which are also covered by the Kyoto Protocol. Under Section 3.1.2, the partner jurisdictions may determine whether any additional greenhouse gases should be covered, allowing for additional flexibility in covered pollutants. Various emissions sources are covered, and coverage extends to transport fuel combustion, which will be covered upstream. Whether and how to include upstream emissions from biofuel and fossil fuel production is to be assessed by the WCI partners prior to the program start, taking into consideration the potential for emissions leakage, the potential role of other policies (such as a low carbon fuel standard), consistent treatment among fuels, and other factors, such as practicality of implementation, Section 1.5. Sources are generally covered if they emit 25,000 or more metric-tons CO_2 p.a., excluding emis-

---

138 *Design Recommendations for the WCI Regional Cap and Trade Program,* Western Climate Initiative (revised ed., March 13, 2009), http://www.westernclimateinitiative.org/the-wci-cap-and-trade-program/design-recommendations.

139 *Design for the WCI Regional Program,* Western Climate Initiative (July 27, 2010), https://wcitestbucket.s3.us-east-2.amazonaws.com/amazon-s3-bucket/documents/en/wci-program-design-archive/WCI-ProgramDesign-20100727-EN.pdf.

140 Further sections without differing citations in this chapter are those of the WCI Design.

sions from eligible biomass,[141] and from certain activities such as general stationary fuel combustion or electronics manufacturing, Section 3.2.1. To allow for the upstream cap detailed below in section b., any fuel supplier within the participating jurisdiction that distributes liquid transportation fuel, petroleum coke, natural gas, propane, heating fuel, or any other fossil fuel sold or imported for consumption in the participating jurisdiction in quantities that when combusted would emit 25,000 metric tons CO_2 or more p.a., excluding emissions from combustion of eligible biomass, is covered beginning 2015, Section 3.2.3. Whether such a fuel supplier passes the threshold is based on the source's highest verified emissions during any year after January 1, 2009.

b. Cap

Section 2 contains interesting proposals for the point of regulation. The WCI Recommendations opt mostly for a downstream cap, *cf.* Section 2.1, under which certain industrial sources (with emissions over a defined threshold) will be regulated at the point of emission. In contrast, emissions from residential, commercial, and certain industrial fuel combustion (with emissions under a threshold) and transportation fuel combustion will be covered upstream, i.e., at the point where the combustion fuels enter commerce in the relevant jurisdictions. This picks up arguments displayed in Chapter C.VI.1.e, according to which upstream coverage is the most efficient regulatory approach as regulation at the point of production/import is both the most complete and least cumbersome administratively.

The emissions threshold is set out in Section 3.1: entities or facilities with emissions of 25,000 metric tons of carbon dioxide equivalents p.a. or more are covered. The program's aggregate cap equals the sum of the WCI partner jurisdictions allowance budgets, Section 6.1. Section 6.1.3 implements a declining cap. Section 6.6 puts restrictions on adjustments of the respective regional cap defined in the WCI Recommendations. This may not be adjusted, except as necessary to account for changes in the WCI membership, changes in scope or thresholds, or changes in data that was used to determine the cap and subsequently found to be incorrect

141 WCI Design, *supra* note 139, Definition 2.30: "Each Partner jurisdiction will define eligible biomass in its discretion, provided it must be carbon neutral. CO_2 emissions from combustion of eligible biomass are not included in the Partner jurisdiction's Cap-and-Trade Program, except for purposes of reporting."

or inaccurate. Within the regional cap, each jurisdiction has an individual allowance budget that is derived from its individual emissions goal. The caps are set in multiple stages. For 2012, each partner jurisdiction's allowance budget is based on the best estimate of expected emissions for covered sources, Section 7.2. In this estimate, population growth, economic growth, voluntary and mandatory emissions reductions, and other factors are considered. Each WCI partner has to make a 1 percent contribution of their 2012 allowance budget into a fund to allow for such adjustments in other jurisdictions. This is an example of burden-sharing in a "climate club."

In 2015, the respective allowance budget was adjusted by adding the best estimate of expected emissions from transportation fuels and residential, commercial, and industrial fuels, i.e., the sectors and industries that were added to the WCI coverage in 2015, Section 7.2.1. From 2015–2020, the trajectory for each WCI partner jurisdiction's annual allowance budget for covered sectors will remain constant from the year of initial coverage (2012 for some sources and 2015 for other sources) to 2020, Section 7.2.2. The same restrictions on adjustments displayed above apply to adjustments of the partner jurisdiction's allowance budget. WCI Partner jurisdictions are obliged to recognize allowances issued by other jurisdictions so that all WCI allowances are of equivalent use and fungible throughout the WCI region, regardless of which WCI Partner jurisdiction has issued the allowances, Section 7.5.

c. Allocation of allowances

Allowances (also called compliance instruments)[142] in Section 5 issued to participants equal one metric ton of carbon dioxide equivalents. A portion of the revenue created from the allocation of allowances (e.g., in the event of an auction of allowances) has to be dedicated to certain public purposes, such as energy efficiency and renewable energy incentives

142 WCI Design, *supra* note 139, definition 2.17. Compliance instruments are allowances, offset certificates, or approved program compliance units, i.e., a compliance instrument from an approved trading program that may be used for compliance purposes in the Partner jurisdiction's Cap-and-Trade program, subject to any limitations set out in this detailed program design, https://wcitestbucket.s3.us-east-2.amazonaws.com/amazon-s3-bucket/documents/en/wci-program-design-archive/WCI-ProgramDesign-20100727-EN.pdf (last visited January 11, 2020).

and achievement. Interestingly enough, the WCI does not allow the usage of revenue for the correction of (economically) distortionary taxes, such as labor taxes, an idea that has been proposed by economists. However, Section 8.3 allows jurisdictions to use the remaining amount of revenue, i.e., the amount that is not used for public purposes, as they see fit. Jurisdictions must either allocate or retire all allowances in their allowance budgets by the end of a compliance period. Consequently, banking on a state level does not exist. One exception exists: Section 8.10 provides for a reserve or minimum price, which shall be established for a portion of the auctioned allowances. This is intended in order to manage the risk of inadvertently setting the program cap higher than intended relative to emissions covered by the program, i.e., overallocation as defined above. This reserve will generally equal 5 percent of the allowances issued by any jurisdiction. If such allowances are not auctioned above the reserve or minimum price, a fraction of those unsold allowances will be retired. However, the not-retired fraction will be "banked" and can be auctioned at a later compliance period. Any jurisdiction that does not participate fully in the auction with the reserve or minimum price must retire the same proportion of its allowance budget as those retired by the jurisdictions that participated in the auction. Auctions feature a purchase limit, which according to the WCI, is to avoid possible market manipulations.[143]

The WCI incentivized sources to reduce emissions even before the first compliance period in 2012. For such reductions, sources were able to obtain "early reduction allowances." Such allowances are not treated differently from regularly allocated allowances, Section 8.11.4. There are no restrictions on the banking of allowances. However, borrowing may not take place, Sections 8.13 and 8.14.

d. Trading

According to the WCI, the WCI cap-and-trade program is designed to harness market forces to spur technological innovation and reduce greenhouse gas emissions at the lowest possible cost.

> *To accomplish this, the WCI Partner jurisdictions are recommending specific policies to ensure fair and equal access to the market, transparent operations and timely public disclosure of critical information to maintain public*

143 *Id.* at 19.

> *confidence, and a market free of manipulation so that prices reflect supply and demand conditions.*[144]

Trading of allowances, or "compliance instrument transfers" in the WCI Design's language, requires a "proposal" of the transfer by the respective authorized account representatives through an online allowance tracking system administered by the competent authorities. In this proposal, a variety of information must be provided, especially information such as the purchase price, Section 7.2.6.1.4. The competent authority is obliged to record the compliance instrument transfer within five business days after an compliance instrument transfer request by moving each compliance instrument from the transferor account to the transferee account as specified by the submission, provided that the transfer is correctly submitted and that the transferor account includes each compliance instrument identified by serial number in the transfer. After this recording, the agency is to notify the parties of the trade.

e. Offset credits and projects

The WCI Recommendations provide for extensive provisions on offsets and emissions reduction projects undertaken to address emissions not included in a cap-and-trade program and inclusion of allowances from other systems. Any of the jurisdictional WCI cap-and-trade systems shall accept offset credits; however, the use of offsets and allowances from other greenhouse gas emissions trading systems is limited to 49 percent of the total emission reductions until 2020. Jurisdictions may set a lower percentage limit at their own discretion, Section 9.2.

Early emission reduction allowances as discussed above can also be obtained by certain emission reduction projects outside of the WCI program's coverage, which gives the "early reduction allowance" mechanism the implications of an offset-program. To be eligible for emissions reduction allowances, the projects must produce a reduction or removal of one metric ton of CO_2 for each emissions reduction allowance without any increase in emissions intensity at the covered source. A reduction is not considered "real" or additional, to use a more commonly used term, if it comes from a decrease in production alone or from a shutdown or a closure of a source or a facility. Instead, the covered source must demonstrate

144 *Id.* at 20.

a reduction in emissions intensity and a reduction in absolute emissions during the eligibility period. A WCI partner jurisdiction may furthermore require sources or facilities to show that emissions reductions are beyond best practice standards. Best practice standards can be defined by the partner jurisdiction for certain types of covered sources. An applicant covered source may be required to prepare an evaluation demonstrating their actions are beyond best practices in their industry, Section 5.2.2.1. In addition to this restriction, the WCI sets out an eligibility period for offset projects. Under Section 5.2.1.3, the program authority can issue emissions reduction allowances for eligible offset projects that reduce emissions on or after January 1, 2008, and prior to January 1, 2012. Such projects must also achieve an emissions reduction that is a surplus to any requirements from existing legislation, regulation, executive orders, and other regulatory obligations.

In addition to emissions reduction allowances, sources can obtain offset certificates. In contrast to early reduction allowances, offset certificates are granted for projects outside of the WCI's coverage, i.e., in not-covered sectors, such as agriculture. An offset certificate represents a reduction or removal of one metric ton of CO_2 equivalents (CO_2e) that results from a clearly identified action or decision. Offset certificates are awarded only for the portion of greenhouse gas emissions reductions or removals that would not have happened under the WCI baseline scenario, Section 8.

f. Compliance

The authority in charge of administering the program under applicable state law is obliged to establish and administer an emissions and compliance instrument tracking system and to establish compliance accounts for each source. Surrenders, deductions, or transfers of allowances are recorded in the tracking system.

If, at the end of the compliance period, each of which lasts three years, sources do not hold sufficient allowances to cover their emissions, they are required to obtain and surrender three allowances for every metric ton of CO_2e not covered by an allowance, i.e., sources have to buy allowances in the required amount on the market. Individual state or provincial laws may establish additional fines, Section 12.3. Sources are required to name account representatives, i.e., a person in charge of the source's account,[145] and, *inter alia,* responsible for submitting, signing, and certifying the source's submission to the authorities, etc.

Compliance liability is extended to source owners and operators, Section 3.3. This is an interesting clause as it produces personal liability for shareholders or directors/employees of entities with limited liability. If the program meets such requirements, a link is established pursuant to procedural linking provisions in the WCI Design.

d. Linking

Due to its intended multi-state character, linking provisions are central to the WCI. Linking with other programs is permissible only if they satisfy certain requirements, such as the implementation of a binding and annually declining aggregate total GHG emissions cap, which provides for the transparent allocation of allowances and provisions to avoid the double counting of emissions or allowances in the electric sector, Sections 9.1.1 and 9.1.2. Linking is established by mutual recognition of compliance instruments as well as synchronized retiring of allowances to disqualify subsequent use in another system. Furthermore, the programs must ensure that the tracking system (or systems) permit the transfer of compliance instruments from one jurisdiction to another, that a jurisdiction will record when a compliance instrument is transferred out of its tracking system, and that the system can be counted on to sever the linking relationship should severance be necessary, Section 9.2. If the program does not satisfy the requirements discussed above, the WCI Design allows for the establishment of a unilateral link to such program:

> *Unilateral linking can be accomplished by allowing sources with a compliance obligation to surrender compliance instruments from an approved trading program. The same criteria can be applied in determining whether*

145 WCI Design, *supra* note 139, definition 2.7. Authorized account representative. For a covered source and each covered unit at the source, the natural person who is authorized by the owners and operators of the source and all covered units at the source, in accordance with section 4.3.1, to represent and legally bind each owner and operator in matters pertaining to the Partner jurisdiction's cap-and-trade program or, for a general account, the natural person who is authorized, under 7.2.2.2, to hold, transfer, retire or cancel or otherwise dispose of compliance instruments held in the general account.

> *to approve the external trading program. In the case of a unilateral link to an external program that generates offsets but is otherwise not a cap-and-trade program, the partner jurisdiction will apply only those criteria that are relevant to offset programs. In the case of unilateral links, the partner jurisdictions will develop a suitable mechanism to ensure the validity of external compliance units and to make sure those units can only be used once for compliance in any program,*

Sections 9.3.1 and 9.3.2 WCI Design.

2. Assembly Bill 32

Assembly Bill 32, also known as the "Clean Air Act 2006," was famously signed into California state law by Governor Arnold Schwarzenegger and ultimately created a state level cap-and-trade system for greenhouse gases with broad coverage across all industry sectors. In contrast to the Acid Rain Program,[146] which only concerned the energy sector, Assembly Bill 32 provided the basis for the first economy-wide mandatory emissions reduction regulation in the U.S., and mandated the California Air Resources Board (CARB)[147] to adopt rules and regulations in an open public process to achieve the maximum technologically feasible and cost-effective GHG emissions reductions. California Code, Health and Safety Code § 38560. CARB aims at reducing California's emissions to 1990 levels by 2020, which would amount to a 15 percent reduction from average 2005 emissions levels.[148]

Due to growing concern amongst environmental justice groups regarding cap-and-trade systems as well as political concerns in the process of enacting the bill,[149] Assembly Bill 32 (AB 32) does not mandate CARB to enact a specific cap-and-trade system according to legislative design but, *inter alia*, allows CARB to design and enact a cap-and-trade system to reduce greenhouse gas emissions. This was likely an attempt to shift political accountability to a "faceless" executive authority. Another result of such

146 *Cf.* Chapter E. I. Acid Rain Program.

147 Some secondary source authors cited in this thesis refer to CARB as ARB.

148 California Air Resources Board, *Climate Change Proposed Scoping Plan ES-1* (2008, revised January 2018), http://www.arb.ca.gov/cc/scopingplan/scopingplan.htm, (last visited January 11, 2020).

149 Alice Kaswan, *Climate Change and Environmental Justice: Lessons from the California Lawsuits*, 5 San Diego J. Climate & Energy Law 5 (2013-2014).

a political struggle is the many provisions in AB 32 requiring CARB to consider low-income neighborhoods and other social justice implications of any proposed regulation. Despite such efforts, AB 32 and CARB's regulations were subject to various lawsuits and a Title IV complaint to the EPA, litigating, *inter alia,* violations of federal civil rights regulations.[150] While neither the courts nor the EPA found any civil rights violations with AB 32, the lawsuits and the Title IV complaint highlight the importance of environmental justice considerations in any environmental legislation.[151] Not only is the balancing of social interests with environmental and economic considerations mandated by the principle of sustainable development, it is also key for the acceptance of environmental legislation by affected citizens.

Another key part of AB 32 was the implementation of a mandatory reporting system for emissions. Mandated by AB 32, CARB promulgated and enacted the "Mandatory Reporting Regulation" in December 2007. The regulation is applicable to a broad range of industrial facilities, fuel suppliers, and electricity importers. In particular, coverage also extends to sources that are not covered by the California cap-and-trade program discussed below.

As will be discussed later in this chapter, such mandatory reporting requirements have important implications for the cap-and-trade program as, for example, reliable emissions data collected in the years 2008–2011 could be used for the determination of the cap-and-trade program's cap.

---

150 For an overview of litigation against the program *cf.* Kaswan, *supra* note 149.

151 The proceedings, especially the Title VI complaint Coalition for a Safe Environment v. California Air Resources Board, August 6, 2012, Docket number(s): 09R-12-R9, also offer a good insight into environmental justice groups' concerns regarding cap-and-trade programs and their effect on disadvantaged and marginalized communities. For example, the Coalition for a Safe Environment argued that offset provisions ultimately increase pollution in communities of color. This reoccurring argument is based on the assumption that even in an effective cap-and-trade system, any achieved emissions reductions do not occur locally but only over the full geographic coverage. Consequently, communities within close distance to large emitters may not feel the effect of the achieved emissions reductions. And, as the Coalition for a Safe Environment puts forward, such communities are mostly communities of color. According to the Coalition, minority communities constitute nearly 35 percent or more of the affected population within six miles of a GHG-emitting facility. Of this, African-Americans make up 87 percent more of the population inside the six-mile zone than in the comparison population outside the zone, while Latinos and Asians represent nearly 34 percent and 30 percent more of the population inside the zone of impact than outside.

3. California's cap-and-trade program

CARB has promulgated its regulations in 17 CCR Article 5, Sections 95801 to 96022. The program is designed to contain three compliance periods.[152] The first compliance period began on January 1, 2013, and ended December 31, 2014. The second compliance period started on January 1, 2015, and ended on December 31, 2017. The third compliance period started on January 1, 2018, and will end on December 31, 2020. In July 2017, California extended the cap-and-trade program to 2030.

a. Coverage

The program covers the known greenhouse gases carbon dioxide (CO_2), methane (CH_4), nitrous oxide (N_2O), sulfur hexafluoride (SF_6), hydrofluorocarbons (HFCs), perfluorocarbons (PFCs), nitrogen trifluoride (NF_3), and other fluorinated greenhouse gases, 17 CCR § 95810.

Entities are covered under the program if their emissions exceed a certain threshold and if they fall within the processes or operations listed in 17 CCR § 95811, e.g., iron and steel production, electricity delivery, and suppliers of natural gas, distillate fuel oil, liquefied petroleum, and natural gas. Following the WCI Design and WCI Design Recommendations, the general applicability threshold for a facility is 25,000 metric tons or more of CO_2 p.a. Specific rules for the determination of the threshold for individual types of sources exist. For example, the threshold for electricity generating facilities is based on the annual emissions of the facility from which the electricity is generated. The threshold for an electricity importer is based on the annual emissions from each of the electricity importer's sources of delivered electricity. The threshold for a fuel supplier is 25,000 metric tons or more of CO_2 annually from the emissions of GHG that would result from full combustion or oxidation of the quantities of the fuels that are imported and/or delivered to California. Entities may choose to opt in to the program if they fall within the enumerated industry types or sectors but do not meet the emission threshold for mandatory coverage, 17 CCR § 95813(a). Such "opt-in entities" may be eligible to receive

152 17 CCR 95802(a)(72): "Compliance Period" means the three-year period for which the compliance obligation is calculated for covered entities except for the first compliance period. The compliance obligation for the first compliance period only considers emissions from data years of 2013 and 2014.

free allowances; however, opt-in participation may not affect the overall allowance budget. At the end of any given compliance period, an opt-in entity may choose to opt out of the program provided its annual emission levels for any data year remain below the inclusion thresholds discussed above. This prevents opt-in entities from selling allowances and subsequently leaving the program unpunished if they afterwards do not have sufficient allowances for their respective emissions. An entity choosing to opt out of the program must either fulfill its compliance obligations by retiring allowances amounting to actual emissions or surrender allowances equivalent to all the directly allocated allowances it has received from the budget years for the compliance period in question, 17 CCR § 95813(g). In addition to covered entities and opt-in entities, the program provides rules on "voluntarily associated entities," i.e., entities or individuals that intend to hold allowances and participate in the trading of allowances. This allows interested individuals to participate in allowance trading and, for example, to retire allowances for charity reasons. Such individuals must have their primary residence in the U.S., 17 CCR § 95814(a)(2). Individuals with a criminal conviction in the five previous years constituting a felony in the United States are ineligible for registration and participation in the program, 17 CCR § 95834(a)(4).

If an entity received allocation of a vintage allowance subsequent to the calendar year that the facility ceased operation, the facility shall return to the executive officer the number of allowances equal to the directly allocated allowances for the corresponding budget years in which it had no production, 17 CCR § 95812(f)(4).

b. Cap

The program's cap is defined by the amount of allowances available for allocation and specified in table 6-1 to 17 CCR § 95841:

For the first compliance period, 162.8 million allowances (equaling 162.8 million tons of greenhouse gases) were allocated for the year 2013 and 159.7 for the year 2014.

In the second compliance period, 395.5 million allowances were allocated for the year 2015, 382.4 for 2016 and 370.4 for 2017. Statistically, this is a 2 percent decline in allotted allowances from the previous compliance period, as the increased number of 395.5 million allowances, equaling 395.5 million metric tons of greenhouse gases, is rooted in a significant increase in coverage.

For the third compliance period, CARB allocated 358.3 million allowances for 2018, 346.3 for 2019, and 334.2 for 2020. This is a 15 percent reduction between 2015 and 2020.

Emissions data[153] shows total emissions of CO_2e in the first compliance period amounting to 144.5 million tons of CO_2e. This is 11.24 percent under the initial cap of 162.8 million tons from the first compliance period. Compared to previous actual emissions of the covered sources, this is a reduction of 3.8 percent.[154] Overall emissions, i.e., including emissions from sources that are not covered under the program as reported under California's Mandatory Reporting Requirements did not change significantly from 2012 to 2013.[155] As covered sources have reduced their emissions, this can only be explained by an increase of emissions emitted by sources not covered by the program. This is a strong indicator of emissions leakage.

c. Allocation of allowances

California's program provides two general types of allowances: "California Greenhouse Gas Emissions Allowances" and offset credits issued by CARB, both characterized as compliance instruments. In addition, the program recognizes certain allowances issued by other programs that have been approved by CARB. Generally, each compliance instrument represents a limited authorization to emit up to one metric ton in CO_2 of any GHG covered by the program.

Participating entities receive free allowances pursuant to complicated mathematical formulas set out in the program. Such formulas take into account, *inter alia*, the aggregate amount of allowances allocated to the same industry, various emissions benchmarks, and actual emissions and decline over time. To generalize, the formula can be understood as grandfathering with certain individual- and industry-specific adjustments to the baseline.

---

153 *Mandatory GHG Reporting—Reported Emissions; 2013 GHG Facility and Entity Emissions*, California Air Resources Board (CARB) (November 2014), https://ww2.arb.ca.gov/mrr-data; last accessed January 11, 2020.

154 Katherine Hsia-Kiung, Emily Reyna & Timothy O'Connor, *Carbon Market California, A Comprehensive Analysis of the Golden States Cap-And-Trade Program/Year Two 2014*, Environmental Defense Fund (2015), http://www.edf.org/sites/default/files/content/ca-cap-and-trade_1yr_22_web.pdf (last visited January 11, 2020).

155 *Id.*

The program allows for the distribution of a defined percentage of allowances into special accounts, some of which are designated for auctioning allowances. The percentage of such special allocation ranges from 0.5 percent to 10 percent for the auction holding account. The program furthermore provides for special distribution of allowances as a form of subsidy to address the danger of emissions leakage. For this, the program defines "assistance factors," according to which subsidized entities receive additional allowances pursuant to a formula. The assistance factor is generally based on the individual industries' perceived leakage risk. For this purpose, industries are classified as high, medium, or low leakage industries. Assistance factors are dependent on this classification: Under 17 CCR § 95870, about 90 percent of allowances will be freely allocated to all industry sectors, regardless of leakage classification in the first compliance period. Beginning in the second compliance period, medium leakage industries will receive a free allocation of 75 percent, whereas low leakage industries receive "only" 50 percent of their allowances for free. Beginning with the third compliance period, free allocation drops to 50 percent and 30 percent for medium and low leakage industries respectively. Free allocations to the high leakage industry stay consistent at 100 percent through all three compliance periods.

However, the aggregate amount of allowances made available for industry support under such a formula may not exceed the aggregate amount of allowances made available for distribution into special accounts, e.g., for auctioning or for sale from the reserve account.

Auctioned allowances can be classified into two types: current vintage and future vintage allowances, wherein "vintage" defines the year assigned to the allowance. Correspondingly, current vintage allowances can be used starting with the year they are purchased, whereas future vintage allowances can be used for three years—one compliance period—after they are auctioned. Future vintage allowances designated for auctioned are withdrawn from a special Auction Holding Account in which 10 percent of allowances for the budget years 2015 to 2020 are deposited, *cf.* 17 CCR § 95870(b).

Auctioning generally takes place on designated dates. For example, beginning in 2013 and through 2014, the auctions were conducted on the twelfth business day of the second month of each calendar quarter in California or a jurisdiction operating an approved greenhouse gas emissions trading system to which California has linked, 17 CCR § 95910(a)(2). In addition to this, numerous specific forms of auctioning exist, such as the auctioning of allowances from the previous year. Auctioning consists of a single round of bidding with sealed bids.

The auction administrator announces a price floor, defined as "Auction Reserve Price." No allowances will be sold for bids under this price floor. The price floor was 10 USD per allowance in 2012 and will be raised by 5 percent p.a. plus the rate of inflation as measured by the most recently available twelve months of the Consumer Price Index for All Urban Consumers, 17 CCR § 95911(c)(3). In addition to the Auction Reserve Price, an auction purchase limit exists. This is defined as the maximum number of allowances offered at each quarterly auction that can be purchased by the same participant or group of associated entities. This differs depending on the mentioned forms of auction and participating entities. While no participant may purchase more than 15 percent of the current vintage allowances sold at any auction, such a limit for non-covered entities, e.g., brokers or individuals, amounts to 4 percent, or 40 percent for certain electricity distribution units. The limit for purchases of future vintage allowances amounts to 25 percent, 17 CCR § 95911(c).

Aside from the auctioning process, allowances can also be purchased from the reserve. Participants in linked greenhouse emissions trading systems may not purchase allowances from the reserve. Prices for such allowances are defined in the program. The aggregate amount of allowances is divided into tiers. Allowances from the first tier are offered at 40 USD per allowance, allowances from the second tier are offered at 45 USD per allowance, and allowances from the third tier are offered for 50 USD per allowance, 17 CCR § 95913(f)(3). In calendar years subsequent to 2013, allowances from each tier are offered at prices equal to those from the previous calendar year increased by five percent plus the rate of inflation as measured by the most recently available twelve-month value of the Consumer Price Index for All Urban Consumers, 17 CCR § 95913(f)(4). Allowances will be made available at the highest price tier of the Allowance Price Containment Reserve if the number of accepted bids at the highest price tier exceeds the number of allowances in that tier.

Generally, the program aims to reduce free allocation of allowances to about 50 percent of the allowance budget over the subsequent compliance periods.

d. Trading and banking

aa. Regulatory environment

17 CCR § 95921 provides provisions on the trading of allowances. The program generally sets out mere procedural provisions—for example, on the information provided in the course of a transfer of allowances, such as the type of transaction agreement. The program defines three types of transactions: over-the-counter agreements for the sale of allowances for which delivery will take place no more than three days from the date the parties enter into the transaction agreement, over-the-counter agreements with a longer delivery period, and exchange agreements for the sale of compliance instruments through any contract arranged through an exchange or the Board of Trade. In addition to such procedural requirements, the program also contains some prohibitions on trading. For example, a participant in the program cannot acquire allowances and hold them in its holding account on behalf of another entity. The program also has rules designated to prohibit market manipulations, such as "cornering" of the allowance market.[156]

The program allows for limited banking. While allowances do not expire after a given time frame, 17 CCR § 95922(c), the program puts restrictions on how many allowances a participant may hold, *cf.* 17 CCR § 95920. Such a limit applies to all participants or associated entities and concerns all allowances that are not held in the participant's limited-use holding account or the exchange clearing holding account. Penalties may be applied whenever the holding limit is exceeded or transfer requests are filed with the accounts administrator that would violate the holding limit, 17 CCR § 95920(b)(6). Generally, the holding limit is calculated with a formula that takes into account the annual allowance budget and the base emissions.[157] A limited exemption from the holding limit exists for allowances in a participant's compliance account. Allowances up to a certain number that are held in the compliance account are not factored into the above formula. The limited exemption is calculated as the sum of the

156 "Cornering" the market is a colloquial term used to describe a method of price manipulation by acquiring large amounts of the traded commodity.

157 17 CCR § 95920(d): Holding Limit = 0.1*Base + 0.025*(Annual Allowance Budget – Base), in which "Base" equals 25 million metric tons of CO_2e and "Annual Allowance Budget" is the number of allowances issued for the current budget year.

annual emissions data reports received in 2012 and 2013 that have received a positive or qualified positive emissions data verification statement for emissions that generate a compliance obligation. Beginning in 2015, the limited exemption is to be increased on November 2 of each year by the amount of emissions that generate a compliance obligation and are included in the emissions data report received that have received a positive or qualified positive emissions data verification statement. However, the limited exemption will be reduced on November 2 of the calendar year following the end of a compliance period by the sum of the entity's compliance obligation over that compliance period.
Entities may submit a petition to adjust the limited exemption based on a factual basis. For corporate associations, the total number of allowances held by a group of entities with a direct corporate association must total a sum less than or equal to the holding limits.

The program also provides provisions on limited borrowing. This is allowed only to satisfy an excess emissions obligation, 17 CCR §§ 95856(b)(A) and (b)(B). This puts limits on borrowing, but allows participants with excess emissions obligations intra-period borrowing, something that might be purposefully utilized by sources, which can create an excess emissions obligation to achieve the basis for such borrowing.

bb. Data

Market data can be divided into two classes: auctioning (primary market) and transactions among participants (secondary market). The secondary market encompasses transactions regarding current and future vintage allowances, current and future greenhouse gas offsets, and future contracts, i.e., contracts to deliver valid allowances and offsets in the future.[158]

158 Katherine Hsia-Kiung, Emily Reyna & Timothy O'Connor, *Carbon Market California, A Comprehensive Analysis of the Golden States Cap-And-Trade Program/Year One 2012-2013*, ENVIRONMENTAL DEFENSE FUND 11, (2014), http://www.edf.org/sites/default/files/content/ca-cap-and-trade_1yr_22_web.pdf (last visited January 11, 2020).

(1) Auctioning data

ARB provides extensive data on its quarterly auctions.[159] In 2013, a total of 81,052,928 current vintage allowances, i.e., allowances to be used from 2013 onwards, were offered in ARB's auctions. Participants purchased 100 percent of these allowances. The floor price in the quarterly auctions amounted to 10 USD in November 2012 and 10.71 USD in February, May, August, and November 2013. The settlement price in November 2012 (the first auctioning date) was 10.09 USD, so only 0.9 USD above the floor price. In February 2013, the settlement price was 13.62 USD before it increased to 14.00 USD in May 2013. It subsequently dropped to 12.22 USD in August 2013 and 11.48 USD in November 2013.

Numbers for future vintage allowances, i.e., allowances to be used in the years 2015 and 2016, are slightly different. A 100 percent purchase rate of offered allowances was only achieved in the last two quarterly auctions. The first auction in November 2012 only saw a purchase rate of 14.1 percent. Over the entire year 2013, a total of 77,690,000 future vintage allowances were offered, and only 36,651,000 allowances, i.e., roughly 47 percent, were purchased.

Auctioning in 2014 shows similar results. In total, 82,029,805 current vintage allowances were auctioned with a 100 percent purchase rate. The floor price was 11.34 USD. Allowances were sold for 11.48 USD in February 2014, 11.50 USD in May and August 2014, and 12.10 USD in November 2014. November 2014 was the first linked auction with the cap-and-trade system established in Quebec. With an average price of 11.645 USD, this is a slight decrease from the average price of 12.282 USD in 2013. Regarding future vintage allowances, data shows an average purchase rate of 78.5 percent, which is a drastic increase from the previous year.

Total auctioning proceeds amount to 2.65 billion USD, and 902 million USD were used for projects in California's Greenhouse Gas Reduction Fund (GGRF). The GGRF invests in clean technology and provides at least 25 percent of its proceeds to disadvantaged communities disproportionally affected by pollution.[160]

---

159 Data compiled by the California Air Resources Board, *Auction Information*, https://ww3.arb.ca.gov/cc/capandtrade/auction/auction_notices_and_reports.htm (last visited January 11, 2020).

160 Kiung et al., *supra* note 154, at 3.

(2) Secondary market data[161]

During the first half of 2013, the average daily volume of trades made across all futures contracts [...] was about 372,900. In the second half of 2013, up to the end of November, this daily average increased to about 408,000 (an increase of about 9 percent). The average daily volume for the year overall was 389,100 allowances. The allowance price for current vintage prices in 2013 fluctuated. The daily settlement price reached a high of approximately 22.5 USD in August 2011 immediately following the opening of the market and dropped sharply to about 14 USD in December 2011. After an increase to approx. 18–19 USD in June 2012, the price dropped to about 11.50 USD between October and December 2012, the first auction. In 2013, the price stabilized under the 12 USD mark, which is close to the auctioning price of 11.48 USD achieved in the November 2013 auction.[162]

With the beginning of 2014, average weekly trading volume more than doubled from 2013 through the first half of 2014 and then increased again by almost 33 percent in the second half of 2014.[163] Price stability increased as well. Over the 2014 period, the average allowance price moved to the lowest level reached in 2013 and stayed around the 12 USD mark.

The future vintage allowance price shows similar trends. Prices for future vintage allowances sold in 2013 experienced a strong decline in their daily settlement price. With a high of 14.75 USD, prices dropped to approximately 12.60 USD following the third auction in 2013. In 2014, the market volume for future vintage allowances increased. The year 2013 saw contracts for about 25 million future vintage allowances, whereas in 2014, contracts for more than 77 million vintage allowances (again, for two and three years in the future) were recorded.[164] This is an increase of about 208 percent.

---

161 CARB does not publish secondary market data. The data discussed here has been compiled using market data provided by the Intercontinental Exchange (IE), a U.S. based network of exchanges and clearing houses for financial and commodity markets. The IE is considered to be the largest trading exchange of compliance instruments under the program. While the data may be considered as representative, uncertainties regarding the reliability of the data exist.

162 Kiung et al., *supra* note 154, at 11 ff.

163 Kiung et al., *supra* note 154, at 14.

164 *Id.*

e. Offset credits and projects

aa. Regulatory environment

California's cap-and-trade program recognizes "ARB offset credits" and "registry offset credits." Offset credits may only be used to up to 8 percent of an entity's entire compliance obligation, *cf.* 17 CCR § 95856(h)(1)(A). CARB offset credits are defined as a tradable compliance instrument issued by CARB that represents a GHG reduction or GHG removal enhancement of one metric ton of CO_2e. The GHG reduction or GHG removal enhancement must be real, additional, quantifiable, permanent, verifiable, and enforceable, 17 CCR § 95802(14). 17 CCR § 95802(a)(4) defines "additional" to mean, "in the context of offset credits, greenhouse gas emission reduction or removals that exceed any greenhouse gas reduction or removals otherwise required by law, regulation or legally binding mandate, and that exceed any greenhouse gas reductions or removals that would otherwise occur in a conservative business-as-usual scenario." This ties offset credits to a business-as-usual scenario that has often been criticized for being prone to uncertainty and error.[165]

In contrast to such offset credits, "registry offset credit" means a credit issued by an Offset Project Registry[166] for a greenhouse gas reduction or greenhouse gas removal enhancement of one metric ton of CO_2. The GHG reduction or GHG removal enhancement must be real, additional, quantifiable, permanent, verifiable, and enforceable and may only be issued for offset projects using Compliance Offset Protocols. CARB is entitled to determine whether a registry offset credit may be removed, retired, or cancelled from the Offset Project Registry system and issued as an CARB offset credit, 17 CCR § 95802(326).

To ensure the environmental integrity of the cap-and-trade program, both types of offset credits must fulfill extensive requirements to be approved by CARB under the program. Such requirements generally concern data collection and monitoring procedures for greenhouse gas emis-

165 Alan Ramo, *The California Offset Game: Who Wins and Who Loses*, 20 Hastings West-Northwest J. Envtl. L. & Pol'y 109, 125 (2014).

166 17 CCR § 95802(250): "'Offset Project Registry' means an entity that meets the requirements of section 95986 and is approved by ARB that lists offset projects, collects Offset Project Data Reports, facilitates verification of Offset Project Data Reports, and issues registry offset credits for offset projects being implemented using a Compliance Offset Protocol." As of 2015, the American Carbon Registry and the Climate Action Reserve are the only approved registries.

sion systems and mechanisms to address emission leakage. The program sets out protocols to be followed by the respective industry. Protocols currently exist for the forestry and dairy industry, ozone depleting substances projects, and urban forestry. Such projects have to take place in the U.S., Canada, or Mexico. A framework for international expansion is in place.

Notably, the program places the burden of invalidity of an offset credit on the buyer ("buyer liability"), *cf.* 17 CCR § 95985(h)(1), i.e., if an offset credit is invalidated by CARB, which can happen within defined, rather long timeframes provided for in the program, generally the buyer has to replace the offset credit.

bb. Data

The offset market started rather slowly with a total of 3,239,096 offset credits issued by November 2013 and almost no recorded trades, *inter alia*, due to the limited number of approved offset projects. Beginning in 2014, CARB approved various offset projects, increasing the number of offset projects to about 13.6 million allowances.[167] However, subsequent events raised uncertainty about the offset market stability. For example,

> [i]*n May 2014, CARB initiated an investigation of ODS offset credits generated by the company Clean Harbors on the grounds of potential non-compliance with environmental laws. During the investigation, over four million credits were taken out of the market to prevent them from being traded. After a thorough review, CARB invalidated about 2% of the offsets that were called into question, representing less than 1% of the total offsets market at the time (see "ODS Offset invalidation," page 25). The investigation and subsequent invalidation process took about five months from start to finish, during which time activity on the offset market decreased.*[168]

f. Compliance

All covered participants are subject to the program's mandatory reporting requirements (MRR) set out in 17 CCR § 95850. However, the program features a phase-in of compliance obligations for certain industries. For

167 Kiung et al., *supra* note 154, at 15 ff.
168 *Id.* at 16.

example, the compliance obligation for suppliers of gas and other specific fuels began only in the program's second compliance period, i.e., on January 1, 2015, *cf.* 17 CCR § 95850.

Participating entities must name a single primary account representative and at least one, but not more than four, alternate account representatives.

CARB administers a complicated tracking system. For each participating entity in the program, CARB creates multiple accounts in the system. Each entity receives a holding account. "Holding Account" or "General Holding Account" means an account created for each covered entity, opt-in covered entity, or voluntarily associated entity to hold compliance instruments, 17 CCR § 95802(182). For the majority of covered entities that receive their allowances by way of direct allocation, CARB creates a limited use holding account. Such an account functions as a holding account, but an entity may not transfer allowances from other accounts into this account and may not transfer allowances from the account into other accounts than the auction holding account.[169] Each entity further receives a compliance account. In this account, allowances are transferred to fulfill an entity's compliance requirements. Allowances in the compliance account may not be removed from the compliance account. Voluntarily associated entities that provide "clearing" services, i.e., brokers, receive an exchange clearing holding account, which allows such a participant to transfer allowances. Some entities also receive an annual allocation holding account, which allows entities to transfer allowances into the compliance account. In addition to such accounts, CARB will create multiple accounts that remain under its control—for example the auction holding account into which allowances are transferred to be sold at auction or the retirement account into which CARB transfers allowances from compliance accounts or from holding accounts under the control of CARB for the purpose of permanently retiring them. Alternatively, entities can voluntarily retire compliance instruments by transferring the allowances to the retirement account, 17 CCR § 95831(b)(3).

Under certain conditions, entities are required to disclose corporate associations, 17 CCR § 95833. Corporate associations exist, for example, if entities hold shares or call options for shares in other entities. If California

169 "Auction" is defined as the process of selling California Greenhouse Gas Allowances, along with allowances from External Greenhouse Gas Emissions Trading Systems with which California has linked its Cap-and-Trade Program by offering them up for bid, taking bids, and then distributing the allowances to winning bidders, 17 CCR 95802(a)(22).

links to one or more GHG emissions trading programs, entities must disclose any direct and indirect corporate associations with entities registered with those linked programs as well. In 2013, accounts for entities in corporate associations were consolidated, unless entities opted out of such consolidation.

Emissions from certain source categories and from certain fuel types count towards the individually applicable reporting threshold under 17 CCR § 951,[170] but do not count towards a participant's compliance obligation. This concerns, *inter alia*, CO_2 emissions from the combustion of certain biomass-derived fuels, such as wood and waste pallets, or biodiesel. Consequently, affected entities are required to calculate and report emissions from such sources but do not need to surrender allowances for such emissions. Arguably, this combines market-based regulation with traditional C&C regulation, as entities do not need to hold allowances for such emissions that are covered under non-market-based regulation.

The program differentiates between annual and triennial compliance obligations. Participants must annually provide allowances for 30 percent of their actual emissions in the previous year and triennially surrender one allowance for each metric ton of greenhouse gas emissions. The program sets out an order in which allowances will be retired by the CARB from the participants compliance accounts: Offset credits will be retired first; however, they may only be used to up to 8 percent of the entire compliance obligation, *cf.* 17 CCR § 95856(h)(1)(A). Allowances purchased from the reserve are retired next followed by any non-vintage allowances, i.e., any allowances that are not assigned to a different compliance year. Then, allowances issued by CARB and other recognized programs are retired, with earlier vintage allowances retired first, 17 CCR § 95856(h).[171]

The participant's compliance obligation for any excess emissions, i.e., actual emissions that are not covered by allowances,[172] is calculated as four times the participant's excess emissions, 17 CCR § 95857(b)(2). Up to 25 percent of such excess emissions may be covered by offset credits, whereas at least 75 percent may only be fulfilled with regular allowances.

---

170 17 CCR § 9510–95158 contain the Regulation for the Mandatory Reporting of Greenhouse Gas Emissions, which establishes a mandatory greenhouse gas reporting and verification system for the state of California.

171 *See* 17 CCR § 95856(h)(D) for current calendar year's vintage allowances and True-up allowances.

172 17 CCR § 95857(b)(1).

The program provides for a special compliance obligation in the event of emissions underreporting by participants.

On the first compliance date of November 3, 2014, CARB recorded a 100 percent compliance rate.[173] However, CARB also issued close to 1 million USD in fines for misreporting emissions to Chevron U.S.A, Inc., Chevron North America Exploration and Production Company, and Southwest Gas Corporation.[174]

d. Linking

Generally, an allowance or other compliance instrument issued by an external greenhouse gas emissions trading system can be used to meet the compliance requirements under the program if the external greenhouse gas emissions trading system and the compliance instrument have been approved pursuant to the approval rules and procedures in the program. 17 CCR § 95941 defines requirements for such approval by CARB. An allowance issued by an approved external greenhouse gas emissions trading system is not subject to the quantitative usage limit, 17 CCR § 95942(b). Offset credits do, however, fall within such a limit, 17 CCR § 95942(c).

As of 2015, the program accepted linkage with the cap-and-trade program established by the Government of Quebec, which was enacted January 1, 2014, *cf.* 17 CCR § 95943.

4. Analysis

a. Environmental analysis

California regulators consider the program a success in reducing emissions to the desired level.[175] However, the reviewed environmental data indicates a less positive outcome, especially in the early years of the program. During the year 2013, the first compliance year, participants reduced their emissions output by 3.8 percent compared to previous years, which amounts to a reduction of 5.53 million metric tons of CO_2 equivalents. This 3.8 percent reduction brings emissions to a level of 11.24 percent

173 Kiung et al., *supra* note 154, at 17.
174 Kiung et al., *supra* note 154, at 25.
175 Kiung et al., *supra* note 154, at 12.

under the cap for the first year. This very clearly indicates that the baseline in the first year was much too generous, i.e., allowances were overallocated and the program failed at achieving its maximum performance.

An even bigger problem surfaces when such a reduction is compared to the data provided by the MMR for the entire industry in the state of California, i.e., participants in the program and Californian sources that are not participants, for example because they are too small to be covered by the program. The data[176] reveals that in the entire area covered by the MMR, no overall emissions reduction was measured. Seeing that covered participants reduced their emissions by 3.8 percent, we can infer that smaller sources outside of the program's coverage have increased their emissions output by the same amount. We have defined this issue as "emissions leakage" in Chapter D.VI.9.

This means that the program, despite extensive provisions aimed at avoiding emissions leakage by providing industry assistance, was not successful at avoiding leakage as it arguably failed at producing measurable emission reductions when emissions outside the program's coverage are taken into account.

b. Economic analysis

California's economy remained largely unaffected by the program's enactment. In fact, California's gross domestic product (GDP) increased by over 2 percent in 2013. California added 491,000 jobs during the first year-and-a-half of the state's cap-and-trade program, a growth of almost 3.3 percent which surpasses the overall national growth rate of 2.5 percent during the same year.[177]

Economic growth in California coupled with no overall increase in emissions has been termed as "breaking the link between emissions and economic growth."[178] From a historical perspective, economic growth is typically accompanied by a proportionate growth in emissions. In today's largely fossil fuel-based economy, such a connection is not surprising: with an increase in economic activity, such as production or transport, fossil fuel emissions increase as well. California has been credited with "demonstrating a different, more efficient path that breaks the link between eco-

---

176 CARB, *supra* note 153.
177 Kiung et al., *supra* note 154, at 10.
178 Kiung et al., *supra* note 154, at 7.

nomic and emissions growth by creating a more efficient, lower-carbon economy that produces more while burning fewer fossil fuels, a trend that will be essential to scale up globally."[179] Though it is true that California's GDP increased since the depression in 2009, emissions have decreased steadily since the beginning of 2008,[180] which cannot be attributed to the cap-and-trade program as it was implemented in 2013. Rather, we can find the cause of such a reduction in CARB's general command-and-control legislation following AB 32, such as the adoption of the scoping plan in December 2008. And while no reliable data exists on industry changes in California, we can still make the educated guess that such development may have also been supported by a general change of industry in the State of California, as non-industrial, non-carbon based technology companies—for example in California's Silicon Valley—now make up a solid portion of the state's GDP.

c. Market analysis

Initial market data indicates few trades between participants. Indeed, the "secondary market" under the program remains rather small, encompassing only 2.3 percent of allowances sold by auction in 2013. While the market size has increased in the subsequent year, such small secondary market volume raises doubts about the efficiency of the market. The small volume especially raises concerns about market liquidity, which may, however, only materialize at later stages as the data suggests an overallocation at the program's early stages.

Such overallocation is shown in the environmental data discussed above in Section 4.a. as well as in the steep price drop after the initial auction of allowances and the low demand for future vintage allowances, which suggests that participants are not concerned about the impending tightening of the cap. Such price drops are typical for the reviewed programs and can ultimately be traced to an overallocation which results in an initial overestimate of prices.

While such results are not encouraging, the regulatory environment for the market is at least theoretically efficient when measured against the theoretical optimum discussed in Chapter D. For example, the auction purchase limit prohibits participants from utilizing a dominant market

179 *Cf.* note 178

180 Kiung et al., *supra* note 154, at 6, referring to data provided by the CARB.

position to inhibit the independent allocation. Regardless, the market data discussed above indicates that this was not achieved. For example, the low purchase rate of future vintage allowances in 2013 auctions shows participants' uncertainty regarding future developments and allowance prices. However, as will be discussed later, the positive influences of linkage with Quebec is visible.

d. Offsets and environmental justice

CARB intended to set up an efficient and secure way of creating and trading offset credits with the implementation of the offset market. The offset structure was intended to avoid the complicated and vulnerable process set out in the Kyoto Protocol and the issues arising from "empty" certificates that do not actually represent emission reductions (colloquially known as "hot air"). To address this issue, the program contains substantial and procedural provisions as displayed above. According to some studies, the implementation of offset credits will result in a reduction of 15 tons per day of combustion-generated soot and 61 tons of oxides of nitrogens, which are credited with producing smog. The estimated health benefits for the California population by 2020 are estimated to be an avoidance of 780 premature deaths, 12,000 incidents of asthma and lower respiratory symptoms, and 77,000 work loss days.[181] To address the uncertainty and manipulation issues with offset certificates discussed above, CARB has opted for an expansive administrative procedure intended to "establish the eligibility and additionality of projects using standard criteria, and quantify greenhouse gas reductions and greenhouse gas removal enhancements using standardized baseline assumptions, emission factors, and monitoring methods," 17 CCR § 95972 (a)(9). Even though CARB has intended for offset credits to only be used to fulfill 8 percent of a participant's compliance, it has been pointed out that mathematically, offset credits could cover all of the expected reductions from cap-and-trade by 2020:

> *Meanwhile, ARB's final regulations set the 2020 allowance budget at offsets that are allowed in 2020 are therefore about 27 MMTCO2E.o'. Under the 4% international offset cap, half of that amount may be allocated to international offsets, that is, about 13.5 MMTCOE, by 2020. Thirteen and one-half MMTCOE of international offsets is 75% of the 18 MMTCO2E of*

181 Ramo, *supra* note 165, at 124.

> *reductions now anticipated under cap-and-trade to come from power plants, refineries and the other capped sources. Domestic offsets from farms, forests, and City tree planting and other approved sources of domestic offsets could completely eliminate any reductions from the capped sources expected to come from cap-and-trade. In effect, offsets could be more than the entire cap-and-trade ballgame, and if a significant number are not real, they would jeopardize the program's effectiveness.*[182]

Consequently, such market design has been subject to litigation in Citizens Climate Lobby v. ARB.[183] This litigation mostly concerned whether CARB's process of approving offset projects with a "standard additionally mechanism" violated AB 32. As displayed above, approval of an offset project by CARB requires that any emission reductions are "additional" to the emission reductions achieved by the program. As discussed, this is essential to the environmental integrity of the program, or, as the District Court noted, non-additional offsets will "undercut [...] the cap-and-trade program because they substitute [...] illusory reductions, those that would have occurred anyway, for real reductions that the capped sources should have undertaken." The rules as promulgated by CARB do not require CARB to evaluate each proposed offset. Rather, CARB evaluates whether the proposed offset project exceeds the business-as-usual performance, which means that a proposed offset will be accepted if the proposed project exceeds standard emissions reduction behavior in the relevant industry. An example produced in the litigation referred to dairy companies: as such companies rarely employ manure digesters, a technology used for producing biogas from waste, any installation of such would automatically lead to an acceptance of the allowance credit. The petitioners, an environmental and civil justice interest group, argued that such a procedure did not adequately ensure the environmental integrity of the program and thus violates CARB's mandate in AB 32.[184] The court rejected the argument and noted that project-based offset mechanisms,

182 Ramo, *supra* note 165, at 128.

183 Citizens Climate Lobby v. California Air Resources Board, 43 ELR 20024, No. CGC-12-5195544 , (Cal. Super. Ct., Jan. 25, 2013).

184 Cal. Health & Safety Code § 38565: "The state board shall ensure that the greenhouse gas emission reduction rules, regulations, programs, mechanisms, and incentives ... direct public and private investment toward the most disadvantaged communities in California and provide an opportunity for ... community institutions to participate in and benefit from statewide efforts to reduce greenhouse gas emissions."

such as the Clean Development Mechanism employed in the Kyoto Protocol, lead to even more inaccuracies, difficulties, and costs. Thus, the chosen-standards approach promulgated by CARB would lead to more accurate and efficient results.

This litigation also provides some insight into how environmental justice considerations can affect perceptions of a regulatory framework and its efficiency. The takeaway is that regulatory efficiency does not always lead to socially just results. While AB 32 requires funds acquired from emissions trading to be used for community benefit, the jury is still out on the success of such an approach.

e. Offsets and market design

Apart from the discussions surrounding the environmental and civil justice considerations of the offset market design, California's cap-and-trade design illustrates the importance of market design for the successful implementation of an offset market. As a result of the market design promulgated by CARB, the offset credit market took a while to develop. The low demand for offset credits as displayed above stands out. This might have been a result of the generally low allowance prices that did not incentivize offset projects but also could be the program's choice for buyer liability. As such potential liability increases costs and risks faced by the buyer, participants might have been reluctant to accept the market with corresponding effects on demand for offset credits. This was likely amplified by the rather long invalidation time frame of, *inter alia*, eight years, *cf.* 17 CCR § 95985(b), which increases the uncertainty faced by buyers regarding the validity of their allowance purchases.

5. Conclusion

Per the above analysis, the program was not effective in achieving emissions reductions across California. While the program achieved emissions reduction from covered sources, overall emissions did not decrease due to emissions leakage. This is surprising, as compared to all other programs reviewed so far, California's program provides the most extensive rules to address emissions leakage. We can therefore conclude that the industry assistance model promulgated in the program was not entirely successful. A reason might be uncertainty regarding future allowance prices coupled with unlimited banking, which provided an incentive to shift production and bank allowances to hedge against future price increases. A solution could be a coupling of the industry assistance allowance allocation with limited banking provisions that incentivize sources to utilize allowances received for free as a means of industry assistance rather than banking such allowances and shifting production to smaller sources outside of the cap-and-trade program's coverage.

Another reason for the sub-maximal reduction of emissions was the overallocation of allowances. This is interesting as in contrast to other administrators, CARB had actual reliable emissions data for the covered sources due to the prior implementation of California's mandatory reporting requirements in 2008, whereas other programs (such as the Illinois ERMS) had inaccurate emissions data, which contributed to overallocation. Overallocation in California's program can thus not be traced to inaccurate emissions data. Thus, the overallocation was most likely a result of a less-than-stringent cap, despite the program's phase-in of coverage. As in other programs, overallocation continues to be a problem for environmental effectiveness, often as a result of lax caps most likely due to political compromises. While this seems to be a fundamental argument against the effectiveness of cap-and-trade programs, upon first sight it ultimately refutes a common point of criticism from cap-and-trade skeptics arguing that cap-and-trade systems are suffering from a lack of accurate monitoring, reporting, and verification of emissions as well as usage of historical data supplied by emitters themselves.[185] California's cap-and-trade program shows that the political process is more likely to interfere with an accurate cap than inaccurate emissions data as it transforms the process of setting the cap from a rational, numbers-based approach into one of political bargaining.

However, this is not an argument in favor of emissions trading, but points to an inherent systematic issue present in emissions trading that will be discussed later.

In terms of market design, the program features many design elements identified as economically preferable in order to achieve the independent and efficient allocation of allowances. While CARB grants a significant amount of free allowances as a form of industry assistance, the phase-in of mandatory auctioning is efficient as it supports allocation of allowances to participants that value them most. Also noteworthy are the rules pro-

185 Brittany A. Harris, *Repeating the Failures of Carbon Trading*, 23 Pacific Rim L. & Pol'y J. 766 (2014).

hibiting market participants from utilizing a market dominating position. As discussed earlier, this can otherwise influence the market and inhibit independent allocation.

The offset market performed not ideally. It can be inferred that offset seller liability might be preferable, at least during a phase-in period to build trust in the allowance market. Another detrimental factor is the long timeframe in which an invalidation of offset allowances could occur. A shorter time frame for invalidation seems beneficial for market performance as it reduces uncertainty. Noteworthy as well are the provisions addressing the problem of offset projects' potential impact on low-income communities, which can result from emissions shifting to industrial areas. As a result of litigation by interest groups such as the Citizens Climate Lobby, utilization of such provisions in future programs is likely to increase.

6. The WCI as an example for bottom-up regulation

For the purpose of the review conducted in this thesis, the WCI is a good example for a bottom-up emissions trading system as it involves federal states coming together to regulate emissions from a bottom-up perspective. Notably, coverage of the program extends to the same greenhouse gases also covered by the Kyoto Protocol, namely carbon dioxide, methane, nitrous oxide, hydrofluorocarbons, perfluorocarbons, and sulfur hexafluoride. This exemplifies that parties were aware of the Kyoto Protocol regulation and may have sought to create an alternative approach.

The WCI as a conference produced certain recommendations, such as the Design Recommendations for the WCI Regional Cap-and-Trade Program in 2008,[186] and a Design for the WCI Regional Program.[187] However, the WCI did not establish a binding program nor a binding emissions cap. The emissions reduction goal of 15 percent set out in the WCI design documents is based on the aggregate emission reduction goals of each party to the initiative. Ultimately, parties are free to set their cap at their own discretion. Correspondingly, the emissions cap set out in the WCI documents resembles the reduction pledges as undertaken by the Kyoto parties in the Copenhagen Amendment.

186 WCI, *supra* note 139.
187 WCI, *supra* note 139.

With that, the WCI has multiple features of bottom-up regulation as it depends entirely on state action, and the WCI as a private, legal, non-profit corporation has no authority itself. While the WCI design documents provide for harmonization potential, states are not obliged to follow the recommendations.

As of now, California and Quebec have enacted cap-and-trade programs following the WCI design. Following the ideas of coalition forming and linking discussed above, California and Quebec's program have been linked. As of 2015, California's program accepts linkage with the cap-and-trade programs established by the Government of Quebec, which was enacted January 1, 2014, *cf.* 17 CCR § 95943. November 2014 was the first linked auction with the cap-and-trade system established in Quebec.

It is possible that some of the observer states will join the initiative at some point, allowing the WCI system to grow further. This exemplifies the idea of growing local cap-and-trade systems as a policy alternative to the top-down approach taken in the Kyoto Protocol. Necessary for this is that the WCI creates enough of a "pull factor" to incentivize other states to join. Whether this seems plausible will be discussed below.

7. Lessons from the WCI for a post-Kyoto world

While it suffers from issues that many cap-and-trade programs have in common, such as lax emissions caps and an overallocation of allowances, the WCI and the respective trading systems in California and Quebec exemplify multiple points that are relevant for the idea of bottom-up linkage as an alternative policy approach.

(1) State actors are willing to address the climate change issue without federal "top-down" regulation. Arguably, states may even be more motivated to enact regulation as they have more freedom to regulate according to the specific needs and prerequisites found in their states, maybe even preempting federal legislation. Of course, this also raises questions of "greenwashing" by evading top-down regulation.

(2) We see that coalition forming in the form of linking ensued. Even though such linking took place at a slow pace, this is a valuable insight as it exemplifies the theoretical idea of a growing trans-jurisdictional emissions trading system developing from bottom-up regulation.

(3) In terms of market data, the linking of California's system with Quebec's system resulted in an increase in allowance prices, from 11.50 USD to 12.10 USD. Not only the auctioning prices, but the market volume for

future vintage allowances increased in 2014. The year 2013 saw contracts for about 25 million future vintage allowances, whereas contracts for more than 77 million vintage allowances (again, two and three years in the future) were recorded in 2014.[188] This is an increase in trade of about 208 percent. This price increase exemplifies multiple facts: Linking caused an increase in demand but, more importantly, in sources' certainty regarding future prices. As prices always reflect participants' expectations of the future, a price increase is a market signal regarding participants' expectations of future market performances and prices—i.e., participants in California and Quebec believed that the linked programs would remain in place and that the carbon price would rise. This shows another positive effect of linkage: it solidifies certainty in the regulatory process.

(4) The reviewed data suggests that the regulation had no adverse impact on the California economy. This likely influenced Quebec's decision to link systems. However, considering the lack of environmental efficiency the program has shown, does it matter that linking ensured? As argued above in relation to international cooperation, it does. Even inefficient regimes can have an impact if they provide incentives for other regions to join. The impact of institutionalizing should not be underestimated. Especially with a flexible mechanism such as emissions trading, reasons for environmental inefficiency can, at least theoretically, be corrected as they become known.

188 Kiung et al., *supra* note 154, at 14.

F. Conclusion: Lessons from U.S. emissions trading

The analysis in Chapter E reveals an underwhelming performance of emissions trading systems. It appears to be a sound academic theoretical concept, and there are some examples of successful trading, but from a practical perspective based on empirical review, the many inherent design issues and practical problems with existing systems display great issues with the application of this academic concept.

In summarizing the experiences from U.S. emissions trading, the following discussion separates two distinct lessons we can learn from the U.S. policy experiences discussed above. Lesson number one concerns the environmental effectiveness of emissions trading as a regulative tool, while lesson number two concerns the potential of such systems for growth and linkage from the "bottom-up."

I. Conclusion: Does emissions trading work?

Aside from the ARP,[1] whose relevance for the issue of climate change is limited due to the comparatively simple nature of acid rain as well as its more regional and visible impact, none of the emissions trading systems reviewed above can be considered successful at both reducing emissions to the intended level and establishing a functioning market.

The ERMS,[2] a trading system with limited relevance to climate change, did achieve the emissions reductions intended by regulators, but failed to establish a functioning market for its emission permits. Among other issues with the program, the ERMS was overallocated with resulting low certificate prices. As a consequence of such low certificate prices, no significant trading or incentive to invest in abatement technologies resulted from the program, and achieved emission reductions were lower than what could have been achieved at maximum performance. All other trading programs reviewed show a similarly disappointing outcome.

1 *Cf.* p. 150 in this text.
2 *Cf.* p. 165 in this text.

Regarding the RGGI,[3] the available information is not sufficient to prove that emissions reductions occurred as a direct result of the RGGI rather than of outside effects. In view of the significant overallocation present in the RGGI, the predominant influence of such outside effects is likely, as emission reductions are unlikely to occur if allowance prices are low. This conclusion again shows the value of the economic analysis of such a system. Consequently, the RGGI also cannot be considered a successful example of emissions trading. This result is mirrored by the WCI.[4] While sources covered by the program did reduce their emissions slightly, overall emissions were not reduced as a result of emissions leakage, despite express provisions intending to avoid this. In addition to significant emissions leakage, the WCI was also overallocated, again preventing maximal environmental efficiency and the establishment of a functioning market.

Overallocation is both the common theme of almost all reviewed programs and their greatest design flaw. As overallocation generally results in low emission prices, an overallocated system can neither achieve a maximum of reductions nor establish a functioning market. Sources can easily purchase readily available allowances at low prices and thus have no incentive to reduce emissions or invest in abatement technology. So while some emission reductions may be achieved—for example, as a result of initial uncertainty about future prices—emissions trading in an overallocated system will not result in optimal environmental performance. A system relying on market performance to achieve effective emission reductions cannot achieve effective reductions without market performance. This mirrors generally accepted economic dogma: market and planned economies are incompatible.[5] Policymakers cannot establish a functioning market from scratch by allocating allowances[6] if the allocation generally does not follow market logic: As the reviewed emissions trading systems empirically prove, allowance allocation remains arbitrary regardless of the allocation method.[7] The ARP used grandfathering to allocate allowances but additionally allocated allowances via auctioning or "substitute provisions," thus further diluting the relationship between baseline and allocated allowances. The ERMS also relied on grandfathering but used the aver-

3 *Cf.* p. 182in this text.
4 *Cf.* p. 205 in this text.
5 Bartling/Luzius, Grundzüge der Volkswirtschaftslehre, 2014, Kapitel B III 1.
6 See also Junker, *supra* note 18 in Chapter A.
7 See p. 118 for academic discussion of the systematic issues present in current allocation models.

age of two seasonal allotment periods with the highest emissions during 1991, 1995, and 1996. The RGGI Model Rules do not provide for rules on allocation but the large majority of involved states have chosen to auction. Despite these auctions, which have been identified in theory as a superior allocation method above, the program was overallocated as a result of the definition of the amount of allowances allocated to the participating states (i.e., the state allowances budget). The WCI opted for allocation based on a complicated formula taking into account, *inter alia*, an aggregate amount of allowances allocated to the same industry, various emission benchmarks, and actual emissions.[8] Each of these programs, regardless of the allocation method of choice, allowed policymakers to influence the baseline based on non-quantitative reasons, i.e., regulative choices independent of a rigorous math-based allocation. This is noteworthy, as proponents of emissions trading argue against C&C regulation based on the argument that pollution targets promulgated in C&C rulemaking are arbitrary and oriented by what is deemed to be politically achievable.[9] As the programs reviewed above show, this can also be said about emissions trading. Given the empirical evidence on overallocation in emissions trading, the lack of aggressive declining caps or other adjustment mechanisms[10] is surprising. Of the reviewed systems, only the RGGI and the WCI feature a declining cap.[11] These are newer systems, which supports the theory that regulators have learned from the overallocation issues present in the early systems. However, the adjustment provisions in the RGGI and the WCI repeat the same design flaw of the initial allocation by using an arbitrary, politically defined reduction that is not tied to market performance. The RGGI cap declines by 2.5 percent per year, starting with the year 2015. In the years 2015 to 2018, the cap declines by 2.5 percent each year to reach a reduction of 10 percent below 2009 levels in 2018. Additionally, the RGGI states lowered caps by a total of 140 in 2014 to

---

8 *Cf.* p. 216 in this text.

9 *See* Dieter Helm, *Economic Instruments and Environmental Policy*, 36 Econ. & Soc. Rev. 210 (Winter 2005) and p. 92 in this text.

10 *Cf.* for more information on adjustment mechanisms Lesley K. McAllister, *The Overallocation Problem in Cap-and-Trade: Moving Toward Stringency*, 43 Colum. J. Envtl. L. (2009).

11 The EPA was not granted authority to implement a declining cap into the CARP; this requires congressional action. Congressional efforts to lower the cap were unsuccessful, *cf.* McAllister, *supra* note 10, at 441.

account for banked allowances.[12] Consequently, the tightening follows the initial political plan using an arbitrarily determined absolute number and not market dynamics. The California implementation of the WCI uses a similar approach by featuring a cap that declines annually by 3 percent from 2015 through 2020. Again, the decline follows an initial political plan, not market dynamics. This further consolidates the disconnect of arbitrary allocation in the first step and the expected free market forces in the second step.

Another interesting topic is the monitoring of emissions data: the review of enacted U.S. emissions trading systems shows that compliance mechanisms in such emissions trading systems rely on self-reporting by the covered sources both for the determination of the baseline as well as for ongoing monitoring and compliance obligations. While, for example, the RGGI Model Rules state that monitoring equipment must be certified by the administrative agency, such reliance on cooperation from the covered sources is problematic. When there is uncertainty as to which input data is correct, companies have an incentive to use data that results in a favorable end—for example, by inflating their initial baseline as the review of the ERMS suggests. The outcome of the California cap-and-trade system suggests a similar issue.

To a certain degree, these conclusions mirror the European Emissions trading System's (EUTS) results during the timespan reviewed in this thesis. The EUTS was established in 2005 by Directive 2003/87/EC of the European Parliament and of the Council of October 13, 2003, and amended from time to time. From its outset, the EUTS was designed to run in three phases, with Phase 1 from 2005 until 2007 as a "learning and experimenting" phase, Phase 2 from 2008 to 2012, and Phase 3 from 2013 to 2020. In February 2017, the European Parliament approved (with some amendments and changes) the Commission's suggestion to introduce a Phase 4 from 2021 to 2030.[13] While much of it is disputed between

12 The RGGI states have subsequently announced a 30 percent decline in emissions by 2023, *cf.* press release, RGGI Inc. (August 23, 2017), https://www.rggi.org/docs/ProgramReview/2017/08-23-17/Announcement_Proposed_Program_Changes.pdf.

13 Council Directive 2003/87/EG, (October 12, 2003) Official Journal of the European Union (L275/32).

scholars, results from the EUTS are often defined as "disappointing,"[14] and while the system is established and has had time to mature, many questions remain unanswered.[15] For example, the environmental integrity of the EUTS is questionable at best. Initially, the EUTS aimed at achieving emissions reductions of 40 percent below 1990 levels by the year 2013. While the EUTS corresponds with reduced emissions, relevant legislation and the recession years in 2008 render a detailed analysis of direct EUTS results impossible. Valid information, however, shows that during Phase 1, no emission reductions were achieved as a result of emissions trading.[16] In fact, emissions of covered sources increased by 0.68 percent in 2007.[17] In Phase 2, some reductions were achieved, but given the drastic price decrease from roughly 25 to 30 Euro in 2008 to under 3 Euro in 2013, the oversupply of certificates is obvious. Market data suggests a surplus of 955 million certificates. In order to achieve the Paris Agreement target, the price per ton of carbon would have to be between 16 and 73 USD.[18] Scholars suggest that the recorded emissions reductions were mostly a result of the decline in Eastern European industrial production and the recession in 2008.[19] Given this price development and market situation, covered sources had no incentive to reduce emissions or even trade allowances. A cap-and-trade market was not established. This shows the importance of the availability of accurate data, allocation methods, and market design. Interestingly enough, many design features (theoretically) identified as necessary for efficient emissions trading have subsequently been implemented into the EUTS for the current and following phases. For example, the allocation method has been changed from grandfathering, which was identified as rewarding "dirty" production measures on page 118, to benchmarking. In addition to that, allowances are to be

14 Kreuter-Kirchhof, Charlotte, Klimaschutz durch Emissionshandel? Die jüngste Reform des europäischen Emissionshandelssystems, Europäische Zeitschrift für Wirtschaftsrecht (EuZW) 2017, 412; Wegener, Bernhard W., Die Novelle des EU-Emissionshandelssystems, Zeitschrift für Umweltrecht (ZUR), 2009, 283.

15 *Zenke/Vollmer*, in Danner/Theobald, Energierecht, Rn. 332-336, 91. EL January 2017.

16 Press release, European Commission (May 23, 2008), IP/08/787.

17 *Id*. Mostly as a result of unavailable or incomplete data, which made the allocation of allowances guesswork rather than a data-driven process.

18 Kreuter-Kirchhof, *supra* note 14, at 414.

19 *Cf.* Wegener, *supra* note 14, at 284.

auctioned from the start of Phase 3 on a feature that was identified as superior to the previous free allocation on page 120 f.[20]

II. Growth and linkage potential

The experiences with the WCI in particular show that a Kyoto Protocol-style, top-down regulation is not necessarily required for the creation of local emissions environmental policies aimed at addressing an international problem.

With the WCI, state actors acting out of their own self-interest[21] decided to establish regulations, such as trading programs. to reduce emissions in a cost-efficient way. In some cases, linkage occurred, which supports the idea of coalition forming. However, we can also see that the development of a joint market took considerable time, which might not be available in the context of global warming.

However, we also see that state actors see an incentive to join existing emissions trading systems. This is an interesting fact as it supports the idea that a growing bottom-up emissions trading could emerge without the influence of a binding international agreement. This might even have influence on shaping a larger, top-down regulation. For example, the ultimately defeated Waxman-Markey bill (H.R. 2454) proposed a federal cap-and-trade system that would have prevented states from operating emissions trading programs during the first six years of the federal program. However, WCI, RGGI, and the Midwest Greenhouse Gas Reduction Accord (MGGRA) were

> *explicitly seeking to influence, and even be replaced by national systems. The WCI design recommendations state that "the WCI Partner jurisdictions have designed a program that can stand alone, provide a model for, be integrated*

20 *Cf.* note 14 for detailed information on the EUTS reform.

21 Of course, federal regulation likely played a motivating role in the decision to create the respective trading systems. State actors might especially be interested in creating regulation to "pre-empt" federal regulation in which states have less influence.

into, or be implemented in conjunction with programs that might ultimately emerge from the federal governments of the United States and Canada."[22]

In contrast to such findings, dropouts occurred as well—for example, New Jersey's decision to leave the RGGI. While such decisions are always influenced by policy decisions and shifts in political opinions, they provide valuable lessons for linking potential. As discussed, for system linking to be efficient, systems must have the potential to form climate clubs. In the case of New Jersey, Gov. Christie explained New Jersey's decision to leave the RGGI as being due to the program's malfunction and the resulting increased energy costs.[23] In the context of club forming, this means that the RGGI was not able to establish a system that was beneficial for all members in order to eliminate the free-rider issue posed by climate change. In view of the above analysis of the RGGI regulative environment and its performance, this is not surprising. For one, the overallocation of allowances prevented the establishment of a functioning market. So while membership in the RGGI comes with costs—for example, administrative expenses and of course industry impact—the malfunctioning market did not provide enough benefits to offset those costs. Additionally, the RGGI does not provide for provisions penalizing members for leaving. To summarize, the RGGI did attempt to form a climate club, but did not develop enough "pull-factors" to establish such a club.

Such drop-outs are mirrored on an international level. Relating to the Paris Agreement, the U.S. formally resigned from the Agreement on August 4, 2017.[24] While this cannot be analyzed without taking into account the policy shift intended by the Trump Administration, the resignation illustrates that the bottom-up approach utilized in the Paris Agreement was not effective in forming a cohesive club and did not provide the necessary "pull-factors."

---

22 Matthew Bramley, P.J. Partington & Dave Sawyer, *Linking National Cap-and-Trade Systems in North America Clean Energy and Climate Action: A North American Collaboration* 11 (The Pembina Institute and the International Institute for Sustainable Development, Discussion paper, December 2009).

23 *Cf.* note 136 in Chapter E.

24 United Nations, *Depositary Notification of U.S. withdrawal from the Paris Agreement*. Ref. C.N.464.2017 .TREATIES-XXVII.7.d (August 4, 2017).

III. Optimizing Design: Fixing a broken system?

1. Systematic issues with emissions trading

As discussed above, the practical experiences with emissions trading show that it has not been an efficient approach to reduce emissions. The experiences with U.S. emissions trading systems show that none of the systems were able to establish a fully functioning market for emissions certificates from the outset. In reviewing practical experiences with emissions trading, we can infer whether these malfunctions are an inherent conceptual issue, or whether they are rooted in individual design choices made by regulators.

The main issue present in emissions trading is the overallocation of allowances. All of the reviewed systems, except for the ARP, were overallocated. While this can be attributed to a lack of available reliable data in some instances, the example of the WCI shows that even with available reliable data, regulators were not able (or willing) to determine a stringent cap. While some scholars argue that initial overallocation is an acceptable strategy to gain support for emissions trading in early stages of a trading system,[25] this points towards an inherent systematic issue in emissions trading, i.e., the failure to establish an accurate baseline even where reliable data is present. This is remarkable as proponents of emissions trading argue that market-based instruments are superior to C&C regulation in situations where information is imperfect. In reality, cap-and-trade does not work even if information is reliable.

This is due to a fundamental fallacy present in all current emissions trading systems: they are, in fact, not "market-based" instruments.[26]

As discussed above, emissions trading allows for arbitrary pollution targets oriented by what is deemed to be politically achievable in the same way as C&C regulation does according to its critics.[27] The experiences with emissions trading show that the determination of baselines and the

---

25 *See*, for example, Danny Ellerman, *US Experience with Emissions Trading: Lessons for CO2 Emissions Trading*, *in* Emissions Trading for Climate Policy: US and European Perspectives 90 (Bernd Hansjurgens ed., 2005).

26 *Cf. also* Wustlich, Guido, Ökonomisierung im Umweltrecht, Zeitschrift für Umweltrecht (ZUR), 2009, Heft 11, 515 (520) arguing that emissions trading utilizes a mixture between C&C style planning and economic mechanisms.

27 *See* Dieter Helm, *Economic Instruments and Environmental Policy*, 36 Econ. and Soc. Rev. 210 (Winter 2005) and page 92 in this text.

allocation of allowances remain a political choice.[28] As Beckmann and Fisahn correctly point out, this ultimately transforms the process into a question of bargaining power: each covered source tries to obtain a maximum amount of allowances in order to avoid emissions abatement or R&D costs.[29] Not only do sources have significant political bargaining power in the process of public opinion forming—for example, by threatening job losses or increasing prices for consumers—regulators also rely on emissions data supplied by the sources themselves to determine the cap. As the process of promulgating C&C regulation shows, this is the case throughout all types of regulation and may therefore just be part of the political reality that shapes law. Consequently, it can be concluded that emissions trading is not an economic instrument, but a policy choice that combines several types of regulation.

This, however, turns into a problem when policymakers misjudge this reality and assume a working market where none exists. This is a systematic issue visible in emissions trading: it implies a market logic where none is present. In terms of environmental efficiency, this is harmful. As the German Federal Administrative Court pointed out, traditional environmental C&C-style emission limits are not designed to be exactly met. As limits are based on imperfect information, C&C regulation generally contains a safety margin, for example, in the event that a cap was set too high.[30] Emissions trading follows the opposite logic. The cap set by regulators defines the available emissions budget, which will be used to its full extent. If this cap is determined in a way that does not follow market

---

28 As stated even by proponents of emissions trading, *see* for example *Weinreich* in Landmann/Rohmer, Umweltrecht, Vorbemerkung, Rn. 11, 82. EL Januar 2017.

29 Beckmann, Martin A., Fisahn, Andreas, Probleme des Handels mit Verschmutzungsrechten - eine Bewertung ordnungsrechtlicher und marktgesteuerter Instrumente in der Umweltpolitik, Zeitschrift für Umweltrecht (ZUR), 2009, Heft 6.

30 Winter, Gerd, Das Klima ist keine Ware, Zeitschrift für Umweltrecht (ZUR) 2009, Heft 6, 289 (296) referring to a decision by the German Federal Administrative Court, dated February 17, 1984 (BVerwG v. 17 Februar 1984, BVerGE 69, 37, 43) stating that: "the applicable emission caps contain residual risks which, on the one hand, are due to the measurement method used and, on the other hand, are based on imperfect information about the harmfulness of certain immissions, their long-term effects and possible synergistic effects. Precautions must therefore be taken if there are sufficient grounds for assuming that immissions may *potentially* lead to harmful environmental effects and thus - even if the respective causal relationships cannot yet be clearly determined in detail - there is a suspicion of danger."

logic, the system fails and prevents environmental integrity. Ironically, this effect might be the only real "market-based" part of emissions trading: by setting a cap, regulators transform the usage of a natural resource into a commodity with economic value. It follows market logic to use such a commodity; everything else would be economically irrational behavior. So, when the FCCC proudly announces that "[c]arbon is now tracked and traded like any other commodity,"[31] they are correct in a fatal way: carbon has been turned into a readily available and thus cheap commodity. The "carbon market" has lost sight of its initial goal. This is supported by statements regulators have made in publications. For example, an EPA program administrator stated that "[g]overnment should refrain from trying to participate in, control, or fine tune the market, particularly since many changes, such as restructuring, may occur outside the regulator's purview. This focus should provide the certainty, efficiency, and stability desired by all and necessary for optimal market performance."[32] If no market exists for the reasons discussed above, this rationale leads to an inefficient regulatory system that fails to achieve its objective.

A solution to the overallocation is to set caps based on the feasibility principle, i.e., basing caps on the "lowest achievable emissions rate."[33] This approach is superior to the currently observable model of basing caps simply upon political decisions but does not break the disconnect between planning emission caps and the market dynamic. The empirical evidence—especially from the California Cap-and-Trade program—shows that the feasibility principle, which was used by CARB to determine the emissions cap in California's cap-and-trade program, *cf.* California Code, Health and Safety Code § 38560 (introduced by AB 32), can result in a tighter cap then other determination methods. However, it did not fully prevent overallocation or create a functioning market, respectively. The empirically proven disconnect between political planning and market economy mirrors a generally accepted economic dogma: market economy and planned economy are incompatible.[34]

---

31 *Cf.* United Nations Framework Convention on Climate Change, Statement on website, http://unfccc.int/kyoto-protocol/mechanisms/emissions-trading/items/2731.php (last visited January 11, 2020).

32 Brian J. McLean, *Evolution of Marketable Permits: The US Experience with Sulfur Dioxide Trading*, 8 (1/2) Intl. J. Env't. and Pollution 19-36 (1997).

33 *Cf.* the discussion above on p. 99.

34 Hartwig Bartling, Franz Luzius Grundzüge der Volkswirtschaftslehre, Einführung in die Wirtschaftstheorie und Wirtschaftspolitik, 17. Auflage 2014, Kapitel B III 1

In theory, a declining cap could over time eliminate overallocated allowances, but this tightening process only works long term, which minimizes the environmental effectiveness of declining caps. Additionally, the option of implementing declining caps is not a strong argument in favor of emissions trading over C&C regulation, as successive tightening of inflated baselines is also possible in traditional C&C regulation. The empirical evidence collected above—or example, regarding California's cap-and-trade program on pages 227 ff.—furthermore shows that even declining caps tend be arbitrary in enacted systems.

Following from this systematic issue is a deficiency regarding the cost effectiveness of emissions trading both for states as well as for covered sources: So far, no in-depth economic studies on the cost efficiency of enacted emissions trading systems have been conducted. Some scholars suggest that emissions trading generally is less costly than traditional C&C regulation;[35] however, while this might be true, any costs, regardless of how low they are, are too high for an ineffective regulation. On the state level, monitoring and other trading infrastructure require significant public investment. In Germany, for example, the competent authority required 11 million Euro in 2007, mostly for the creation of the EUTS trading infrastructure.[36] Regarding covered sources, monitoring duties imposed by emissions trading systems often require considerable investment, just like trading infrastructure needed by covered sources. Given the generally disappointing outcome of the reviewed systems, such imposed costs are too high.[37]

A further issue is emissions leakage. For example, despite extensive provisions aimed at avoiding emissions leakage, the California cap-and-trade was not able to avoid leakage. However, emissions leakage does not fol-

---

35 Gabriel Chan, Robert Stavins, Robert Stowe & Richard Sweeney, *The SO2 Allowance Trading System and the Clean Air Act Amendments of 1990: Reflections on Twenty Years of Policy Innovation*, 65 Nat. Tax J. 419, 424 (2012). For stakeholder opinions see Bryant Walker Smith, *Stakeholder Reaction to Emissions Trading in the United States, the European Union, and the Netherlands*, 25 J. Land Use & Envtl. L. 137-155 (2009).

36 *Cf.* note 29.

37 Other than traditional C&C regulation, emissions trading is costly both for the administrating public body and the covered source. This leads to an interesting climate justice side issue: the consumer is burdened twice—as a taxpayer paying for the establishment of trading infrastructure as well as a consumer burdened with the rollover of compliance costs. Such a rollover is especially problematic if the costs being rolled over include the value of the certificates, as such are often allocated for free (*cf.* also the "windfall profit" issue discussed above).

low from a design issue inherent in emissions trading systems. All of the reviewed systems contained limited coverage, either geographically or industry-based. Limiting industry coverage—for example, to larger sources with bigger emissions output or certain industries—certainly simplifies the process of implementing the system and determining the cap. It also prevents smaller sources or sensitive industries from being burdened with the costs associated with regulation. However, even considering extensive industry aid provisions as utilized in the WCI, such limited coverage is an open invitation for emissions leakage towards non-covered sources. This is a design issue that, at least in theory, can be avoided by extending coverage. To summarize, instead of using industry assistance to avoid leakage, regulators should aim at establishing complete coverage or supplement emissions trading systems with command and control regulation that reduces incentives to "import" from non-covered sources. Regarding geographical coverage, this is of course limited by the given jurisdiction. In view of the issues with bottom-up linking discussed in this thesis, this makes a case for top-down regulation.

As discussed above, many design features (theoretically) identified based on empirical evidence in this thesis as necessary for efficient emissions trading have subsequently been implemented into the EUTS for the current and following phases. For example, the allocation method has been changed from grandfathering, which was identified as rewarding "dirty" production measures on page 118, to benchmarking. In addition to that, allowances are to be auctioned from the start of Phase 3 on, a feature that was identified as superior to the previous free allocation on page 1208 f.[38]

The conclusion above shows that even absent a binding top-down regulation, local regulative approaches can emerge from the bottom-up. This, however, increases the pressure on the individual design elements of a given cap-and-trade system. For example, with the possibility of cross-jurisdictional emissions trading systems, state participants have an incentive to promulgate less stringent caps, i.e., to allocate more allowances than necessary. This can be addressed with provisions on limited banking and retirement of allowances. In addition to that, national emissions trading shows a strong tendency to move towards more stringent caps as in the case of overallocation, and allowance prices decrease drastically. This sends a strong signal to regulators, who can react by tightening the cap.

This topic also highlights the importance of design compatibility between systems, especially regarding design elements with pricing impact,

38 *Cf.* note 14 for detailed information on the EUTS reform.

such as safety valves. For example, the EU decided to not implement a safety valve, whereas different systems, such as the RGGI, might contain one. Such incompatibility can impede the linking process as it, *inter alia*, requires additional regulative adjustments of the respective systems.

Even though it was shown that trading systems might evolve without explicit linking provisions, linking design is key to allowing for the organic growth of trading systems and to incentivize linkage between systems. In that regulators will be faced with a conflict between the primary objective of linking (i.e., the reduction of costs) and other linking implications on a systems environmental and economic performance. For example, linking with another system generally reduces the regulator's influence on the system as, for example, price fluctuations in other systems affect the allowance price in linked systems.[39] Optimized linking provisions can be a solution for some, but not all, negative effects of linkage. For example, exchange rates can be used to offset drastic allowance price differences between systems. Such exchange rates can even be implemented as a flexible provision: the rule could be drafted in a way that only a certain price difference triggers the exchange rate. This is important, as scholars perceive allowance price differences between systems to "be a key determinant of the cost savings from linking, and of linking's emissions and distributional impacts."[40]

Apart from price differences, there are many other design factors that can impact linked systems and thus the decision whether or not to link. These design factors are, for example, the given system's coverage and whether a downstream or upstream is used, the allowance allocation method, and offset rules. To summarize, Bramley, Partington, and Sawyer argue that the cap-and-trade design elements "that most need to be harmonized to allow linking are cap type, limits on use of offsets, borrowing, mechanisms to constrain the carbon price, and quality of enforcement. Stringency (measured by the carbon prices in the un-linked systems), and offset types and standards also likely need to be harmonized to allow linking."[41]

Thus, some cap-and-trade systems might be designed in a way more conducive to linking than others. This is where "harmonizing" comes

39 Judson Jaffe & Robert N. Stavins, *Linking U.S. Cap-and-Trade System for Greenhouse Gas Emissions: Opportunities, Implications, and Challenges* 10 ff (Reg-Markets Center, Working Paper 08-01, January 2008).

40 Jaffe & Stavins, *supra* at 24.

41 Bramley et al., *supra* note 22, at 1.

in. Regulators could, for example, use an umbrella agreement to harmonize emissions caps. This would facilitate linkage between systems and discourage governments from setting less stringent caps than they would absent linkages.[42] Unfortunately, the agreement on caps has, as discussed in the context of the Kyoto Protocol, proven to be the most difficult part of policy negotiations for many state actors. However, in a harmonized, bottom-up approach as discussed in this paper, there is more flexibility than in a strict bottom-up approach. For example, some jurisdictions could agree on a binding cap, whereas others could only obligate themselves to reduce emissions by a certain percentage each trading period.

Furthermore, this thesis contains reviews of multiple emissions trading systems using subsidy systems to support either member states, such as the ARP, or certain industries, such as California's cap-and-trade system. This is a powerful tool, which could be used very effectively in the context of bottom-up regulation. For example, a portion of a state's auctioning proceeds could, similar to the California system, go into a fund designated to subsidize other jurisdictions in case they join the trading system. This could provide a strong incentive to join, even for jurisdictions that would otherwise be opposed to emissions reductions for economic reasons.

2. A case for harmonized sectoral bottom-up regulation?

Sawa takes this idea one step further and makes a case for harmonized bottom-up regulation under which sectoral approaches would be employed to establish national emissions targets, and governments would internationally pledge to implement policies and measures to achieve the targets. [43] Indeed, a sectoral approach would especially be helpful at encouraging developing countries to enact regulation. Governments of emerging countries are often hesitant to enact economy-wide regulation due to the fear of stunting economic growth. A sector-based trading system, instead of economy-wide regulation, could avoid such conflicts. Of course, that would not help if a given government considers the respective sector to be especially important for economic development and therefore seeks to protect the sector from any potential disadvantages. However, an international

42 Jaffe & Stavins, *supra* at 24.

43 Akihiro Sawa, *A Sectoral Approach as an Option for a Post-Kyoto Framework* (Harvard Project on International Climate Agreements Discussion Paper 2008-23, December 2008).

sectoral-emissions trading system would be an incredibly efficient tool to address emissions leakage in the sector. Sawa furthermore argues that "[a] sectoral approach promotes consensus by contributing to the establishment of equitable economy-wide reduction targets."[44]

Ultimately, while there are some advantages to sectoral trading, there are several arguments against going forward with such a regulatory approach. As stated above, various countries have already enacted emissions trading systems, virtually all which feature economy-wide regulation. For such countries, "reducing" their systems to a sectoral approach will not be feasible nor, from an environmental perspective, desirable. Furthermore, a national regime of both economy-wide systems and sectoral systems is likely to inhibit linkage as it poses additional design and comparability challenges.

To conclude, harmonized bottom-up trading with the possibility of "just" enacting sectoral emissions trading could provide great incentives for the creation of a "growing" system with the result of a global "climate club" but would not eliminate the systematic issues inherent with the trading of emissions.

3. Implications from international law

The above findings show that empirically, most major emissions trading systems have not operated as expected. Arguably, this failure is due to an inherent systematic issue. In view of such shortcomings, it is necessary to look at the role of international law and whether it has an effect on the continued use of emissions trading as compliance systems. As discussed, the Paris Agreement contains language only on international emissions trading systems, stating in Article 6 para. 2, that

> *[p]arties shall, where engaging on a voluntary basis in cooperative approaches that involve the use of internationally transferred mitigation outcomes towards nationally determined contributions, promote sustainable development and ensure environmental integrity and transparency, including in governance, and shall apply robust accounting to ensure, inter alia, the avoidance of double counting, consistent with guidance adopted by the Conference of the Parties serving as the meeting of the Parties to this Agreement.*

---

44 *Id.* at 4.

Regarding emissions trading on a national level, however, Article 4 para. 2 of the Paris Agreement implicitly gives the parties full discretion regarding their national policy approaches in order to achieve desired emissions reductions. Emissions trading on a national level is therefore still possible without any further express restrictions from the Agreement. However, the accepted principles of international law restrict nation states' discretion to further rely on emissions trading in order to achieve their intended emissions reductions.

International law, regardless of whether it is binding or customary international law, is not directly applicable in all individual states but influences domestic legal policy through multiple angles.[45] In Germany, binding international law is considered equal to federal law that applies directly in courts and preempts any conflicting state legislation, *cf.* Article 25 of the German Constitution. Customary international law is covered by such a clause. In contrast, the role of international law in the U.S. legal system is more complicated. Written international law, such as rules following from treaties joined by the U.S., is considered "Supreme law of the Land" by Article VI, Clause 2 of the U.S. Constitution and thus binds the U.S. states as well as preempts conflicting state legislation.[46] However, the U.S. Constitution supersedes any conflicting international treaty, even after the Senate ratifies the treaty.[47] However, more relevant for the purpose of reviewing the influence of the principles of international law on the future of emissions trading is international law's influence on the interpretation of national regulation. The European Court of Justice, for example, has long held that in interpreting national regulation that implements international obligations, such as those following from international law, "objectives, principles and provisions" of international law must be considered, even if the state is not a party to the agreement that shaped such international law.[48] In the U.S., the effect of customary, i.e., non-treaty-based, international law on the domestic legal system is disputed between the "modernist" school, which considers such international law as essentially federal law, and the "revisionist" school, which argues that in the absence of congressional legislation or a U.S. treaty,

45 The role of international law for domestic law is unclear and subject to debate in many states. For the purpose of this thesis, such discussion does not need be replicated at length. The following paragraph focuses on the effect of international law for the interpretation of domestic law.

46 *Cf.* Ware v. Hylton, 3 U.S. (3 Dall.) 199 (1796).

47 *Cf.* Reid v. Covert, 354 U.S. 1 (1957).

48 European Court of Justice, Case C-154/02, Jan Nilsson, 2003 Slg. I-12 39.

rules of customary international law are generally not federal law and will therefore generally be governed by state law.[49] However, there is consent that customary international law may be used to interpret U.S. national law. In its *Murray v. The Charming Betsey* Case, the Court stated, that "an act of Congress ought never to be construed to violate the law of nations if any other possible construction remains."[50] This doctrine is now known as the "Charming Betsey Doctrine" and remains an accepted canon of statutory interpretation in the U.S.[51]

As discussed on the pages 62 ff., relevant international environmental law as it relates to emissions trading is defined especially by the Principles of Sustainable Development, Prevention, and Due Diligence. The Principle of Sustainable Development obliges public actors to balance ecological, economic, and social interests.[52] The Principle of Prevention obliges public actors to ensure that activities within their jurisdiction and control respect the environment of other states or of areas beyond national control. States therefore are required to exercise due diligence in order to prevent environmental damage in other states. As put by the ICJ in its Pulp Mill Case: "A State is thus obliged to use all means at its disposal in order to avoid activities, which take place in its territory [...] causing significant damage to the environment of another State."[53] The Principle of Due Diligence obliges states to act with due diligence with respect to all activities that take place under the jurisdiction and control of a nation state. According to the ICJ, Due Diligence "entails not only the adoption of appropriate rules and measures but also a certain level of vigilance in their enforcement and the exercise of administrative control applicable to

49 *Cf.* Gary Born, *Customary International Law in United States Courts*, 92 WASH. L. REV. 1641 (December 2017); Carlos M. Vazquez, *Customary International Law as U.S. Law, A Critique of the Revisionist and Intermediate Positions and a Defense of the Modern Position*, 86 NOTRE DAME L. REV. 1495 (2011); Michelle M. Kundmueller, *Application of Customary International Law in U.S. Courts: Custom, Convention, or Pseudo Legislation*, 28 J. LEGIS. 359 (2002).

50 Murray v. The Charming Betsey, 6 U.S. (2 Cranch) 64 (1804); *cf.* Restatement (Third) of Foreign Relations Law of the Unites States, § 114 (1987) stating that "[w]here fairly possible, a United States statute is to be construed so as not to conflict with international law or with an international agreement of the United States."

51 *Cf.* Hartford Fire Insurance Co. v. California, 509 U.S. 764 (1993) with a dissent by Judge Scalia.

52 *Cf.* page 64 f.

53 *Cf.* page 70 f.

public and private operators."[54] Read together, these and other principles of international environmental law constitute a binding substantive and procedural framework that states must consider when interpreting their national laws and deciding on as well as administering their national compliance programs aimed at reducing emissions. In view of the Principle of Sustainable Development, states do have a right to economic development even at the price of compromising environmental concerns. The required balancing of ecological, economic, and social interests does, however, prohibit states from ignoring environmental concerns. In implementing environmental regulation, states may therefore not forgo environmental concerns in favor of economic development. While the Principle of Prevention and the Due Diligence Principle also do not prohibit states from engaging in economic activity, they are required to adapt the appropriate rules and measures. Arguably, such binding principles prohibit states from using compliance instruments that have a proven record of deficiency if other options exist.

Pertaining to international emissions trading, this follows from Article 6 of the Paris Agreement: the Paris parties may only engage in international trading if environmental integrity is ensured.

IV. Emissions trading decision making

During the introduction to the topic on page 90, the question was raised whether emissions trading is the policy tool of choice when regulators have "no better idea." And indeed, in view of the empirical evidence suggesting the failure of emissions trading in practice, it is necessary to ask why regulators stay focused on this policy instrument. This is primarily a question of political science. However, a legal analysis can offer some contribution to this discussion.

For one, the implications of the generally positive experiences of the ARP has shaped much of the discussion on emissions trading, as discussed above on pages 164 ff. Regulators have expressly cited the ARP as reason for their interest in emissions trading. However, as also discussed on these pages, the ARP is not a good model for approaches against climate change, which differs significantly from Acid Rain and thus requires alternate policy approaches. This is not addressed in the policy debate.

54 *Cf.* page 81 f.

A further explanation can be found in the history of emissions trading. Looking at past policy discussions (even further back than the first positive experiences with the ARP, which laid the foundation of today's perception of emissions trading),[55] studies focused on the interaction of political and social opinion forming and their influence have suggested that the reliance on market-based instruments, which are at the core of U.S. environmental regulation, are a result of the perceived injustices after the period in U.S. policy coined as the "New Deal."[56] According to these studies, the U.S. public and interest groups felt that government authorities, which were given new and strong administrative competencies during the "New Deal" after a long period of *laissez-faire* politics, abused their powers in favor of large corporations and to the detriment of small business and the general population. As a result, the CAA was "created in a climate of great distrust of both agencies and industries"[57] and restricted the agency's competencies to regulate the very issue they were supposed to regulate. Agencies have thus taken on a "banker-accountant"-role.[58] Given this setting, emissions trading might have seemed appealing to agencies. This goes beyond "a blind trust in the market" ideology, a criticism that has often been raised regarding emissions trading. However, this cannot be denied either. A policy-focused study conducted by Meidinger identified as a key factor for the rising popularity

> *the development and spread of a particular form of regulatory culture. Promoted primarily by recent graduates of law and public policy programs, this culture emphasizes that: (1) while science is critical to understanding the impacts of regulatory policies it cannot form the basis for choosing them, (2) regulatory decisions are inherently and necessarily just compromises among contending interests, (3) the goal of the regulatory agency is thus a stable, predictable framework within which the pull and haul of interests can take place and through which compromises can be implemented, and (4) the content and legitimacy of regulatory policies should be based as much as possible on the interests and compromises of private parties.*[59]

---

55 *Cf.* page 164 ff.

56 Errol Meidinger, *On Explaining the Development of "Emissions Trading" in U.S. Air Pollution Regulation*, 7 L. and Pol'y 447, 450 f. (1985).

57 *Id.*

58 Kruger *in* EMISSIONS TRADING, INSTITUTIONAL DESIGN, DECISION MAKING AND CORPORATE STRATEGIES 17 f. (Ralf Antes, Bernd Hansjürgens & Peter Letmathe, eds., 2008).

59 *Cf.* note 56.

Apart from such ideological tendencies, Meidinger further concludes that the dominance of trading-focused approaches also results in "significant part to the inherent complexity of air pollution regulation, which limits effective discourse to a very small group of experts, and to the organizational location of the regulatory entrepreneurs promoting it."

Due to cultural differences, the ideological reasons advanced as a hypothesis for the North American tendency towards emissions trading can hardly explain the European Union's or China's tendency towards emissions trading. Apart from the force of institutionalization discussed above on page 37 f., which can explain the European attempts at emissions trading in view of the Kyoto parties' focus on emissions trading, the most likely explanation is the greatest strength of emissions trading: it's potential for "club-forming" discussed in the following chapter.

V. Conclusion: Can "bottom-up" trading work?

Climate Change is a global issue. In order to effectively approach its root causes, emissions abatement is needed in every nation state across the globe, including the emerging countries as major emitters with an expectation of increasing emissions.[60] For any future approach to be successful, it needs to be both environmentally effective and able to eliminate the free-rider issue imminent in a localized (bottom-up) approach. For bottom-up trading, this requires the formation of climate clubs in the form of linking. To summarize academic work about bottom-up linking and real-life experiences with emissions trading in the U.S., emissions trading systems can grow by linkage and coalition forming. Such bottom-up linkage can be a viable alternative to a top-down approach as utilized by the Kyoto Protocol. Compared to such regulation, the bottom-up approach has various advantages:

For example, the Kyoto Protocol's "top-down" approach was modeled after the Montreal Protocol, which was highly successfully at regulating

60 The emerging countries (for a discussion of the feasibility of such classification *cf.* also the discussion in Chapter C footnote 36) account for more than half of the worldwide emissions from fossil fuels. For example, China emitted 10.9 Gt CO^2 in 2017, double the US emissions in that time. For a recent data analysis of worldwide GHG emissions from fossil fuels see, M. Muntean, D. Guizzardi, E. Schaaf, M. Crippa, E, Solazzo, J.G.J Olivier, & E. Vignati, *Fossil CO2 Emissions of all World Countries - 2018 Report* (Office of the European Union, EUR 29433 EN, 2018).

the use of ozone depleting substances.[61] However, as discussed above, the premises are very different, and ozone depletion is a relatively simple issue compared to climate change. Ozone depletion is caused by a relatively small class of artificial gases used by a relatively small class of industry sectors. Through research and development, alternatives for such gases were found and widely utilized shortly after enactment of the Protocol. Climate change, on the other hand, can be traced to a variety of GHG emitted across various industries and private households. Alternative technology replacing the combustion of fossil fuels is hard to utilize. Indeed, "[o]n present trends, for another 20 years, the world will continue installing carbon-intensive infrastructure, such as coal power plants, with a 50-year lifetime."[62] A national bottom-up approach has (irrespective of the regulative method used) the theoretical potential to be more flexible and efficient. A regime addressing climate change must necessarily be flexible, as on the one hand, perception and understanding of climate change evolves, and on the other hand, impact assessment for industry and sources change. However, flexibility is only a means to an end. If flexibility does not result in an efficient outcome, it does not add value.

Furthermore, with the exceptions of the "TWAIL" scholars cited above,[63] there seems to be a general consensus that to be effective, a post-Kyoto regime needs to include all major emitters, irrespective of GDP. Correspondingly, scholars argue that the Kyoto Protocol's emphasis on the developed Annex I countries is not an effective approach to climate change.[64] Indeed, estimates project that developing countries will account for 75 percent of emissions growth in the next twenty-five years.[65] (For projections of greenhouse gas emissions growth in developing countries, *see also cf.* Exhibit 4.) A bottom-up approach could, as discussed above in the context of coalition forming, incentivize developing countries to create their own emissions trading system, especially considering the advantages of cap-and-trade for development discussed above. This happened in the case of China: once a major emitter refusing to cut emissions in the Kyoto

---

61 Rafael Leal-Arcas, *Top-Down Versus Bottom-Up Approaches for Climate Change Negotiations: An Analysis*, 6 The IUP J. Governance & Pub. Pol'y 16 (December 2011).

62 Gwyn Prins & Steve Rayner, *Time to Ditch Kyoto?* 449 Nature 974 (2007).

63 *Cf.* Makau Mutua, *What is TWAIL?* 94 Proceedings of the 94th Annual Meeting of the American Society of International Law 31(2000).

64 Leal-Arcas, *supra* at 50 f.

65 U.S. Energy Information-Administration, International Energy Outlook 2014, http://www.eia.gov/forecasts/ieo/pdf/0484(2014).pdf (last visited January 11, 2020).

negotiations, it has now set up its own emissions trading regime, which could potentially be linked to other programs. In particular, a bottom-up structure can eliminate the "burden-sharing" element that often stands in the way of international agreements, as states are ultimately self-interested actors.

In addition to that, linking amongst existing trading systems has a significant distributional effect.[66] This especially provides incentives for research and development, which is considered the main success factor in driving emissions reductions.[67]

As of now, there are major risks associated with this approach. For example, reliance on a market emerging from the bottom-up could slow down multinational, cooperative approaches such as the Kyoto Protocol and result in a non-homogenous climate governance. However, cap-and-trade creates incentive for countries to enact regulation.[68] "International pledges grow out of, and reflect, domestic policies, rather than being superimposed on them."[69] Thus, the biggest issue remains the uncertainty towards how long such a program would need to evolve and whether, given the above conclusions on the efficiency of emissions trading, be environmentally efficient. One could argue that slow incremental progress might not even be environmentally problematic as the biggest emitters worldwide already have emissions reductions systems in place that would allow for linking. Indeed, it can be argued that

> *[i]n case of climate change, the temporal factor should not be a real concern if the 20 major GHG emitters, responsible for around 80 % of GHGs in 2008, are on board from the beginning. An incremental expansion to the rest of the UNFCCC membership will not really be detrimental to the global warming effect, as the rest of the UNFCCC membership is only responsible for around 20 of global emissions.*[70]

This argument, however, does not consider that while such emitters have systems in place, they are not environmentally efficient, as discussed in this thesis.

In addition, one may consider whether strict bottom-up approaches are more susceptible to lobbying or industry influence than strict (especially

---

66 Jaffe & Stavins, *supra* note 39, at 13.
67 Prins & Rayner, *supra* note 62, at 973.
68 Leal-Arcas, *supra* note 61, at 29.
69 Daniel Bodansky, *A Tale of Two Architectures*, 43 Ariz. St. L.J. 16 (2011).
70 Leal-Arcas, *supra* note 61, at 24 f.

multi-national) top-down systems. For example, industry influence could multiply with many different systems in place, and even "small" lobbying efforts could have an exponential effect. However, this argument can also be reversed: significant industry influence on many and various state actors might be harder to gain than on one single multi-national regulative body. Furthermore, the existence of many systems might be able to partially cushion the negative effects lobbying might have on one specific system. Arguably, lobbying effects should therefore not be considered in the discussion regarding top-down vs. bottom-up systems.

An interesting development in the EUTS displays the importance of linking and the significance of institutionalization discussed here. While the EUTS cannot be considered a success,[71] it shows a clear tendency towards centralization of key features. The process in which the EUTS cap is determined demonstrates this. In Phases 1 and 2, member states used grandfathering to allocated certificates based on national allocation plans. Such national allocation plans determined the cap for every member state, and thus cumulatively the cap for the EU-ETS. With the 2009 reform, this procedure was significantly centralized. Starting with Phase 3, the cap is no longer set by member states in national allocation plans but by the European Commission. The cap has been set to 2,04 bln. tons of CO_2 and will be reduced by 1.74 percent per year starting from 2014. From 2021 on, the annual reduction is increased to 2.2 percent.[72] This can be understood as a reaction to a deficient system, but also as an example of the progression caused by institutionalization. One caveat, however, prohibits the generalization of this lesson to emissions trading outside of the EU-ETS. The European system was, from the beginning, designed to undergo increasing centralization.[73] Additionally, it cannot be seen outside of the general political development of the European Union, which displays a shift towards the centralization of many important policy decisions. Both factors weaken any national opposition towards centralization.

The central question, therefore, is whether bottom-up linking of emissions trading systems has the potential to form a global-climate club. According to majority scholarship, the conditions necessary for club for-

71 *Cf.* the discussion on page 237 f.

72 *See* Directive 2009/29/EC of the European Parliament and of the Council of April 23, 2009 amending Directive 2003/87/EC so as to improve and extend the greenhouse gas emission allowance trading scheme of the Community. OFFICIAL JOURNAL OF THE EUROPEAN UNION L 140/63, (June 5, 2009).

73 Wegener, *supra* note 14, at 285.

mation include (i) a public-good-type resource that can be shared, (ii) that the cooperative arrangement, including the dues, is beneficial for each of the members, (iii) that non-members can be excluded or penalized at relatively low cost to members and (iv) that the membership is stable in the sense that no one wants to leave."[74]

As discussed above, the atmosphere and other natural resources affected by climate change have a public-goods character. Real life experiences with emissions trading in the U.S., such as New Jersey leaving the RGGI, indicate that emissions trading might not have strong enough pull-factors to fulfill these requirements, most likely because of its systematic deficiencies. The requirement of a shared emissions trading system being beneficial for all members could in theory be fulfilled by linked emissions trading systems. The theoretical benefits of linked markets have been reviewed and displayed empirically earlier in this thesis and include, *inter alia*, better distribution of emission certificates and thus cheaper prices as well as reduced transaction costs and, most importantly as seen in the case of the WCI, increased certainty amongst participants as a result of larger markets. In practice, however, this is dependent on a functioning system whose emergence seems doubtful considering the empirically proven systematic issues inherent in emissions trading. Especially the disconnect between the costs and lacking results discussed above eliminates any potential pull factors.

In addition, an isolated bottom-up trading system implemented in a singular state does not have the potential to penalize non-members for not joining its system. This would require additional legislation, for example by linking bottom-up trading systems with trading agreements. None of the reviewed systems includes such a mechanism. Instead, some of the reviewed systems rely on regulators' perceived inherent interest in linking systems. While this is intuitive in view of the advantages of linked systems discussed above, this requires the existing wish of other public entities to implement an emissions trading system. Especially in view of the free-rider problem discussed above, if they do not intend to implement emissions trading systems or another type of emissions abatement regulation, this perceived incentive falls short. Another factor indicating the failure to effectively approach the free-rider issue is the overallocation of allowances in virtually all reviewed systems. While a lack of reliable data and general systematic issues may play a role, the failure to impose stringent caps

74 *Cf.* William D. Nordhaus, *Climate Clubs to Overcome Free-Riding*, 105 Am. Econ. Rev. 1339 (2015).

may also be rooted in regulators' fear of hurting the local economy and providing advantages for competitors outside of the respective system's coverage, therefore encouraging emissions leakage. This points towards the general flaw of local bottom-up regulation in view of a shared resource.

If club-forming is considered a necessary prerequisite for an effective climate change approach, the above displays the advantages of (international) top-down approaches. While bottom-up approaches eliminate the international law requirement of unanimity and therefore have greater chances of being implemented, they do not effectively eliminate the free-rider issue. This remains a critical advantage of top-down approaches.

In addition to such a deciding point, the following systematic advantages of top-down systems are not present in bottom-up approaches.

As a direct result of club-forming, a global top-down approach can afford to be more aggressive in mandated emissions reductions, as no emissions leakage or free-rider issues exist. This is especially important as climate change is a time-sensitive issue that needs immediate solutions.

Furthermore, a centralized, global, top-down approach can reduce uncertainty and provide a more reliable market environment for market participants. This is especially important as certainty and long-term planning possibilities can incentivize R&D and especially much-needed adaptation research.[75] Related to that, emissions monitoring and institutional oversight would be less costly and potentially more effective as resources could be bundled globally.

A global approach is most effective at preventing emissions leakage as it establishes a level playing field for all economic actors and removes the possibility of physically moving locations to unregulated areas. If such a global approach uses a market-based approach, such as emissions trading, a larger market will allow for more effective emission abatements and reduce transaction costs if regulators avoid overallocation.

To summarize, (isolated) bottom-up systems have a higher chance of being implemented than a global top-down system and have certain desirable effects, such as the institutionalization of emission reductions, but ultimately they lack the ability to form climate clubs and thus provide an effective response to the free-rider issue imminent in climate change. Top-down approaches are therefore favorable. As one scholar puts it, "what may look good from a short-term political perspective may contradict

75 Elinor Ostrom, *A Polycentric Approach for Coping with Climate Change*, 15 ANNALS ECON. & FIN. 97–134 (2014).

longer-term objectives."[76] However, global top-down approaches must put a bigger focus on encouraging club forming. The reliance on market-based instruments, such as emissions trading, is not sufficient. What is necessary, *inter alia*, is linkage of emissions reduction systems with free-trade deals, which has been successful in the Montreal Protocol and can provide the incentive needed to form a club.

76 *Cf.* William Hare et al., *The Architecture of the Global Climate Regime: A Top-down Perspective*, 10 CLIMATE POLICY 600-614 (2010).

G. What U.S. emissions trading teaches us about emissions trading, bottom-up regulation, and linkage in an international context

As concluded above, emissions trading cannot be considered a successful compliance tool.

Paradoxically, the arguments proposed by its supporters in favor of emissions trading, such as the proposed efficiency in view of imperfect information and the self-correcting nature of economic instruments, can be put forward against emissions trading. The many flaws reviewed above suggest that emissions trading is too complex, with too much room for error, and has lost sight of its initial goal, i.e., the reduction of emissions. Especially even if reliable information is available, the determination of a functioning baseline seems impossible, most likely because of the political process connected with it. This hurts environmental efficiency more than in traditional C&C legislation (which also depends on political bargaining) because it prevents the underlying mechanisms of emissions trading from functioning as intended. Thus, one of the main arguments in favor of emissions trading, i.e., the ability to function even in view of imperfect information, seems contradicted.

In addition to such findings regarding the effectiveness of emissions trading systems, we can infer that the reviewed bottom-up regulation has not developed the pull-factors necessary to form a climate club, potentially as a result of emissions trading as a compliance tool. The working hypothesis stating that collective action issues relating to global goods can only be solved globally remains in place.[1] Bottom-up regulation may be "better than nothing" and can provide certain advantages, especially those resulting from the process of institutionalization, but cannot ensure an effective approach to climate change. The Paris Agreement and its reliance on bottom-up regulation without substantial rules to encourage club formation is thus not a "reasonable gamble,"[2] but a perpetuation of a dysfunctional policy approach.

---

1 *Cf.* Elinor Ostrom, *A Polycentric Approach for Coping with Climate Change*, 15 ANNALS ECON. & FIN. 97–134 (2014).

2 Meinhard Doelle, *The Paris Agreement: Historic Breakthrough or High Stakes Experiment?* 6 CLIMATE LAW 1-20 (Special Issue 1-2, 2016).

Considering the international principles that govern international environmental law,[3] especially Article 6 para. 2 of the Paris Agreement[4] and the Principle of Due Diligence and the Principle of Sustainable Development, policymakers may no longer rely on the continued experimentation with economic instruments and hope for the emergence of an international emissions trading system. Instead, international law requires policymakers to use alternatives to the non-functioning system of emissions trading.[5]

3 *Cf.* page 62

4 The Paris Agreement to the United Nations Framework Convention on Climate Change, art. 6 2, Dec. 12, 2015, T.I.A.S. No. 16-1104 states that
[p]arties shall, where engaging on a voluntary basis in cooperative approaches that involve the use of internationally transferred mitigation outcomes towards nationally determined contributions, promote sustainable development and ensure environmental integrity and transparency, including in governance, and shall apply robust accounting to ensure, inter alia, the avoidance of double counting, consistent with guidance adopted by the Conference of the Parties serving as the meeting of the Parties to this Agreement.

5 *Cf.* the similar discussion regarding the influence of international environmental law on the binding nature of targets in the Paris Agreement: Ekardt, Felix, Das Paris Abkommen zum globalen Klimaschutz, Chancen und Friktionen - auf dem Weg zu einer substantiellen EU-Vorreiterrolle? in: Neue Zeitschrift für Verwaltungsrecht (NVwZ) 2016, 355.

References

Books

Aldy, Joseph E. and Robert Norman Stavins, eds., *Post-Kyoto International Climate Policy: Implementing Architectures for Agreement* (Cambridge University Press 2009).

American Law Institute, *Restatement (Third) of Torts: Liability for Physical and Emotional Harm* (American Law Institute 2005).

Antes, Ralf, Bernd Hansjürgens, and Peter Letmathe, eds. *Emissions Trading, Institutional Design, Decision Making and Corporate Strategies* (Springer 2008).

Baldwin, Robert, Martin Cave, and Martin Lodge, *Understanding Regulation: Theory, Strategy, and Practice* (Oxford University Press 2d ed. 2011).

Baumol, William, *Welfare Economics and the Theory of the State* (London School of Economics and Political Science 1952).

Brohé, Arnaud, Nick Eyre, and Nicholas Howarth, *Carbon Markets: An International Business Guide* (Earthscan 2009).

Chevalier, Julien, *Econometric Analysis of Carbon Markets: The European Union Emissions Trading Scheme and the Clean Development Mechanism* (Springer 2012).

Cowen, Tyler, "Public Goods" in *The Concise Encyclopedia of Economics*, David Henderson ed. (Liberty Fund Inc. 2008).

Daly, Herman E. and John Cobb, *For the Common Good, Redirecting the Economy toward Community, the Environment, and a Sustainable Future* (revised), (Beacon Press 1994).

Dow, Kirstin and Thomas E. Downing, *The Atlas of Climate Change* (University of California Press 3d ed. 2011).

Durlauf, Steven N. and Lawrence E. Blume, eds. *The New Palgrave Dictionary of Economics*, (Palgrave 2nd ed. 2008).

Ellerman, A. Denny, Paul L. Joskow, Richard Schmalensee, Juan-Pablo Montero, and Elizabeth M. Bailey, *Markets for Clean Air: The U.S. Acid Rain Program* (Cambridge University Press 2000).

Ellerman, Denny A. "US Experience with Emissions Trading: Lessons for CO_2 Emissions Trading," *in Emissions Trading for Climate Policy: US and European Perspectives* 78-95, B. Hansjürgens, ed. (Cambridge University Press 2005).

Fink, Arlene, *Conducting Research Literature Reviews: From the Internet to Paper* (Sage Publications 2d ed. 2005).

Hollo, Erkki, Kati Kulovesi, and Michael Mehling, eds., *Jus Gentium, Comparative Perspectives on Law and Justice: Climate Change and the Law* (Springer 2013).

Hammersley, Martyn, "What is Social Research?" in *Principles of Social and Educational Research: Block 1*, Martyn Hammersley, ed. (The Open University 1993).

Hanley, Nick and Clive L. Splash, *Cost-Benefit Analysis and the Environment* (Edward Elgar Pub. 1993).

Hill, Marquita K., *Understanding Environmental Pollution* (Cambridge University 3d ed. 2010).

Humphreys, Stephen, ed., *Human Rights and Climate Change* (Cambridge University Press 2009).

Hunter, David, James Salzman, and Durwood Zaelke, *International Environmental Law and Policy* (Foundation Press 4th ed. 2011).

Hutchinson, Terry, *Researching and Writing in Law* (Thomson Reuters 2018).

Kapp, William K., *The Social Costs of Private Enterprise* (Schocken 1964).

Leyh, Gregory, ed., *Legal Hermeneutics: History, Theory, and Practice* (University of California Press 1992).

McConville, Mike and Wing Hong Chui, eds., *Research Methods for Law* (Edinburgh University Press 2017).

McKenzie, Richard B. and Dwight R. Lee, *Microeconomics for MBAs: The Economic Way of Thinking for Managers* (Cambridge University Press 2d ed. 2010).

Nordhaus, William D., "Paul Samuelson and Global Public Goods, A Commemorative Essay for Paul Samuelson," *in Samuelson Economics and the Twenty-first Century*, Szenberg, Michael, Lall Ramrattan, and Aron A. Gottesman, eds. (Oxford University Press 2006).

Pigou, Arthur C., *The Economics of Welfare* (Macmillan & Co. 1920).

Roosa, Stephan A., *Sustainable Development Handbook* (Fairmont Press 2010).

Sagoff, Mark, *The Economy of Earth: Philosophy, Law and the Environment* (Cambridge University Press 2d ed. 2008).

Sands, Philippe and Jaqueline Peel, *Principles of International Environmental Law* (Cambridge University Press 3d. ed. 2012).

Shavell, Steven, *Foundations of Economic Analysis of Law* (Harvard University Press 2004).

Speth, James Gustave, *The Bridge at the End of the World: Capitalism, The Environment, and Crossing from Crisis to Sustainability* (Yale University Press 2009).

Tietenberg Thomas, ed., *Emissions Trading Programs* Volume I (Routledge 2001).

Tietenberg, Thomas H., *Emissions Trading: Principles and Practice*, (Routledge 2d ed. 2006).

Tinbergen, Jan, *Shaping the World Economy: Suggestions for an International Economic Policy* (Twentieth Century Fund 1962).

Tschirhart, John T., "Transferable Discharge Permits and Profit-Maximizing Behavior," *in Economic Perspectives on Acid Deposition Control,* Thomas D. Crocker, ed. (Butterworth-Heinemann 1984).

Weishaar, Stefan, *Emissions Trading Design: A Critical Overview*, New Horizons in Environmental and Energy Law Series (Edward Elgar Publishing Ltd 2014).

Selected Articles

Ackerman, Frank and Lisa Heinzerling, *Pricing the Priceless: Cost-Benefit Analysis of Environmental Protection,* 150 U. Pa. L. Rev. 1553 (May 2002).

Adler, Jonathan H., *Fables of the Cuyahoga: Reconstructing a History of Environmental Protection*, 14 Fordham Envtl. L. Rev. 89 (2002).

Baldursson, Fridrik M. and Nils-Hendrik von der Fehr, *Price Volatility and Risk Exposure in Market-Based Environmental Policy Instruments,* 48 J. Envtl. Econ. & Mgmt. 682 (2004).

Basiago, A.D., *Economic, Social, and Environmental Sustainability in Development Theory and Urban Planning Practice*, 19 The Environmentalist 145 (1999).

Berger, Sebastian, *The Making of the Institutional Theory of Social Costs: Discovering the K.W. Kapp and J.M. Clark Correspondence*, 72 Am. J. Econ. & Soc. 1106 (November 2013).

Bodansky, Daniel, *A Tale of Two Architectures*, 43 Ariz. St. L.J. 697 (2011).

Bodansky, Daniel, *The Legal Character of the Paris Agreement*, 25 Rev. Eur. Comp. & Int'l Envtl. L. (2016).

Bohringer, Christoph and Andreas Löschel, *Climate Policy Beyond Kyoto: Quo Vadis? A Computable General Equilibrium Analysis Based on Expert Judgments*, 58 Kyklos 467 (November 2005).

Born, Gary, *Customary International Law in United States Courts*, 92 Wash. L. Rev. 1641 (December 2017).

Carlson, Curtis, Dallas Burtraw, Maureen Cropper, and Karen L. Palmer, *Sulfur Dioxide Control by Electric Utilities: What Are the Gains from Trade?* 108 J. Pol. Econ. (December 2000).

Chan, Gabriel, Robert Stavins, Robert Stowe, and Richard Sweeney, *The SO_2 Allowance Trading System and the Clean Air Act Amendments of 1990: Reflections on Twenty Years of Policy Innovation*, 65 Nat'l Tax J. 419 (2012).

Coase, Ronald H., *The Problem of Social Cost*, 3 J. L. & Econ 1 (1960).

Coates, John C. IV, *Cost-Benefit Analysis of Financial Regulation: Case Studies and Implications*, 124 Yale L.J. 882 (January-February 2015).

Cooley, David M. and Jonas J. Monast, *Carbon Offsets and Environmental Impacts: NEPA, The Endangered Species Act, and Federal Climate Policy*, 28 Pace Envtl. L. Rev. 378 (Winter 2011).

Dahlman, Carl J., *The Problem of Externality*, 22 J. L. & Econ. 141 (1979).

Dehm, Julia, *Carbon Colonialism or Climate Justice? Interrogating the International Climate Regime from a TWAIL Perspective*, 33 Windsor Yearbook of Access to Justice 129 (2017).

Doelle, Meinhard, *The Paris Agreement: Historic Breakthrough or High Stakes Experiment?* 6 Climate Law 1-20 (2016).

Driesen, David M., *Distributing the Costs of Environmental, Health, and Safety Protection: The Feasibility Principle, Cost-Benefit Analysis, and Regulatory Reform*, 32 BC Envtl. Aff. L. Rev. 1 (2005).

Economic Times Commentary, "Environmental Issues: Time to Abandon Blame-Games and Become Proactive," *Economic Times*, December 15, 2012.

Ellerman, Denny A. and Barbara Buchner, *Over-Allocation or Abatement? A Preliminary Analysis of the EU Emissions Trading Scheme Based on the 2005-06 Emissions Data*, 41 Envtl. & Resource Econ. 267 (2008).

Epstein, Lee and Gary King, *Empirical Research and the Goals of Legal Scholarship: The Rules of Inference* 69 U. Chi. L. Rev. 1 (2002).

Evans, David A. and Joseph A. Kruger, *Where are the Sky's Limits? Lessons from Chicago's Cap-and-Trade Program*, 49 Envtl. Sci. & Pol'y (2007).

Falkner, Robert, Stephan Hannes, and John Vogler, *International Climate Policy After Copenhagen: Towards a "Building Blocks" Approach*, 1 Global Policy 252 (2010).

Fell, Harrison, Ian A. MacKenzie, and William A. Pizer, *Prices versus Quantities versus Bankable Quantities*, 34 Resources & Energy Econ. 607 (2012).

Gaines, Sanford, *Emerging Principles of International Environmental Law*, 26 Tex. Int'l L.J. 463 (1991).

Goffman Joseph, *Title IV of the Clean Air Act: Lessons for Success of the Acid Rain Emission Trading Program*, 14 Nr. 2 Penn St. Envtl. L. Rev. 177 (2005-2006).

Goldberg, Donald, *As the World Burns: Negotiating the Framework Convention on Climate Change*, 5 Geo. Int'l Envtl. L. Rev. 239, 244 (1993).

Goodland, Robert and Herman Daly, *Environmental Sustainability: Universal and Non-Negotiable*, 6 Ecological Applications 1002 (1996).

Hahn, Robert W. and Roger G. Noll, *Barriers to Implementing Tradable Air Pollution Permits: Problems of Regulatory Interactions*, 1 Yale J. on Reg. 63 (1983).

Hahn, Robert W., *Market Power and Transferable Property Rights*, 99 Q. J. Econ. 753 (1984).

Hahn, Robert W. and Robert N. Stavins, *The Effect of Allowance Allocations on Cap-and-Trade System Performance*, 54 J. L. & Econ. S267 (2011).

Hanemann, Michael, *The Role of Emission Trading in Domestic Climate Policy*, 30 Energy J., Special Issue 2: Climate Change Policies after 2012 79 (October 2009).

Hardin, Garrett, *The Tragedy of the Commons*, 162 Science 1243 (1968).

Hare, William, Claire Stockwell, Christian Flachsland, and Sebastian Oberthür, *The Architecture of the Global Climate Regime: A Top-down Perspective*, 10 Climate Pol'y 600 (2010).

Harris, Brittany A., *Repeating the Failures of Carbon Trading*, 23 Pacific Rim L. & Pol'y J. 766 (2014).

Helm, Carsten, *International Emissions Trading with Endogenous Allowance Choices*, 87 J. Pub. Econ. 2737 (December 2003).

Helm, Dieter, Cameron Hepburn, and Richard Mash, *Credible Carbon Policy*, 19 Oxford Rev. Econ. Pol'y 438 (2003).

Helm, Dieter, *Economic Instruments and Environmental Policy*, 36 Econ. & Soc. Rev. 205 (Winter 2005).

Huber, Bruce R., *How did RGGI do it? Political Economy and Emissions Auctions*, 40 Ecol. L. Q. 59 (2013).

Hunter, David, *Implications of the Copenhagen Accord for Global Climate Governance*, 10 Sustainable Dev. L. & Pol'y, 4-15, 56-57 (Spring 2010).

Joyner, Christopher C., *Common but Differentiated Responsibilities*, 96 Proceedings Am. Soc. Int'l L. 358 (2002).

Junker, Kirk W., *A Focus on Comparison in Comperative Law*, 52 Duq. L. Rev. 69 (Winter 2014).

Junker, Kirk W., *Ethical Emissions Trading and the Law*, 13 U. Balt. J. Envtl. L. 149 (2005-2006).

Kaswan, Alice, *Climate Change and Environmental Justice: Lessons from the California Lawsuits*,. 5 San Diego J. Climate & Ener. L. 2 (2013-2014).

Klassen, Ger and Andries Nentjes, *Sulfur Trading under the 1990 CAAA in the US: An Assessment of First Experiences*. 153 J. Inst. & Theoretical Econ. (JITE) 384 (June 1997).

Kundmueller, Michelle M., *Application of Customary International Law in U.S. Courts: Custom, Convention, or Pseudo Legislation*, 28 J. Legis. 359 (2002).

Larsen, Kari and Vanessa Tanaka, *Emissions Trading Schemes across the U.S.*, Practical Law Article 9-381-2351 (2008).

Leal-Arcas, Rafael, *Top-Down Versus Bottom-Up Approaches for Climate Change Negotiations: An Analysis*, 6 IUP J. Governance & Pub. Pol'y 7 (December 2011).

Malik, Arun, *Further Results on Permit Markets with Market Power and Cheating*, 44 J. Envtl. Econ. & Mgmt. 371 (2002).

McAllister, Lesley K., *The Overallocation Problem in Cap-and-Trade: Moving Toward Stringency*, 43 Colum. J. Envtl. L. 395 (2009).

McLean, Brian J., *Evolution of Marketable Permits: The US Experience with Sulfur Dioxide Trading*, 8 (1/2) Int'l J. Envt. & Pollution 19 (1997).

Meidinger, Errol, *On Explaining the Development of "Emissions Trading" in U.S. Air Pollution Regulation*, 7 Law & and Pol'y 447 (1985).

Misiolek, Walter S. and Harold W. Elder, *Exclusionary Manipulation of Markets for Pollution Rights*, 16 J. Envtl. Econ. & Mgmt. 156 (1989).

Montero, Juan-Pablo, Jose Miguel Sanchez, and Ricardo Katz, *A Market-Based Environmental Policy Experiment in Chile*, 45 J. L. & Econ. 267 (2002).

Montgomery David W., *Markets in Licenses and Efficient Pollution Control Programs*, 5 J. Econ. Theory 395 (1972).

Murry, Brian C., Maniloff, Peter T., and Evan M. Murry, *Why have Greenhouse Emissions in RGGI States Declined? An Econometric Attribution to Economic, Energy Market, and Policy Factors*, 51 Duke Envtl. & Energy Econ. 581 (September 2015).

Newell, Richard G., William A. Pizer, and Daniel Raimi, *Carbon Markets 15 Years after Kyoto: Lessons Learned, New Challenges*. 27 J. Econ. Persp. 134 (Winter 2013).

Nordhaus, William D., *Climate Clubs to Overcome Free-Riding*, 105 Am. Econ. Rev. 1339 (2015).

Notes, *Causation in Environmental Law: Lessons from Toxic Torts*, 128 Harv. L. Rev. 2256 (June 9, 2015).

Nye, John V., *The Pigou Problem*, 31 Regulation 32 (Summer 2008).

Oates, Wallace E. and Diana L. Strassmann, *Effluent Fees and Market Structure*, 24 J. Pub. Econ. 29 (1984).

Ostrom, Elinor, *A Polycentric Approach for Coping with Climate Change*, 15 Annals of Econ. and Fin. 97 (2014).

Owen, David G., *Problems in Assessing Punitive Damages Against Manufacturers of Defective Products*, 49 U. Chi. L. Rev. 1 (Winter 1982).

Parry, Ian W. H. and Kenneth A. Small, *Does Britain or the United States Have the Right Gasoline Tax?* 95 Am. Econ. Rev. 1276 (2005).

Postel, Sandra L, Gretchen C. Daily, and Paul R. Ehrlich, *Human Appropriation of Renewable Fresh Water*, 271 Science 785 (1996).

Prins, Gwyn and Steve Rayner, *Time to Ditch Kyoto?* 449 Nature 973 (2007).

Ramo, Alan, *The California Offset Game: Who Wins and Who Loses*, 20 Hastings West-Northwest J. Envtl. L. & Pol'y 109 (2014).

Salzman, James and J.B. Ruhl, *Gaming the Past: The Theory and Practice of Historic Baselines in the Administrative State*, 64 Vand. L. Rev. 1 (2010).

Samuelson, Paul A., *The Pure Theory of Public Expenditure*, 36 Rev. Econ. & Stat. 387 (1954).

Schmalensee, Richard and Robert N. Stavins, *The SO_2 Allowance Trading System: The Ironic History of a Grand Policy Experiment*, 27 J. Econ. Persp. 103 (Winter 2013).

Smith, Bryant Walker, *Stakeholder Reaction to Emissions Trading in the United States, the European Union, and the Netherlands*, 25 J. Land Use & Envtl. L. 137 (2009).

Smith, S., *Environmental and Public Finance Aspects of the Taxation of Energy*, 14 Oxford Rev. Econ. Pol'y 64 (1998).

Stavins, Robert N., *Transaction Costs and Tradeable Permits*, 29 J. Envtl. Econ. & Mgmt. 133 (1995).

Svendsen, Gert Tinggaard, *U.S. Interest Groups Prefer Emission Trading: A New Perspective*, 101 Pub. Choice J. 109 (1999).

Swift, Byron, *U.S. Emissions Trading: Myths, Realities and Opportunities*, 20 Nat. Res. & Envt. 3,4 (2005).

Trotignon, Raphael, *Combining Cap-and-Trade with Offsets: Lessons from the EU-ETS*, 12 Climate Pol'y 273 (2012).

van de Kerkhof, Martijn, *The Trail Smelter Case Re-examined: Examining the Development of National Procedural Mechanisms to Resolve a Trail Smelter Type Dispute*, 27 Utrecht J. Int'l and Eur. L. 68 (2011).

Vazquez, Carlos M., *Customary International Law as U.S. Law, A Critique of the Revisionist and Intermediate Positions and a Defense of the Modern Position*, 86 Notre Dame L. Rev. 1495 (2011).

Victor, David G. et al., *The Kyoto Protocol Emission Allocations: Windfall Surpluses for Russia and Ukraine*. 49 Climatic Change 263, 264 (2001).

Wara, Michael, *Measuring the Clean Development Mechanism's Performance and Potential*, 55 UCLA L. Rev. 1759 (2008).

Weitzman, Martin, *Prices vs. Quantities*, 41 Rev. Econ. Stud. 477 (1974).

Werksman, Jacob and Kirk Herbertson, *The Aftermath of Copenhagen: Does International Law have a Role to Play in a Global Response to Climate Change?* 25 Md. J. Int'l L. 109 (2010).

Wing, Ian Sue, Denny A. Ellerman, and Jaemin Song, *Absolute vs. Intensity-based Emissions Caps*, 3 (Supplement 2) Climate Pol'y S7-S20 (2003).

Government Documents

Carbon Pollution Emission Guidelines for Existing Stationary Sources: Electric Utility Generating Units No. 205; 80 Fed. Reg. 64661 (October 23, 2015).

Department of the Interior, Geological Survey 1987, *Acid Rain*, Water fact sheet, Open-file report, 87-399.

U.S. Environmental Protection Agency, *Renewable Fuel Standard Program: Standards for 2017 and Biomass Based Diesel*, 81 Fed. Reg. 89746 (December 12, 2016).

U.S. Environmental Protection Agency, *Endangerment and Cause or Contribute Findings for Greenhouse Gases Under Section 202(a) of the Clean Air Act, Final Rule*, 74 Fed. Reg. 66496 (December 15, 2009).

Reports and Papers

Bramley, Matthew, P.J. Partington, and Dave Sawyer, *Linking National Cap-and-Trade Systems in North America Clean Energy and Climate Action: A North American Collaboration* (The Pembina Institute and the International Institute for Sustainable Development, Discussion Paper, December 2009).

Burns, Douglas A., Jason A. Lynch, Bernhard J. Cosby, Mark E. Fenn, and Jill S. Baron, *National Acid Precipitation Assessment Program Report to Congress 2011: An Integrated Assessment* (Office of the President of the United States, 2011).

Cooper, Richard N., *Alternatives to Kyoto: The Case for a Carbon Tax* (Harvard University, Discussion Paper, 2006).

Haites, Erik, *Harmonization between National and International Tradeable Permit Schemes* (OECD Global Forum on Sustainable Development: Emissions Trading and Concerted Action for Tradable Emissions Permits, Synthesis Paper, 2003).

Heitzig, Jobst, *Bottom-Up Strategic Linking of Carbon Markets: Which Climate Coalitions Would Farsighted Players Form?* (FEEM Working Paper No. 48, June 5, 2013).

Herold, Martin, *The Significance of Monitoring Capabilities to Decide about the Scope of a Carbon Market*, Presentation at 1st Global Carbon Market Forum on Monitoring, Reporting, Verification, Compliance and Enforcement Session II.(May 19, 2008).

International Panel on Climate Change (IPCC): *Climate Change 2007: Mitigation. Contribution of Working Group III to the Fourth Assessment Report of the Intergovernmental Panel on Climate Change* (B. Metz, O.R. Davidson, P.R. Bosch, R. Dave, and L.A. Meyer, eds., 2007).

International Panel on Climate Change (IPCC), 2007. *Climate Change 2007: Synthesis Report. Contribution of Working Groups I, II and III to the Fourth Assessment Report of the Intergovernmental Panel on Climate Change* (R.K. Pachauri and A. Reisinger, eds., 2007).

International Panel on Climate Change (IPCC), *Climate Change 2014: Synthesis Report. Contribution of Working Groups I, II and III to the Fifth Assessment Report of the Intergovernmental Panel on Climate Change* (R.K. Pachauri and L.A. Meyer, eds., 2014).

International Panel on Climate Change (IPCC), Annex III: Glossary, *Climate Change 2013: The Physical Science Basis. Contribution of Working Group I to the Fifth Assessment Report of the Intergovernmental Panel on Climate Change* (T. F. Stocker, D. Qin, G.-K. Plattner, M. Tignor, S.K. Allen, J. Boschung, A. Nauels, Y. Xia, V. Bex, and P.M. Midgley eds., 2013).

Jaffe, Judson and Robert N. Stavins, *Linking a U.S. Cap-and-Trade System for Greenhouse Gas Emissions: Opportunities, Implications, and Challenges* (Reg-Markets Center Working Paper 08-01, January 2008).

Kosobud, Richard F., Houston H. Stokes, Carol D. Tallarico, and Brian L. Scott, *The Chicago VOC Trading System: The Consequences of Market Design for Performance* (Massachusetts Institute of Technology Center for Energy and Environmental Policy Research, Working Paper #04-019, 2004).

Liao, Chao-Ning and Onal Hayri, *An Economic Analysis of the Emission Reduction Market System in Chicago* (American Agricultural Economics Association [New Name 2008: Agricultural and Applied Economics Association], Annual Meeting Selected Paper, July 28-31, 2002).

Mutua, Makau, *What is TWAIL?* Proceedings of the 94th Annual Meeting of the American Society of International Law 31-40 (2000).

Peñalver, Eduardo M., *Acts of God or Toxic Torts? Applying Tort Principles to the Problem of Climate Change* (Cornell Law Faculty Publications, Paper 730, 1998).

Prins, Gwyn, Isabel Galiana, Christopher Green, Reiner Grundmann, Atte Korhola, Frank Laird, Ted Nordhaus, Roger Pielke Jr, Steve Rayner, Daniel Sarewitz, Michael Shellenberger, Nico Stehr, and Tezuko Hiroyuki, *The Hartwell Paper: A New Direction for Climate Policy after the Crash of 2009* (Institute for Science, Innovation & Society, University of Oxford; LSE Mackinder Programme, London School of Economics and Political Science, 2010).

Ranson, Matthew and Robert N. Stavins, *Linkage of Greenhouse Gas Emissions Trading Systems: Learning from Experience* (Harvard Project on Climate Agreements, Discussion Paper ES 2013-2, November 2013).

Sasson, David, *Business as Usual: A Report to the President on Pending Federal Climate Legislation* (Greenpeace Report, 2009).

Sawa, Akihiro, *A Sectoral Approach as an Option for a Post-Kyoto Framework* (Harvard Project on International Climate Agreements, Discussion Paper 2008-23, December 2008).

Schwarte, Christoph. *"No Harm" Rule and Climate Change* (Legal Response Initiative, Briefing Paper 42, July 2012).

Wing, Ian Sue and Marek Kolodziej, *The Regional Greenhouse Gas Initiative: Emission Leakage and the Effectiveness of Interstate Border Adjustments, Regulatory Policy Program* (Mossavar-Rahmani Center for Business and Government, John F. Kennedy School of Government, Harvard University, Working Paper RPP-2008-03, 2008).

Internet Resources

Baxter, Christopher, *Gov. Christie Announces N.J. Pulling Out of Regional Environmental Initiative*, NJ.com (May 26, 2011; updated March 31, 2019), https://www.nj.com/politics/2011/05/gov_christie_to_announce_nj_pu.html.

Burtraw, Dallas, Karen Palmer, Clayton Munnings, Paige Weber, and Matt Woerman, *Linking by Degrees, Incremental Alignment of Cap-and-Trade Markets*, 13 Resources for the Future (April 2013), https://www.rff.org/publications/working-papers/linking-by-degrees-incremental-alignment-of-cap-and-trade-markets/ (last visited January 11, 2020).

California Air Resources Board, Climate Change Proposed Scoping Plan ES-1 (2008), http://www.arb.ca.gov/cc/scopingplan/scopingplan.htm, revised (last visited January 11, 2020).

California Air Resources Board. *Auction Information,* https://ww3.arb.ca.gov/cc/capandtrade/auction/auction_notices_and_reports.htm (last visited January 11, 2020).

California Air Resources Board, *Mandatory GHG Reporting— Reported Emissions; 2013 GHG Facility and Entity Emissions* (November 2014), https://ww2.arb.ca.gov/mrr-data.

Environmental Protection Agency, *Acid Rain Program*, https://www.epa.gov/airmarkets/acid-rain-program (last visited January 11, 2020).

Environmental Protection Agency, *Sources of Greenhouse Gas Emissions*, http://www3.epa.gov/climatechange/ghgemissions/sources.html (last visited January 11, 2020).

Environmental Protection Agency, *Air Markets Program Data*, http://ampd.epa.gov/ampd/, (last visited January 11, 2020).

Environmental Protection Agency, *Acid Rain Program*, *Progress Reports, 1999–2012,* https://www.epa.gov/airmarkets/acid-rain-program-historical-reports (last visited January 11, 2020).

European Commission, *International Carbon Market*, http://ec.europa.eu/clima/policies/ets/linking/index_en.htm (last visited January 11, 2020).

European Parliament, Briefing, *The EU, A World Leader in Fighting Climate Change* (May 2018), http://www.europarl.europa.eu/RegData/etudes/BRIE/2018/621818/EPRS_BRI(2018)621818_EN.pdf.

Hsia-Kiung, Katherine and Erica Morehouse, *Carbon Market California, A Comprehensive Analysis of the Golden States Cap-And-Trade Program/Year Two: 2014*, published by the Environmental Defense Fund, https://www.edf.org/sites/default/files/carbon-market-california-year_two.pdf (last visited January 11, 2020).

Hsia-Kiung, Katherine, Emily Reyna, and Timothy O'Connor, *Carbon Market California, A comprehensive Analysis of the Golden States Cap-And-Trade Program/Year One 2012-2013*, published by Environmental Defense Fund, http://www.edf.org/sites/default/files/content/ca-cap-and-trade_1yr_22_web.pdf (last visited January 11, 2020).

Illinois Environmental Protection Agency (IEPA), *Emissions Reduction Market System, Annual Performance Review Report – 2000*, http://www.epa.state.il.us/air/erms/apr/2000/aprr-2000-full.pdf (last visited January 11, 2020).

Illinois Environmental Protection Agency (IEPA), *Emissions Reduction Market System, Annual Performance Review Report – 2005*, http://www.epa.state.il.us/air/erms/apr/2000/aprr-2005-full.pdf (last visited January 11, 2020).

Illinois Environmental Protection Agency (IEPA), *Emissions Reduction Market System, Annual Performance Review Report – 2013*, https://www2.illinois.gov/epa/Documents/epa.state.il.us/air/erms/apr/2013/index.pdf (last visited January 11, 2020).

International Carbon Action Partnership, *Emissions Trading Worldwide: Status Report 2019*, 2019, https://icapcarbonaction.com/en/icap-status-report-2019 (last visited January 11, 2020).

International Law Association, *Legal Principles Relating to Climate Change* (2014),

https://www.ila-hq.org/index.php/committees (last visited January 11, 2020).

International Union for Conservation of Nature and Natural Resources, *World Conservation Strategy: Living Resource Conservation for Sustainable Development* (1980), https://portals.iucn.org/library/sites/library/files/documents/WCS-004.pdf (last visited January 11, 2020).

Lehmann, Evan, "Regional Carbon Regulators Could Be Linked if Congress Fails," *ClimateWire* (November 10, 2009), http://www.eenews.net/climatewire/2009/11/10/3/.

Organisation for Economic Development and Cooperation (OECD), *Greenhouse Gas Emissions*, http://dx.doi.org/10.1787/data-00594-en (last visited January 11, 2020).

Organisation for Economic Development and Cooperation (OECD) *Action Against Climate Change: The Kyoto Protocol and Beyond* (1999), https://doi.org/10.1787/9789264173927-en (last visited January 11, 2020).

Martin, Ralf, Mirabelle Muûls, and Ulrich Wagner, *Climate Change, Investment and Carbon Markets and Prices–Evidence from Manager Interviews*, Climate Strategies, Carbon Pricing for Low-Carbon Investment Project, Climate Policy Initiative (2011), https://climatepolicyinitiative.org/wp-content/uploads/2011/12/Climate-Change-Investment-and-Carbon-Markets-and-Prices.pdf (last visited January 11, 2020).

Millennium Ecosystem Assessment, *Living Well Beyond Our Means: Natural Assets and Human Well-Being,* Statement of the MA Board (March 2005), http://www.millenniumassessment.org/documents/document.429.aspx.pdf (last visited January 11, 2020).

Muntean, M., D. Guizzardi, E. Schaaf, M. Crippa, E. Solazzo, J.G.J. Olivier, and E. Vignati, *Fossil CO_2 Emissions of All World Countries - 2018 Report*, Joint Research Center European Commission (November 23, 2018), https://op.europa.eu/en/publication-detail/-/publication/41811494-f131-11e8-9982-01aa75ed71a1/language-en.

Nichols, Mary D., Assistant Administrator for Air and Radiation, U.S. Environmental Protection Agency, *Testimony before Subcommittee on Clean Air, Wetlands, Private Property, and Nuclear Safety, Committee on the Environment and Public Works, United States Senate* (July 24, 1997), https://www.epw.senate.gov/105th/epa_7-24.htm.

Panorama, BBC One, *Climate Chaos: Bush's Climate of Fear* (June 1, 2006), http://news.bbc.co.uk/2/hi/programmes/panorama/5005994.stm.

Pew Center for Global Climate Change, *Summary of the American Power Act* (May 2010), https://www.c2es.org/document/short-summary-of-the-american-power-act-kerry-lieberman/ (last visited April 21, 2020).

Potomac Economics, *Annual Report on the Market for RGGI CO_2 Allowances: 2009*, prepared for RGGI, Inc. on behalf of the RGGI participating states (August 2010), https://www.rggi.org/sites/default/files/Uploads/Market-Monitor/Annual-Reports/MM_2009_Annual_Report.pdf (last visited January 11, 2020).

Potomac Economics, *Annual Report on the Market for RGGI CO_2 Allowances: 2010*, prepared for RGGI, Inc. on behalf of the RGGI participating states (April 2011), https://www.rggi.org/sites/default/files/Uploads/Market-Monitor/Annual-Reports/MM_2010_Annual_Report.pdf (last visited January 11, 2020).

Potomac Economics, *Annual Report on the Market for RGGI CO_2 Allowances: 2011*, prepared for RGGI, Inc. on behalf of the RGGI participating states (May 2012), https://www.rggi.org/sites/default/files/Uploads/Market-Monitor/Annual-Reports/MM_2011_Annual_Report.pdf (last visited January 11, 2020).

Potomac Economics, *Annual Report on the Market for RGGI CO_2 Allowances: 2012*, prepared for RGGI, Inc. on behalf of the RGGI participating states (April 2013), https://www.rggi.org/sites/default/files/Uploads/Market-Monitor/Annual-Reports/MM_2012_Annual_Report.pdf (last visited January 11, 2020).

Potomac Economics, *Annual Report on the Market for RGGI CO_2 Allowances: 2013*, prepared for RGGI, Inc. on behalf of the RGGI participating states (May 2014), https://www.rggi.org/sites/default/files/Uploads/Market-Monitor/Annual-Reports/MM_2013_Annual_Report.pdf (last visited January 11, 2020).

Regional Greenhouse Gas Initiative, *Model Rules for the CO2 Budget Trading Program*, https://www.rggi.org/program-overview-and-design/design-archive/mou-model-rule (last accessed January 11, 2020).

Regional Greenhouse Gas Initiative (RGGI), *CO_2 Data for RGGI Units 2000-2008*, https://www.rggi.org/allowance-tracking/emissions (last visited January 11, 2020).

Regional Greenhouse Gas Initiative, *CO2 Emissions from Electricity Generation and Imports in the Regional Greenhouse Gas Initiative: 2010 Monitoring Report* (August 6, 2010), https://www.rggi.org/sites/default/files/Uploads/Electricity-Monitoring-Reports/2010_Elec_Monitoring_Report.pdf.

Regional Greenhouse Gas Initiative, *CO_2 Emissions from Electricity Generation and Imports in the Regional Greenhouse Gas Initiative: 2011 Monitoring Report* (June 27, 2013), https://www.rggi.org/sites/default/files/Uploads/Electricity-Monitoring-Reports/2011_Elec_Monitoring_Report.pdf.

Regional Greenhouse Gas Initiative, *CO_2 Emissions from Electricity Generation and Imports in the Regional Greenhouse Gas Initiative: 2012 Monitoring Report* (August 11, 2014), https://www.rggi.org/sites/default/files/Uploads/Electricity-Monitoring-Reports/2012_Elec_Monitoring_Report.pdf.

Regional Greenhouse Gas Initiative (RGGI), press release (August 23, 2017), https://www.rggi.org/docs/ProgramReview/2017/08-23-17/Announcement_Proposed_Program_Changes.pdf.

Shapiro, Robert J., *Addressing the Risks of Climate Change: The Environmental Effectiveness and Economic Efficiency of Emissions Caps and Tradable Permits, Compared to Carbon Taxes* (February 2007), http://www.sonecon.com/docs/studies/climate_021407.pdf.

StandardCarbon blog, *Q & A with Mary Nichols*, Chair of the California Air Resources Board, https://www.standardcarbon.com/2010/12/qa-with-mary-nichols-chair-of-the-california-air-resources-board/ (last visited January 20, 2020).

United Nations, *Treaty Collection Homepage*, https://treaties.un.org/pages/ViewDetails.aspx?src=TREATY&mtdsg_no=XXVII-7-d&chapter=27&clang=_en (last visited January 11, 2020).

United Nations, *Plan of Implementation of the World Summit on Sustainable Development*, https://www.un.org/esa/sustdev/documents/WSSD_POI_PD/English/WSSD_PlanImpl.pdf (last visited January 11, 2020).

United Nations, Department for Economic and Social Information and Policy Analysis, *Glossary of Environment Statistics, Studies in Methods*, Series F, No. 67, https://unstats.un.org/unsd/publication/SeriesF/SeriesF_67E.pdf. (last visited January 11, 2020).

United Nations, UNFCCC Legal Affairs Programme, *Information on Ratification Status* http://unfccc.int/paris_agreement/items/9444.php (last visited January 11, 2020).

United Nations Framework Convention on Climate Change (UNFCCC), *Glossary of Climate Change Acronyms and Terms*, https://unfccc.int/process-and-meetings/the-convention/glossary-of-climate-change-acronyms-and-terms (last visited January 11, 2020).

United Nations Framework Convention on Climate Change, *Parties to the Convention and Observer States*, https://unfccc.int/process/parties-non-party-stakeholders/parties-convention-and-observer-states (last visited January 11, 2020).

United Nations Framework Convention on Climate Change (UNFCCC), Secretariat, *Interim NDC Registry*, http://www4.unfccc.int/ndcregistry/Pages/Home.aspx (last visited January 11, 2020).

United Nations Framework Convention on Climate Change (UNFCCC), Ad Hoc Working Group on Further Commitments For Annex I Parties under the Kyoto Protocol, Eleventh session Bonn, 9–11 April 2010, *Views on the need for additional meeting time for the Ad Hoc Working Group on Further Commitments for Annex I Parties under the Kyoto Protocol and the Ad Hoc Working Group on Long-term Cooperative Action under the Convention, and on organization of work of the Ad Hoc Working Group on Long-term Cooperative Action under the Convention* (March 16, 2010), https://unfccc.int/sites/default/files/resource/docs/2010/awglca9/eng/misc01.pdf.

United Nations Framework Convention on Climate Change, *Annual Report of the Executive Board of the Clean Development Mechanism to the Conference of the Parties Serving as the Meeting of the Parties to the Kyoto Protocol* (November 6, 2014), http://unfccc.int/resource/docs/2014/cmp10/eng/05.pdf.

United Nations Framework Convention on Climate Change, *Emissions Trading Greenhouse Gas Initiative, A New Commodity*, https://unfccc.int/process/the-kyoto-protocol/mechanisms/emissions-trading (last visited April 17, 2020).

United Nations Framework Convention on Climate Change, *Clean Development Mechanism: Glossary,* https://unfccc.int/process-and-meetings/the-convention/glossary-of-climate-change-acronyms-and-terms (last visited January 11, 2020).

United Nations Framework Convention on Climate Change, *Clean Development Mechanism, CDM insights, monthly reports*, https://cdm.unfccc.int/Statistics/Public/index.html (last visited January 11, 2020).

U.S. Energy Information-Administration, *International Energy Outlook 2014*, http://www.eia.gov/forecasts/ieo/pdf/0484(2014).pdf (last visited January 11, 2020).

Western Climate Initiative, *Design Recommendations for the WCI Regional Cap and Trade Program, r*evised edition (March 13, 2009), http://www.westernclimateinitiative.org/the-wci-cap-and-trade-program/design-recommendations.

Western Climate Initiative, *Design for the WCI Regional Program* (July 27, 2010), http://www.westernclimateinitiative.org/the-wci-cap-and-trade-program/program-design.

Yale Climate & Energy Institute Blog, Poll: *Americans Support Strong Climate, Energy Policies* (Sept. 9, 2019), https://www.climatechangecommunication.org/wp-content/uploads/2019/09/American-Voters-Support-Climate-Action.pdf.

Other

European Commission, Press release, IP/08/787, (May 23, 2008).

German Language Resources

Beckmann, Martin A., Fisahn, Andreas, Probleme des Handels mit Verschmutzungsrechten - eine Bewertung ordnungsrechtlicher und marktgesteuerter Instrumente in der Umweltpolitik, Zeitschrift für Umweltrecht (ZUR), 2009, Heft 6.

Bohne, Eberhard, Der informale Rechtsstaat, Eine empirische und rechtliche Untersuchung zum Gesetzesvollzug unter besonderer Berücksichtigung des Immissionsschutzes, 1981.

Böhringer, Ayșe-Martina, Das neue Pariser Klimaübereinkommen - Eine Kompromisslösung mit Symbolkraft und Verhaltenssteuerungspotential, Zeitschrift für ausländisches öffentliches Recht und Völkerrecht (ZaörV) 2016, 753.

Czarnecki, Ralph, Verteilungsgerechtigkeit im Völkerrecht, Dogmatik und Umsetzung, in: Schriften zum Umweltrecht, Kloepfer, Michael (Hrsgb.), Band 159, 2008.

Cited as: Czarnecki, Verteilungsgerechtigkeit im Völkerrecht

Danner, Wolfgang, Theobald Christian (Hrsg.), Energierecht, (Loseblatt, 91. EL January 2017).

Cited as: *Author* in Danner/Theobald, Energierecht.

Deutscher Alpenverein, Gletscherrückgang und tauender Permafrost, available online under https://www.alpenverein.de/natur/klimaschutz/ausstellung-klimawandel-klimaschutz/gletscherrueckgang-und-tauender-permafrost_aid_28388.html (last visited January 11, 2020).

Djeffal, Christian, The Iron Rhine Case - A Treaty's Journey from Peace to Sustainable Development, Zeitschrift für ausländisches öffentliches Recht und Völkerrecht (ZaöRV) 2011, 569.

Ekardt, Felix, Das Paris Abkommen zum globalen Klimaschutz, Chancen und Friktionen - auf dem Weg zu einer substantiellen EU-Vorreiterrolle?, Neue Zeitschrift für Verwaltungsrecht (NVwZ) 2016, 355.

Epiney, Astrid, Scheyli, Martin, Strukturprinzipien des Umweltvölkerrechts, 1998

Cited as: *Epiney/Scheyli*, Strukturprinzipien des Umweltvölkerrechts.

Epiney, Astrid, Zur Einführung - Umweltvökerrecht, JuS 2003, 1066.

Frank, Will, Anmerkungen zum Pariser Klimavertrag aus rechtlicher Sicht - insbesondere zu den "(I)NDCs", der 2°/1,5° Celsius-Schwelle und "loss and damage" im Kontext völkerrechtlicher Klimaverantwortung, Zeitschrift für Umweltrecht (ZUR), 2016, 35.

Frank, Will, Überlegungen zur Klimahaftung nach Völkerrecht, Neue Zeitschrift für Verwaltungsrecht (NVwZ)-Extra, 2014.

Hartwig Bartling, Franz Luzius, Grundzüge der Volkswirtschaftslehre, Einführung in die Wirtschaftstheorie und Wirtschaftspolitik, 17. Auflage 2014.

Handelsblatt, January 2, 2017, "Prämie für Elektroautos floppt - Nur 9000 Anträge für E-Auto-Kaufprämie", http://www.handelsblatt.com/unternehmen/industrie/praemie-fuer-elektroautos-floppt-nur-9000-antraege-fuer-e-auto-kaufpraemie/19199008.html (last visited January 11, 2020).

Herdegen, Matthias, Völkerrecht, 13. Auflage, 2014.

Junker, Kirk W., *Fiddling with Trade as Home Burns*, 2.12, Kölner Schrift zum Wirtschaftsrecht, pp. 236-244 (2012).

Kreibich, Nicolas and Wolfang Obergassel, *Carbon Markets After Paris - How to Account for the Transfer of Mitigation Results?* JIKO Policy Paper 01/2016. Wuppertal Institut für Klima, Umwelt, Energie. Wuppertal.

Kreuter-Kirchhof, Charlotte, Das Pariser Klimaschutzübereinkommen und die Grenzen des Rechts - eine neue Chance für den Klimaschutz, Deutsches Verwaltungsblatt (DVBL) 2, 2017, 97.

Kreuter-Kirchhof, Charlotte, Dynamisierung des internationalen Klimaschutzregimes durch Institutionalisierung, Zeitschrift für ausländisches öffentliches Recht und Völkerrecht (ZaöRV), 2005, 967.

Kreuter-Kirchhof, Charlotte, Klimaschutz durch Emissionshandel? Die jüngste Reform des europäischen Emissionshandelssystems, Europäische Zeitschrift für Wirtschaftsrecht (EuZW) 2017, 412.

Landmann, Robert von, Rohmer, Gustav, (Hrsg.) Umweltrecht, Umweltvölkerrecht, (Loseblatt, Stand: 90. Auflage 2019).

Cited as *Author* in Landmann/Rohmer, Umweltrecht, Umweltvölkerrecht.

Marauhn, Thilo, A Global Energy Strategy as a Viable Means for Redressing Climate Change?, Zeitschrift für ausländisches öffentliches Recht und Völkerrecht (ZaöRV), 2003, 281.

Marauhn, Thilo, A Global Energy Strategy as a Viable Means for Redressing Climate Change?, Zeitschrift für ausländisches öffentliches Recht und Völkerrecht (ZaöRV), 2003.

Mayntz, Renate, Vollzugsprobleme im Umweltrecht, 1978.

Peters, Heinz-Joachim, Verwaltungsrechtliche Verfahren zur Anpassung von Vorhaben an den Klimawandel, Zeitschrift Kommunaljurist 2017, 41.

Rehbinder, Eckard, Das Vorsorgeprinzip im internationalen Vergleich, in: Schlacke, Sabine, Franzius Claudio (Hrsg.), Umweltrechtliche Studien, Vol. 12, 2000.

Saurer, Johannes, Purnhagen, Kai, Klimawandel vor Gericht - Der Rechtsstreit der Nichtregierungsorganisation „Urgenda" gegen die Niederlande und seine Bedeutung für Deutschland, Zeitschrift für Umweltrecht (ZUR) 2016, 16.

Sieben, Peter, Was bedeutet Nachhaltigkeit als Rechtsbegriff?, Neue Zeitschrift für Verwaltungsrecht (NVwZ) 2003, 1173.

Tagesanzeiger, Walliser beten für den Gletscher, July 7, 2012, http://www.tagesanzeiger.ch/panorama/vermischtes/Walliser-beten-fuer-den-Gletscher/story/31501391 (27.07.2012,) (last visited January 11, 2020).

Übersohn, Gerhard, Effektive Umweltpolitik: Folgerungen aus der Implementations- und Evaluationsforschung, 1990.

Verheyen, Roda, Lührs, Michael, Klimaschutz durch Gerichte in den USA - 1. Teil: Öffentliches Recht, Zeitschrift für Umweltrecht (ZUR) 2009, Heft 2, 73.

Vitzthum, Wolfgang Graf, Proeßl, Alexander (Hrsg.) Völkerrecht, 6. Auflage, 2013

Cited as: *Author* in in Graf Vitzthum/Proeßl, Völkerrecht.

Volmert, Barbara, Roßnagel, Alexander, Hentschel Anja, Rechtliche Möglichkeiten und Grenzen einer Verknüpfung des europäischen Emissionshandelssystems mit der amerikanischen „Regional Greenhouse Gas Initiative“, Zeitschrift für Umweltrecht (ZUR) 2012, 666.

Wegener, Bernhard W., Die Novelle des EU-Emissionshandelssystems, Zeitschrift für Umweltrecht (ZUR), 2009, 283.

Winter, Gerd, Das Klima ist keine Ware, Zeitschrift für Umweltrecht (ZUR) 2009, Heft 6, 289 (296).

World Energy Council - Deutschland e.V. Energie für Deutschland 2016; Fakten, Perspektiven und Positionen im globalen Kontext, p. 86, http://www.weltenergierat.de/wp-content/uploads/2014/02/61524_DNK_Energie16_D_final_72dpi.pdf (last visited January 11, 2020).

Wustlich, Guido, Ökonomisierung im Umweltrecht, Zeitschrift für Umweltrecht (ZUR), 2009, Heft 11, 515 (520).